POLITICAL TRANSFORMATIONS AND POLITICAL ENTREPRENEURS


First published in 2009 by
PALGRAVE MACMILLAN®
in the United States—a division of St. Martin's Press LLC,
175 Fifth Avenue, New York, NY 10010.

Where this book is distributed in the UK, Europe and the rest of the world, this is by Palgrave Macmillan, a division of Macmillan Publishers Limited, registered in England, company number 785998, of Houndmills, Basingstoke, Hampshire RG21 6XS.

Palgrave Macmillan is the global academic imprint of the above companies and has companies and representatives throughout the world.

Palgrave® and Macmillan® are registered trademarks in the United States, the United Kingdom, Europe and other countries.

ISBN: 978–0–230–61867–1

Library of Congress Cataloging-in-Publication Data

Meydani, Assaf.
Political transformations and political entrepreneurs : Israel in comparative perspective / Assaf Meydani.
p. cm.
Includes bibliographical references.
ISBN 978–0–230–61867–1 (alk. paper)
1. Elections—Israel. 2. Election law—Israel. 3. Prime ministers—Israel—Election. 4. Prime ministers—Election. 5. Pressure groups—Israel. 6. Pressure groups. 7. Political stability—Israel. 8. Political culture—Israel. 9. Israel—Politics and government. 10. Comparative government—Case studies. I. Title.

JQ1830.A95M49 2009
324.9—dc22 2009010767

A catalogue record of the book is available from the British Library.

Design by Newgen Imaging Systems (P) Ltd., Chennai, India.

First edition: December 2009

10 9 8 7 6 5 4 3 2 1

Printed in the United States of America.

*To my wife Marit and my daughters Romy and Alma with love and appreciation*

*To my mother Lea, my father Ben-Zion, and my sisters Inbal and Reut, thank you for always being there.*

# CONTENTS

# FIGURES AND TABLES

## Figures



## Tables

# ACKNOWLEDGMENTS

This book is based on my Ph.D. dissertation (2004): Political Entrepreneurs and Dynamics of Institutional Change: Conceptual Framework and Analysis of Case Studies in Israel (Hebrew), Ben Gurion University, Israel, later on developed and expanded. I would like to thank Gideon Doron, Shlomo Mizrahi and David A. Frenkel for their help in this research. I'm grateful to Gad Barzilai, Arye Naor, David Nachmias, Gideon Rahat, Shimon Shetreet, Itai Sened, Pablo T. Spiller, Arye Carmon, Amnon Rubinstein and Uriel Reichmann for their advice and collaboration. I would also like to thank Naomi Chazan for her time and support. I would like to thank the Academic College of Tel-Aviv-Yaffo for their generous support and especially to Israel Zang, Nehemia Friedland and Dror Amir.

The manuscript would never have reached final form but for the editorial skill and dedication of Nina Reshef. In addition, I would like to thank Farideh Koohi-Kamali, Colleen Lawrie, Robyn Curtis and Asa Johnson from Palgrave Macmillan for their useful advice and support. And finally my thanks to the anonymous readers for useful remarks and to B. Guy Peters for his guidance.

# CHAPTER ONE

## Introduction

The past two decades have seen dramatic changes in Israeli society, captured in its nascent examination of the essence and relevance of the rules by which it is organized. Declarative announcements of reform have been all too frequent in the political arena. Politicians drape their platforms in the banner of reform so frequently that it seems as if "change, reform and more change" is proffered as the miracle cure to all the nation's problems. But is it really? None of the several attempts at reform have left any significant marks. The direct election of the prime minister was enacted in 1992 and repealed in 2001; of the New Public Management reforms belatedly adopted, the few adopted failed in the implementation stage; legislative attempts to pass a constitution are still stalled, with basic laws being amended as if they were ordinary laws. In brief, policy change in many policy domains has been so frequent as to become a major social problem in itself.[1]

In approaching this situation from a theoretical and empirical perspective, this book attempts to provide policy-makers with the tools they need to make policy decisions that are concurrently legitimate and feasible. In particular, the book examines the process by which formal political rules are changed, while emphasizing the involvement and role of political entrepreneurs (or change agents) in formulating and motivating such changes. Such changes are important because they redefine the framework of political debate together with the distribution of power among the players.[2]

Sociopolitical change usually requires vast effort and resources. We therefore expect change to occur when the major players have clear interests in making it happen. However, more often than not, fundamental institutional change entails the concession of political power by the major players in the game. This situation demands that we delve into why politicians and legislators, individuals presumably interested in maximizing their own value and power, would promote and support institutional change that concludes in concession of their political power.

Moreover, as fundamental political rules usually reflect the distribution of power, among social and political actors we would expect any proposed change in the rules to initiate a complex process of social and political bargaining. In order for such bargaining to result in stable institutional change, the players must rely on long-term considerations rather than on the achievement of immediate goals. Yet even here, we find cases in which the players involved in a fundamental institutional change are guided by short-term considerations motivated by the drive to maximize their immediate interests; alternatively, we can find other cases in which institutional change is promoted as a mechanism for the resolution of economic, political or social crises. Yet, both approaches lead to instability. Even when political entrepreneurs seem to be guided by long-term considerations, they often act according to short-term considerations. Therefore, any investigation into the causes of change must ask what motives stimulated or provoked these players to initiate institutional change.

Responding to these questions requires an in-depth analysis that places the players' actions into the wider social-structural, institutional and political context. Therefore, this book examines the broader theoretical questions of why, and under what conditions, do fundamental changes in formal, political institutions transpire? That is, when do the rules of the game change in democratic systems? How are the character and composition of formal institutional change determined? Finally, what factors explain the stability of changes?

The theoretical framework at the heart of this book is examined in the empirical context of the Israeli political system. The formal procedural change explored is the electoral reform determining direct election of the prime minister. This reform comprised two formal institutional changes:

1. *Basic Law: the Government* passed on March 18, 1992—Legislating Direct Election of the Prime Minister Law.
2. *Basic Law: the Government* (amended in 2001) passed on March 7, 2001—repealing the previous 1992 amendment to the law.

To support the book's argument, we compare the Israeli case with four other cases in which laws targeted at procedural change in political institutions were passed in other countries: judicial reform in Argentina in 1993 and 1997, electoral reform in Italy in 1993, and electoral reform in New Zealand in 1993. In New Zealand, a simple plurality election system for the House of Representatives was replaced by a revised mixed system combining single-member districts and proportional representation by means of a referendum;[3] in Italy, election to the Chamber of Deputies was changed from proportional representation to a mixed system combining single-member districts and proportional representation;[4] while in Argentina, a constitutional amendment was passed altering the selection process for Supreme Court Justices and creating a national Judicial Council to administer the judicial branch as well as to regulate lower-level judicial behavior.[5] All four institutional changes restructured the political debate in addition to the power relations maintained between the political players in each society. The cases themselves were chosen after attempting to overcome the difficulties encountered in locating states having a common denominator based on population size, geographic location, culture, social structure and political type of government.[6]

Institutional change in Israel occurs frequently; it is characterized by the short-term time preferences that indicate instability attached to such change. In addressing this instability, the book examines the behavior of various political entrepreneurs. Regarding Israel's Direct Election of the Prime Minister Law, the book treats Professor Uriel Reichmann and the *Constitution for Israel* movement as external political entrepreneurs, whereas Members of Knesset (MK) Uriel Lynn, Amnon Rubinstein, David Libai and Yoash Tsiddon are treated as internal political entrepreneurs. Regarding the law's repeal; the book analyzes the actions of Dr. Arye Carmon, President of the Israel Democracy Institute and the Association for Parliamentary Democracy, as an external entrepreneur and MKs Moshe Arens, Uzi Landau and Yossi Beilin as internal entrepreneurs. Their actions are examined in light of structural and social constraints. In addition, special emphasis is placed on the formation of a belief in the necessity of change in isolation of its substance. This ambiguity has unique significance, addressed later in the book.

The book's central argument points to two main variables that explain the creation and stability of an institutional change:

1. The level of economic and political stability.
2. The character of the political culture, demonstrated by social attitudes toward democratic norms; that is, whether such values comprise the fundamental values of society (henceforth: *fundamental*

*democratic perceptions*) or utilitarian beliefs applied when maximizing other values or interests (henceforth: *procedural democratic perception*).

According to this argument, economic and political instability, together with weak democratic norms, lead change agents to focus on short-term considerations. This model presumes that the timing of the players' moves impacts upon the stability of the change engendered, manifested by the level of its implementation and the intensity of attempts to reverse it. The stability of institutional change is therefore viewed as a function of the initial political and socioeconomic instability together with the popular perceptions of procedural democracy. In such circumstances, analysis of the design of institutional change comprises two phases. The first phase examines what motivates change while the second phase examines the interaction between the players during design of that change.

The first phase emphasizes two variables:

1. *To begin the process of formulating an institutional change, the agent of change must identify a public need to alter the political rules.* The book also discusses the feeling shared by a large segment of society regarding the necessity to change political rules, a variable that explains the drive to implement institutional change. This feeling emerges after a long period of learning, during which society comes to understand that in order to alter the current problematic situation (that is, to formulate policy solutions capable of solving problems), one must act to revise the political rules.[7] This temporal process includes attempts to initiate reforms relying on existing rules, i.e., policy regulations. When such attempts fail (for instance, due to structural centralization), society may come to believe in the necessity of regime change, i.e., political rules. This belief, however, does not encompass new or radical ideas regarding the substance of the political rules (for instance, it does not address the possibility of exchanging a parliamentary system with a presidential one, or revising the parliamentary system itself).

2. *Political entrepreneurs identify a need to modify political rules* A major focus of the model is the involvement of political entrepreneurs who identify a need (or, more accurately, the popular belief in the need) to modify political rules as well as the benefits they—in addition to the public—will derive from that modification. As this belief develops, political entrepreneurs become crucial for their ability to link public dissatisfaction to the proposed institutional change, which they frame as a solution to the problem. In terms of social-choice theory, this link

requires an additional parameter, one representing the cost-benefit functions associated with the various players. The model refers to this choice of solution as *electoral capital*, that is, the assets (e.g., image, material resources and political support) change agents can use to maximize their individual benefits. A political entrepreneur, in his role as an elected official, can, for instance, use these assets to maximize his chances of re-election. The act of supporting a law aimed at revising the electoral system, including the case of the Direct Election of the Prime Minister Law (an assumed reform) can thus be converted into electoral capital under certain circumstances.

Following this logic, a political entrepreneur acts to promote change for ideological reasons but, perhaps more, because of the belief that such actions will maximize his or her political support or his or her public prestige when treated as a goal rather than an asset. However, this does not mean that other players will also adopt the respective institutional change as a source of electoral capital; they will do so only if the political entrepreneur can convince them that similar behavior will likewise further their own objectives. Moreover, a political entrepreneur's ability to identify and accumulate electoral capital depends on various social and structural conditions or constraints that affect the complex interactions conducted with the players during formulation of the change to be implemented. In doing so (i.e., defining the electoral capital and convincing the players), the political entrepreneur transforms the respective social problem into a policy problem.

As defined in this book, a *political entrepreneur* is a person or a group intent on changing political reality by changing the political rules of the game or policy regulation within the existing rules of the game.[8] Political entrepreneurs will therefore be analyzed according to the following parameters:

1. Political Values: Moral and political perceptions.
2. Public Visibility: Reasons for maximizing power and prestige.
3. Affiliation with a specific group and profession.
4. Past experience and learning.
5. Ability to identify and make use of crises to alter public beliefs and preferences.

One of our main hypotheses, therefore, states that structural and cultural conditions motivate political entrepreneurs to promote those institutional changes that express the operative transformation of their fundamental ideologies.

A political entrepreneur can emerge from among the following groups: politicians, bureaucrats, organized interest groups, and other groups of citizens. His interactions with these groups are complex. These four groups, whose identities vary by the specific issue, represent the major players in the design and determination of policy. The precise nature of the institutional change proposed reflects the power relationships and interests characterizing these groups under given structural and cultural conditions. Just how power relations between these players affect the character of the change will be discussed in Part Two of the book. The discussion will progress according to the four analytic levels on which political entrepreneurs initiate action. The first level pertains to the entrepreneurs' actions with regard to their reference groups and designated publics. Asset accumulation, including strategies for garnering public support, will be analyzed. At the second level, entrepreneurs interact with interest groups and policy-makers. The third level deals with the reciprocities maintained between the politicians in Parliament. On the fourth and final level, the involvement of the bureaucratic players in change is investigated.

The State of Israel is currently in the midst of a learning process in which various reforms promoted to solve a range of social problems are being tested. Historically, most reforms of the Israeli system were never implemented; too often, they were replaced before they could yield results. A theoretical and empirical examination of successful implementation of reform is crucial at this point, a period that many researchers have characterized as tainted by a moral vacuum and the deterioration of self-governing capabilities—conditions threatening national stability.

The empirical research will be guided by the theoretical model just sketched. Hence, the process analysis will be based on established theoretical axioms. Use is made of primary as well as secondary sources throughout. Regarding the positioning and actions of the various players, the analysis is based on data gathered from newspapers, articles and personal interviews.

The combination of these two variables—issues and political entrepreneurs—has allowed us to develop a two-tier tool for measuring the structural conditions that influence players' temporal preferences and hence the stability of a given institutional change. For example, both *Israel* and *Argentina* have been characterized by high levels of economic and political instability. Such structural conditions impose short-term time preference on the players. In addition, the political cultures of both states are characterized by instrumental democratic attitudes that also support short-term time frames as far as calculating the lifespan of changes in democratic settings. The combination of these structural and cultural conditions promotes short-term considerations and thus the likelihood of unstable, frequent institutional changes. On the other hand, *New Zealand* has been characterized by a lower level of economic and political instability, structural conditions that do not impose short-term considerations on the players. The country's political culture is also characterized by fundamental democratic attitudes that support a long-term perspective regarding reform, implying more stable and less frequent institutional change. *Italy*, on the other hand, presents a mixture of conditions characterized by greater economic and political instability when compared to New Zealand. Such structural conditions are likely to impose short-term considerations upon the players. However, Italy's political culture is characterized by higher level of fundamental democratic attitudes in comparison to Argentina and Israel; this implies a long-term horizon as far as views of changes are concerned. The respective combination implies a greater receptivity to change than in New Zealand but more stable and less frequent change than in Argentina and Israel.

In all four cases, the involvement of political entrepreneurs is pivotal for the realization of institutional reform. Their activities remain crucial because they identify public attitudes towards change in addition to the readiness for institutional change; they also specify the social problem and identify the solution as the change of political rules. Entrepreneurs' preferences, activities and influence grow in significance when players are guided by short-term perspectives. On the other hand, when the structural and cultural conditions promote long-term perspectives, the interactional complexity characterizing relations among the political players, especially if encouraged by political entrepreneurs, exerts greater influence of the design of institutional change. The path chosen therefore depends on the society's level of economic and political stability in addition to its political culture, both expressed in public attitudes toward democracy. Together, they explain the stability of institutional change.

## Book Structure

The *second chapter* of this book presents a review of the research literature on political rules of the game, drawn from various streams of institutional theory. It includes a summary of the literature about political entrepreneurs and social-choice theory. The general argument will be integrated in the material, with the proposed model's basic axioms explained accordingly.

The *third chapter* applies the theoretical analysis in its explanation of the acceptance and formulation of institutional change in Israel. The empirical case study involves passage of *Basic Law: the Government*, on March 18, 1992, a law also known as the Direct Election of the Prime Minister Law. The chapter deals with the Israeli public's recognition of the preferences for change in political rules. It will focus on the process by which preferences have been formulated since the 1970s. It will show that, due to deep rifts within Israeli society, inadvertently supported by its institutional structure, the government could neither properly attend to institutional problems nor formulate effective public policies. Because of the lack of long-term, coherent policies, the Israeli public adopted alternative political participation patterns that expressed the adoption of exogenous political rules. These patterns led the political system to modify policies according to the momentary whims of the Israeli public.

The formulation of institutional change will be addressed in light of the emergence of political entrepreneurs and player interactions. The chapter describes the beginnings of the Constitutional Reform Movement, with the emergence of Uriel Reichmann and Amnon Rubinstein as salient political entrepreneurs and, at a later stage, Uriel Lynn, David Libai and Yoash Tsiddon in supporting roles. These entrepreneurs identified the problem, defined it and saw passage of a constitution as the solution. As the process developed, they shifted to the issue of direct election of the prime minister, a more attainable structural and process reform.

In the second section of the chapter, the definition and development of fundamental formal change is examined through the history of the Direct Election of the Prime Minister Law. The law will be analyzed according to four levels previously enumerated.

The *fourth chapter* will make use of an institutional theory to explain passage of the law's amendment in 2001, commonly known as Nullification of Direct Election of the Prime Minister Law. The chapter focuses on the public's expectations for change after the late Prime Minister Yitzhak Rabin took office. It also examines the learning process during which the public began to realize that the direct election law was not solving the problem of Israeli government instability. This feeling partially resulted from Benjamin Netanyahu's difficulties in forming a coalition and his inability to govern in light of the actions taken by Knesset members following the law's inauguration.

The beginning of this learning process was characterized by the emergence of additional political entrepreneurs: Yossi Beilin, Arye

Carmon, Uzi Landau and Moshe Shahal. These entrepreneurs redefined the problem and looked to the law's amendment as the solution. Their emergence and actions will be analyzed with the help of several parameters, including moral and political perceptions, maximization of power and motives of personal prestige, affiliation with particular political interest groups and professions, past experience and learning, manipulation of crises and changes in the public's beliefs and preferences.

Following this analysis, the chapter then defines and develops a model for fundamental formal institutional change as demonstrated by the repeal of the Direct Election of the Prime Minister Law. The analysis will again focus on the actions of players such as politicians, bureaucrats, citizens' groups and special-interest groups with respect to how they used their electoral capital to maximize their benefits under the given circumstances. The direct-election law's repeal will also be analyzed according to the four levels.

*Chapters three and four* demonstrate the added value of theoretical analysis and the model. The chapters illustrate how the model allows us to approach an issue in a clear, organized way. It also allows us to explain the logic underlying the behavior of political players. At this level, the model contributes to our understanding of the sociopolitical system, while explaining past processes and predicting future trends.

The *fifth chapter* examines the four comparative case studies of the acceptance of changed formal political rules: those of Argentina in 1993 and 1997, Italy in 1993, and New Zealand in 1993. The findings of the analysis are then compared to the Israeli case. Finally, the *sixth chapter* draws conclusions regarding the suggested structural and procedural models.

# CHAPTER TWO

## *Institutional Change as an Interaction between Political and Social Players—The Role of Political Entrepreneurs*

This chapter surveys the literature relevant to our investigation of institutional change processes, presents the book's main claims and develops a procedural model to analyze formal institutional change. This model will be of special use to us especially when analyzing cases pertaining to the design and ultimate repeal of Israel's law providing for the direct election of the prime minister.

In the first part of this chapter, we present the major tenets of institutional theory, including its sociological facets as well as those flowing from social choice theory. At the start, we should point to the comparative lack of analysis regarding political strategies, political entrepreneurs and social-structural patterns of institutional change, noting as well as the relative dearth of studies about the stability of change. The second part of the chapter elaborates the claims that underpin the book's central thesis. To support our thesis, we present a procedural, multivariate model explaining the process of designing and implementing institutional change by means of political rule-making. The model utilizes social choice theory to analyze how political rules are made by combining two factors: the level of economic and political stability and the type of political culture, characterized by public attitudes to democratic norms. These variables enable us to develop a bivariate scale for the measurement and analysis of the structural conditions that influence the range of institutional behavior and thus the stability of institutional change. These conditions are indispensable for the design of an institutional change process as they constitute the network of coercions and reinforcements that affect the players' behavior in the political sphere. Given the specific structural and cultural conditions, the proposed procedural model stresses two stages in the analysis of political rules and their reform. The first focuses on the social need for institutional change together with the rise of political entrepreneurs; the second examines the interactions between players as elements among the structural and cultural conditions.

## 2.1 Institutional Theory

The book's conceptual foundations rest on Institutional Theory, a unique approach to the study of social, economic and political phenomena. As a distinctive perspective on research, Institutional Theory has penetrated several disciplines, including economics, organizational theory, political science, history, sociology and social choice. Within each field, different aspects of the creation and/or dissolution of organizations are stressed, whether—micro, macro, cognitive, or normative.

The referents of the concept "institution" vary by the given field and its methodologies. For instance, according to sociologists, an institutional is a pattern of conduct, i.e., part of ordinary life, so habitual that its structure and process remain unquestioned (taken for granted).[1] Scholars of political economy, however, define institutions as interactions between individuals governed by rules that allow the players to profit from cooperation.[2] These two variants of institutional theory—the sociological and the political-economic (specifically, social choice theory)—are most pertinent to the issues examined here.

### *Institutional Theory as a Sociology of Organizations*

Institutional theory represents a renaissance in sociology, born of the scholarly reaction to ideas of political collectivism and economic behavior as the straightforward sum of individual choices, treated as a variant of individual property rights in isolation from the behavior's social, political and economic context. Traditional sociology viewed institutions as limiting the ability of actors to behavior according to their individual interests.[3] It regarded institutional change as a local or unique occurrence, initiated by macro-level interactions.[4]

In the 1970s, a new branch of research called the neo-institutional approach began to develop. According to this approach, the environment's effect on organizations and their structure is more complex than previously believed, exerting a more direct influence on the actions and thoughts of organizational actors.[5] Institutionalization came to be viewed as a more strictly cognitive process, taking place on interorganizational and sectoral levels.[6]

Yet, according to Jeffrey Alexander (1987), the transition from the traditional institutional to the neo-institutional approach continued to lack multidimensional depth. Tom R. Burns and Helena Flam (1987) argue that institutions are first and foremost products of human behavior, meaning that rules are to be understood as the products of conflict. In a similar vein, Paul J. DiMaggio and Walter W. Powell (1991) claim that motives of power and interest have received insufficient attention in neo-institutional sociology. They note that little attention has been paid to the question: "How do key workers (actors or players) preserve their dominance or respond to threats in times of crisis or instability?" The way in which gifted entrepreneurs implement multi-institutional strategy has also been neglected.[7]

This book continues this critical institutional stance by attempting to combine political strategies and social-structural patterns to explain institutional change.[8] It stresses the role of political behavior and coping strategies for understanding how formal institutional changes are designed and implemented. By doing so, it turns its analytic lens toward the factors that determine the distribution of power within institutions as well as the organizational strategies adopted by political entrepreneurs to advance their own interests.

## *Institutional Theory in the Study of Social Choice*

As part of their effort to understand social phenomena, political-economists (i.e., scholars who subscribe to the notion of rational choice) offer several definitions for the structured interactions maintained between individuals.[9] According to Jack Knight (1995), institutions are constructed by rules that design social interactions in a way that enables the players to profit from cooperation. Douglas North (1995), who defines institutions as limitations imposed upon human interactions further differentiates between formal rules (constitutions, laws, accepted court rulings, regulations) and informal ones (conventions, norms, codes of behavior). This book deals with the design and determination of formal rules of the game and uses informal rules as variables explaining that institutional change.

The social choice literature, which analyses of the rules of the institutional game, differentiates between policy regulations and political rules. Policy regulations are rules that order or control everyday life. Political rules are rules that define the framework of political discussion, meaning decision-making procedures; these rules consequently define how policy regulations can be changed.[10] Here, we focus on rules of the political type.

The rational-choice literature encompasses a number of theories of institutional change. All begin with the initial supposition that social players are interested in achieving optimal results at minimal cost. The analytic tradition that began with the written works of Ronald Coase (1937, 1960) and continued with Oliver E. Williamson (1975, 1985) took a turn in the writings of economic historians such as Douglass C. North (1981); scholars of law and economics such as Richard Posner (1981); game theorists such as Andrew Schotter (1981); and organizational economists including Alchian, Armen and Harold Demsetz (1972); Grossman, Sanford and Oliver Hart (1987); as well as Richard R. Nelson and Sidney Winter (1982). They all met under the rubric of neo-institutional economy theory. The neo-institutional approach thus added a measure of empirical realism to accepted micro-economic assumptions by recognizing that individual attempts to maximize profit are realized within a constant set of limitations (or institutional priorities). In addition, actors are hampered in their efforts by their limited information and the difficulty of making and later enforcing social institutions.

The neo-institutional, social choice literature has proposed several theories regarding the emergence of social institutions. Throughout them all, rule design and change reflect complex interactions among numerous players, all of whom understand the importance of following stable, elemental rules. Long-term time-preference considerations therefore tend to guide the players in constructing those rules. An additional common claim is that institutions appear in society as a result of the interactions between players. To explain the rules constructed—or the solutions found that maintain the respective interactions—neo-institutionals turn to the economic concept of equilibrium. Each equilibrium achieved constitutes a solution to one type of interaction or social issue, and the players should be able to identify a general equilibrium.[11]

It was Terry Moe (1987) who later criticized the social choice institutional approach for its emphasis on the formal mechanism of legislation and regulation as the primary factors structuring political and social behavior. According to Moe, social choice ignores the informal, dynamic aspect of institutions. He stresses the influence of informal norms on those interactions that lead to political rule change.[12] The sociologists Powell and DiMaggio (1991: 6) concur with Moe: "While some concern is evidenced for how institutions emerge, most of the analyses treat rules and procedures as exogenous determinants of political behavior." This book will attempt to compensate for this deficiency by trying to combine informal norms rooted in a given democratic society with structural issues, i.e., economic and political stability, all of which affect the ability of political actors to choose a certain path of political behavior.

The institutional theorist most pertinent to the issues to be discussed here is Douglas North. According to North (1995), institutional analysis is a confusing undertaking due to the vagueness of the concepts used. He claims that theories regarding institutional changes will be impossible to develop as long as the players and the rules of the game are analytically combined. Individuals, as actors, inherently have the ability, especially as members of an organization, to make decisions that can change the rules of the game, that is, adopt new informal limitations either suddenly or gradually. Therefore, the key to understanding institutional development and change is the behavior of individuals within organizations.

North adds that institutions, as the most taken-for-granted sociocultural entities, affect the power of those interested in implementing change. Neo-classical theory, he continues, ignores the micro-macro interface of behavior, that is, the factors that influence the perception of individuals. This lacuna manifests itself in the assumption that rational human beings indeed know what they are doing as well as what they want. North claims that this assumption is incorrect as it fails to acknowledge the fact that for most of the people belonging to organizations, the information at their disposal is incomplete because the distribution of information is structurally determined. Furthermore, most changes are supplemental; Yesterday's choices are at most today's starting point. This, according to North, explains why revolutions are rare. Even when they take place, time eventually shows that most revolutions are not total transformations of the sociopolitical reality. Not to be neglected is the fact that the informal limitations posed by deeply rooted cultural norms, conventions and codes contribute to the behavioral paths ultimately taken.

Placing itself within the tradition of neo-institutional analysis, this book examines general change in the institutional rules of the game (formal political rules) from the perspective of the individuals who contribute most crucially to the results. Such a perspective, as the preceding has shown, requires a methodology that considers the social, cultural and structural parameters that prevent creation of the behavioral vacuum previously assumed to frame behavior. In the following section, I therefore present the book's primary claims and describe the procedural model proposed to explain the design and implementation of institutional change.

## 2.2 A Procedural Model for Formal Institutional Change Analysis

This chapter presents a procedural model for the design and determination of formal institutional change (rules of the political game) The model hereby stresses informal rules that affect the time preference of those individuals who eventually lead to the equilibrium stated in formal, stable rules of the political game.

We begin with a consideration of the two factors proposed to explain the formation and stability of such an institutional change:

1. The level of economic and political stability.
2. The character of the political culture, which is affected by the attitude of the civilians in a given society toward democratic norms.

A high level of political and economic instability as well as weak democratic norms lead to the enforcement of short-term considerations among the agents of change. The model assumes that the time frame of the players affects the stability of the change, the breadth of its implications, and the strength of the efforts to alter it. The greater the initial political-economic instability and the more procedural the democratic perception, the less stable the institutional change will be.

*Level of Economic Stability* refers to people's perceptions of the government's ability to provide economic public goods such as jobs and an improved standard of living (reduction of poverty). We use measures such as the unemployment rate, poverty forecasts, size of mortgages and frequency of changes in government policy. These variables will be analyzed according to how well they comply with predetermined estimates. Other measures to be examined include secondary variables such as the Arian and Nachmias (2003) Democracy Index and the Gastil (1990) Freedom Index, which include the level of political-economic stability.

*Level of Political Stability* refers to people's perceptions of the government's ability to provide public services based on current rules of the

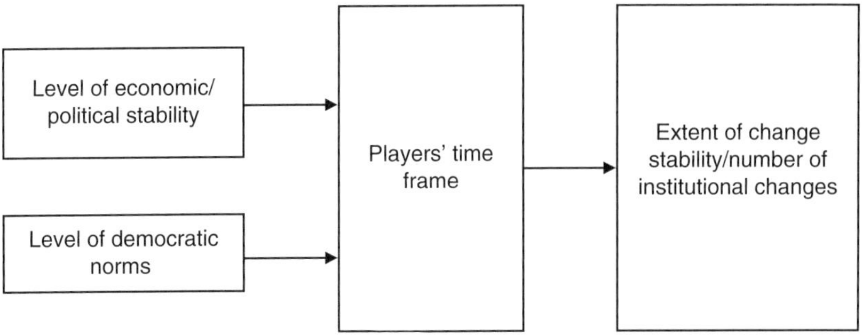


**Figure 2.1** Institutional Change Stability

political game. The measures used are: number of electoral changes in a given election both within political units and between them, the number and size of new parties, the length of governmental or parliamentary office and the frequency of changes in political appointment procedures, such as the process for appointing members of parliament to particular posts. This factor is also analyzed according to the measures cited for the assessment of economic stability.

*Level of Democratic Norms* refers to people's perceptions of the democratic system. Do democratic values constitute the core beliefs regarding the nature of society (essential democracy) or are they considered only as tools for the maximization of other values or interests (procedural democracy)?[13] According to De Haan and Clemens (1995), a country is democratic if there is considerable competition between individuals and organized groups for election and/or appointment to government office. For a nation to be democratic, competition must be free of violence, all sizeable groups can compete, and those political and civil liberties that ensure political participation and competition are embraced. By civil rights we mean that individual rights, such as freedom of the press and the right to organize and demonstrate, are freely exhibited. In democratic societies, these perceptions, developed over time, represent the consensus.[14] Gastil (1990) rates political rights, defined as the extent to which an individual is allowed to participate in or control the decisions made by government policy-makers, from 1 (high) to 7 (low). In order to examine this factor, we again rely on the democracy measure (Arian and Nachmias, 2003) and the freedom measure.[15]

*Players' Time Frame* refers to the players' time frames variances from short term at one end of the scale to long term at the opposite end of the scale. Short-term time frames are associated with the immediate maximization of prestige as well as the probability of being elected. Long-term time frames are associated with intensive discussions, public hearings, and collaboration of interest groups.

By "players" we mean organized or ad hoc interest groups, politicians, and bureaucrats. Political entrepreneurs or change agents can emerge from any of these categories. The level of political-economic stability and the degree of internalization of democratic norms affect an entrepreneur's time frame. Given these initial conditions, the design of an institutional change evolves in two phases. In the *first phase,* the reasons for an institutional change take form. Two factors are stressed in this regard: (1) The change agent's sense of the need to change political rules as a necessary precondition for initiating institutional change design; and (2) The political entrepreneurs who identify the need for a political rule change and their benefits from the change. In the *second phase*, we examine the character and design of basic, formal institutional change. The analysis stresses the actions of various players—politicians, bureaucrats, interest groups and the general public—meant to utilize implementation of the reform as electoral capital when striving to maximize their profit within the structural and social limitations.

The literature in this field posits a variety of structural factors, all of which explain the evolution of what I see as two key issues—*the level of economic and political instability* and *the degree of internalization of democratic norms.* For example, the literature indicates that under certain conditions, systemic centrality can explain the formation of political and economic instability (Arian, Nachmias & Amir, 2003).

Democratic systems vary in their level of systemic centrality (Arian & Nachmias, 2003). Centrality is characterized by the existence of rules that grant power and control to a certain group or groups in the state's decision-making arenas, such as the economic and the political system. Centrality is reflected in the ability to enforce public policy in different spheres. Such powers of enforcement imply the ability to intervene in the decisions made by the lower ranks on the one hand, and the relative immunity from the intervention of others on the other hand. Intervention has enforcement costs, while enforcement has influence costs[16] even if the centralized government is not corrupt and is sufficiently wise not to intervene without a good reason. Under the rubric "influence costs" we include the costs incurred by groups and individuals when attempting to influence decision makers as well as the time and effort decision makers devote to repelling these attempts, all of which lead to inefficient decisions. Paul Milgrom and John Roberts (1990) claim that the more centralized the system, the higher its influence costs, as it must counteract the dissatisfaction of most of its subordinates. Therefore, centrality leads to inefficient decisions in addition to the public's inability to systematically influence those decisions. If such a syndrome lasts long enough, it diminishes the government's ability to provide public services—nongovernability—with the resulting overload of public demands.[17] Demand overload, coupled with nongovernability, eventually creates the impression of political and economic instability. In cases where the public has yet to learn how to design definite beliefs for solving social problems,[18] instability can provoke uncertainty, a condition spurring change agents to focus on immediate policy results. The literature notes that such a learning process requires ingredients such as societal coherence, agreement and public readiness. In such a situation, risk-taking and long-range planning are viewed as unrealistic, a perspective that induces the players to focus on short-term considerations, maximize their immediate interests or initiate institutional change to resolve urgent economic, political and social crises.

In addition, as shown in Figure 2.1, the players' political culture and time frame are directly related. For instance, the more that democratic norms represent a society's core values, the more the populace tends to respect government, law and democratic rules. They will therefore perceive a change in the rules of the game as part of a long-term, legitimate process (fundamental democracy). However, if the society is characterized by an instrumental approach to democratic norms (procedural democracy), the players will act according to short-term considerations reflecting immediate interests and advocating immediate solutions even to complex problems. The resulting institutional change will then be open to manipulation by other immediate interests and problems.[19]

A Political Rule Stability is reflected in the extent of rule implementation and the attempts to change it. Therefore, the greater the initial political and economic stability and the more procedural the democratic perception, the less stable the formal institutional change will be.

In the early stages of institutional change, change agents try to propose political solutions to political and economic instability. Adam Przeworsky (1991) has noted, that due to the system's complexity, individuals living under democratic governments are often uncertain about the relationship between political rules and their societal outcomes. This ambiguity contributes to the rules' stability. However, as William Riker notes, this stability lasts only until beliefs about the need for change take hold. The link between the rules and the outcomes is made by political entrepreneurs who, as stated, define the problem and the solution.[20] From that moment on, institutional change transpires by means of interactions maintained between political players who, being impelled by short- or long-term considerations, operate according to procedural or fundamental democratic norms, respectively.

*To summarize*, the level of political and economic instability as well as the extent to which democratic norms have been internalized affect the time frame within which change agents are prone to act. Given these primary conditions, a formal institutional change design should be analyzed in two stages. The first involves the examination of the causes of institutional change; the second requires an examination of the ways in which the character of that change is determined. The *first stage* stresses the perception of the need for an institutional change as a necessary condition for the design of formal institutional change. This need is identified by political entrepreneurs who link public dissatisfaction with the specific change proposed as a solution. The formal endorsement of an institutional change is the product of complex interactions in which political entrepreneurs play a significant role.

The *second stage* analyzes the interactions between the affected constituencies. The outcome of the combined actions of these factors, at a given point in time, constitutes a formal institutional change. A detailed illustration of the process is found in Figure 2.2.

*The change agents' (political entrepreneurs) sense that there is a need for a change in political rules represents the primary condition for formal institutional change design.*

Movement towards change of formal institutional rules begins when the public senses that the political rules governing institutional behavior are no longer appropriate. Perceptions regarding the depth of instability have implications for development of an active movement toward change. This feeling generally comes about in the aftermath of a learning process during which the public comes to understand that political rules require transformation in order to solve social problems.[21] This learning process begins with attempts to formulate viable policy within the existing rules. When this fails due to, perhaps, political and social centrality, rule reform is perceived as an option. While initial suggestions may favor sweeping revisions, only carefully sculpted ideas ultimately lead to results. For example, in March 2006, a debate arose regarding revision of Israel's parliamentary system of government as an initial step in solving the country's social problems. However, the

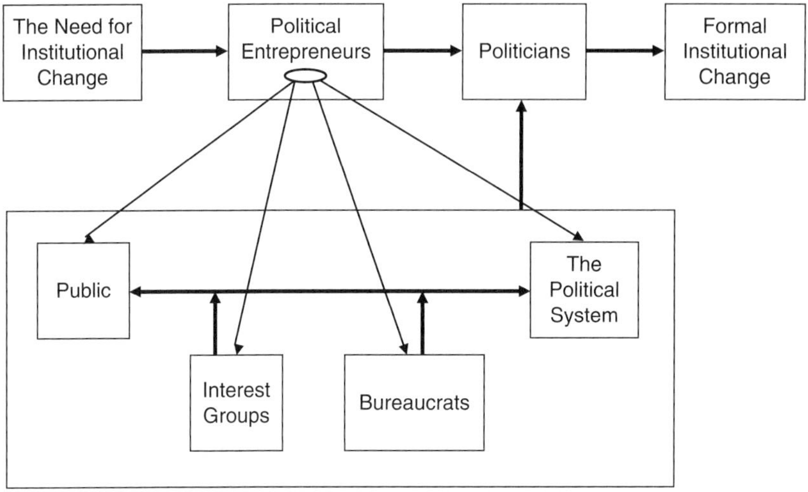


**Figure 2.2** Institutional Change of Formal Political Rules—Process

plethora of proposals presented demonstrated the public's confusion over the issue. No clearly articulated reform has yet to be offered.

## *Political Entrepreneurs*

A "political entrepreneur" is an individual or a group that attempts to alter the political context either through a change in policy or a change in the political rules of the game.[22] A political entrepreneur may come from outside the parliamentary system or from within it (e.g., a member of the parliament).[23] This definition conforms to Olson's (1965) definition of a "privileged group," composed of individuals willing to bear the costs of a societal action irrespective of the other individuals also interested in the outcomes of that action. In Albert Hirshmann's terms, a political entrepreneur is a rational individual who chooses the act of raising his voice instead of exiting the scene. To continue Hirshmann's argument in marketing terms, we might say that a political entrepreneur demonstrates significant product loyalty, the product in this case being the state.

This book stresses the salience of political entrepreneurs in political rule change. Although the public's belief in reform is crucial to initiation of the change process, it is the political entrepreneurs who link public dissatisfaction with the institutional solutions eventually proposed and implemented. In terms of social choice theory, this link introduces cost-benefit calculations into the equation, calculations that identify how much electoral capital can be gained for supporting institutional change. By electoral capital we mean the assets (image, real resources, group support) the entrepreneur might employ to maximize his benefits. In the case of politicians, these assets are clearly related to their electability. To illustrate, support of the legally mandated change in Israel's electoral system, including direct election of the prime minister, was considered electoral capital by some when the issue arose. According to this model, then, an entrepreneur promotes reform in part because the reform's supporters may back him politically or ideologically and/or his identification with the change (or the change itself) may enhance his public prestige.

We cannot, however, ensure that the institutional change proposed by the political entrepreneur will be viewed as electoral capital by other players. The political entrepreneur's ability to transform the idea of reform into electoral capital is related to his ability to spread the understanding that the change he proposes will maximize the other players' chances to be elected and/or enjoy increased prestige. Other societal and structural conditions, as we will demonstrate by means of the case studies, are part of the complex interactions conducted among the players while formulating an institutional change. It is by means of this process and environment that political entrepreneurs translate social problems into policy-related issues.

The discussion on political entrepreneurs is rooted in the literature on interest groups. David S. Truman's (1971) classic political approach posited that interest groups are born of social change attempts. They arise in the face of social injustices and consolidate in order to improve the situation. Olson's (1965) more economics-based approach argued that interest group recruitment is motivated by the quality of the public products offered as well as the promise of rewards to be gained in exchange for membership in the group. Robert Salisbury (1969) extends this economics-based approach when he introduces the concept of entrepreneurs into the political sphere for the first time. These individuals, Salisbury states (1969: 37) offer to sell a variety of commodities ranging from expertise to societal resources in the societal marketplace. Buyers purchase these commodities only if they are rewarded. Entrepreneurs thus make sure that the buyers' rewards are adequate to increase their own rewards.

Leaving the issue of interest group formation aside, this book emphasizes issues pertaining specifically to political entrepreneurs. The discussion will be conducted according to a number of parameters set out in detail in the following as well as in Figure 2.3. These variables have been noted briefly in the social and economic entrepreneurship literature but they are here linked to the political sphere for the first time. They are:

1. The entrepreneur's perception of political value.
2. The entrepreneur's motivation to maximize his power and personal prestige.
3. The entrepreneur's affiliation with his profession and politics.
4. The entrepreneur's past experience and participation in the learning process.
5. The entrepreneur's ability to identify and use crises to alter public beliefs and preferences.

Variables 1 to 4 explain the entrepreneur's behavior, his appearance on the political scene, his definition of the social problem, his view of institutional change as a social problem-solving mechanism and the translation of social problems into issues to be resolved on the policy level.

## *Perception of Political Value*

The entrepreneur's perception of what comprises political value affects the way he chooses to define the social problem and its solution while affecting the strategy he will adopt to achieve his goal. I argue that structural as well as cultural conditions motivate political entrepreneurs

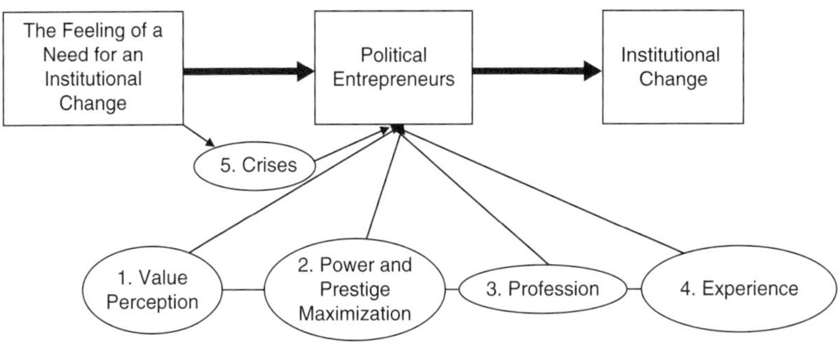


**Figure 2.3** Why Has Institutional Change Taken Place?

to promote institutional change. Such changes reflect the operative transformation of their fundamental ideology.[24]

### *Motivation to Maximize Power and Personal Prestige*

The motivation to maximize one's power and personal prestige is a personality trait that influences the entrepreneur's behavior and explains why he or she would become involved in political activities that do not yield immediate economic benefits but exhibit the potential to do so in the long run. The accompanying prestige may help the political entrepreneur promote his or her goals in the interim.

### *The Entrepreneur's Affiliation with his Profession*

The political entrepreneur's professional affiliation provides him entry into a larger group of people, sharing the same profession and sometime same ideas and way of thinking. Normally professional groups are led by senior members whose ideas and values are adopted by the members of the profession.[25]

### *The Entrepreneur's Past Experience and Previous Learning*

Another variable is the entrepreneur's experience, gained from his own and others' interactions with interest groups over the promotion of various initiatives. Such experience affects the complex considerations of entering into the process of institutional change design. Learning from the successes and failures of themselves and others guides the strategies that political entrepreneurs later adopt. For example, "Gush Emunim," an Israeli political movement, succeeded in encouraging Jewish settlements through lobbying, demonstrations and creating a new reality by establishing facts on the ground. This mode of behavior influenced later interest groups and political entrepreneurs to adopt this same strategy.[26]

### *Entrepreneurs' Ability to Identify and Use Crises to Alter Public Beliefs and Preferences*

The fifth variable refers to the way in which political entrepreneurs affect public attitudes to institutional change by using social crises to promote change, which is meant to be translated into electoral capital.

Political entrepreneurs thus function as essential factors linking public preferences to institutional change, the outcomes of which they harvest for their own advantage.[27]

According to Nisbet (1966: 96), political entrepreneurs label the social situation as intolerable (i.e., as a crisis) and as one that requires collective action to ameliorate its negative effects. According to Berger (1969: 23–24), a crisis is created when there is a disjunction, even if temporary, between the value system (the ideal) and the social system (the real), due to the gap between expectations and reality. This disjunction gives rise to social movements whose goal is to cope with the crisis-engendered chaos.

Based on our knowledge of the character of social problems, an effective procedure to define social problems involves two main phases. First, the entrepreneur must establish that the present situation is threatening, dysfunctional, and intolerable. To accomplish this goal, the entrepreneur must raise the public's consciousness about the issue's importance and transform it into a major topic of public debate.[28] Second, the entrepreneur must offer a solution for the problem,[29] which he proposes as an alternative for the current, detrimental policy. For these steps to be effective, the problem must not be perceived as a necessary evil but as a policy failure to be corrected. That is, the entrepreneur is to adopt a strategy translating the social problem into a policy problem capable of resolution through changes in the political-bureaucratic system.[30]

According to Lindblom (1959), political entrepreneurs prefer promoting policies within the existing framework of rules to changing the system[31] because the cost of the latter is greater than the cost of acting within the existing system. These lower costs reflect the ease with which political entrepreneurs can expose problematic issues within existing social system as a precondition to spurring collective action.[32]

After political entrepreneurs complete this process, the emphasis shifts to the interactions between the other players, on which adoption of the proposed solution depends.

### *Institutional Change Arising from Interactions between Players*

The second phase of the analysis is an examination of the character and design of formal institutional change with an emphasis on the role of these players: politicians, bureaucrats (state employees), interest groups and the political entrepreneurs who use the solution as one form of electoral capital within existing structural and cultural limitations. The proposed model is predicated on studies of the actions and motivations of the numerous players in the political game. The interaction among them based on their specific actions and motivations is the key to understanding the design of political rules.[33] We thus examine the determination and design of political rules from a perspective broader than usually taken; that is, we consider individual, structural and cultural elements in the belief that structural-cultural factors, together with the involvement of the players at a given moment in time, are the main factors necessary for the change of political rules in a democratic system. The analysis also emphasizes the role of political entrepreneurs in overcoming public inertia. Political entrepreneurs generally begin their campaigns by focusing on four segments of the population: politicians, bureaucrats, interest groups and groups of independent civilians, unidentified with any of the three previous groups. The exact nature of the change reflects the power relationships and interests of these four segments and their positions within the structural-cultural framework. We therefore analyze the way in which the interactions—conceived as power relationships—maintained between these factors affect the type of the change introduced.

To support my analysis, I rely on findings obtained from studies on economic entrepreneurship, for the purpose of differentiating between the characteristics of political entrepreneurship and economic entrepreneurs, with special emphasis placed on the differences of the products they each promote. Economic entrepreneurship studies stress personality, ambition, control, autonomy, risk-taking tendencies, ambiguity tolerance, motivation, and vision as well as the strategies conceived and the environment's receptivity to his initiatives.[34]

An additional factor is the political entrepreneur's interactions with his reference group and his environment. Such interactions may include collective action to solve a problem common to the group's members, striving for cooperation between group members and internalization of the change objective, overcoming the gaps in interests between the leader and the group while stressing the entrepreneur's organizing ability, the change's benefits to the group and the rewards of leadership.[35] I likewise draw on findings from social entrepreneurship research that point to the need to activate the public, overcome the government's passive behavior, and use the media and other social resources, as well as definition of the problem.[36]

The character and design of formal institutional change is presented in the following part on four levels, each of which refers to the relevant interactions between the players when designing the change along with the variables that explain the choice of strategies. The *first level* analyzes the actions of the political entrepreneurs with respect to their reference group and the public. The analysis includes a detailed account of the resources and strategies used to recruit public support. The *second level* analyzes the actions taken by political entrepreneurs as they interact with different interest groups and policy-making politicians. The *third level* analyzes the interactions among politicians and between politicians and parliament. On the *fourth and final level*, we discuss the involvement of the bureaucratic players in the process. We include administrative officials at this point because, due to their different interests and positions in the government bureaucracy, they can influence the content and implementation of politician-preferred policy.

### *Level 1: Political Entrepreneurs, Reference Groups and the Public*

Interaction on this level focuses on two features: initial resources and the use of various strategies for recruiting public support.

#### Initial Resource Recruitment

Resource recruitment is crucial whether the entrepreneur comes from outside or inside the parliamentary system. The recruitment strategy adopted is a function of how broadly based the political entrepreneur views the public's involvement in the process. This part of the model, presented in Figure 2.4, stresses the relationship between the entrepreneur, his reference group (i.e., his profession, tribe, ethnic group) and monetary recruitment.

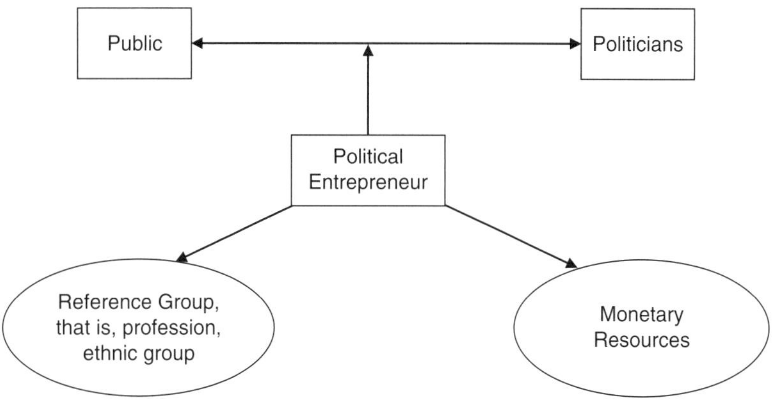


**Figure 2.4** The Entrepreneur and Initial Resource Recruitment

## The Entrepreneur and the Group

According to the literature, the entrepreneur has to approach the public in order to create a social movement. His role is colored by *the different interests separating him and the group's members.* This difference allows two types of players to share the cost of the bargain yet reap sufficient benefits to keep each satisfied.[37] *The entrepreneur's role is defined as coordination between group members, establishment of an organization, recruitment of resources and application of pressure on the government* for the purpose of achieving acceptance of the policy (or *public product*)[38] the group is interested in. If the entrepreneur has power, prestige and (perhaps) a political career, group members enjoy both personal and collective benefits that he or she can provide. The entrepreneur is usually the person who has the time to organize and possesses the necessary verbal and technical skills, personality and access to the media and government clerks. These characteristics led Yael Ishay (1987) to classify entrepreneurial leaders into four categories: the *competitive leader*—for whom the organization's management functions as a political start-up, the *observant leader*—who holds organizational as well as professional roles, the *involved leader*—who receives connections to government officials and business elite, and the *reputational leader*—who acts on the basis of his authority, vision or idea,[39] sense of belonging and social status.

Occasionally, a crisis forces the political entrepreneur to begin a hiatus or period of retreat. During this phase, the entrepreneur reappraises the situation, examines the gaps between the desired outcomes and the existing situation as well as the gap between him and the other group members. *This requires cultivating his relationship with his group and being attentive to their wishes.* The entrepreneur has to be relatively certain that he can deliver the desired policy at a level satisfactory to his group[40] so that they will not be disappointed.[41]

The literature indicates that in most cases, interactions create the collective awareness (identity) that leads to political activity.[42] Marketing activities, however, although needed to promote the project, detract from the time spent forging a collective identity within the group. Following Yael Ishay's notion on interest group, we can say that a political entrepreneur who cannot maintain a collective identity is bound to fail. The expected outcome in such cases is withdrawal of activists and decreasing donations. Such cases can emerge when *the entrepreneur initiates marketing strategies deemphasizing the learning and internalization* experienced by the group members in the course of their recurring interactions.[43]

An interest group's creation is subject to the social problem as well as its solution as defined by the entrepreneur. The entrepreneur must convince the public (as well as politicians and media agents) that his proposed solution is appropriate and acceptable. A well-known, related strategy is that which springs from the *entrepreneur's personality and public persona*. His or her reference group is usually composed of people who have impact on the decisionmakers even when group members do not hold official political or administrative positions. Olson (1965) locates the political entrepreneur within the "privileged group," composed of individuals willing to bear the costs of social action irrespective of the positions taken by other individuals, also interested in the action's outcomes. According to Olson, the uniqueness of an interest group as compared to a general interest or participatory group lies in the fact that fewer resources are required for its integration. Here, we also distinguish between reference groups and privileged groups.

### Recruitment of Profession Reference Groups

Profession is defined as an insulated community where the members' occupation grants them social prestige and full autonomy. The public grants this group autonomy because it acknowledges the group's immense specialized knowledge and the subsequent monopoly it exercises over the practices related to that knowledge.[44] The more prestigious a certain profession is in the eyes of the public, the more difficult it will be for the political entrepreneur to change to its organizational features.[45]

Profession groups are recruited in order to maximize public resources. Association with a profession lends an aura of legitimacy to the political entrepreneur's activities by attesting to the appropriateness of the offered solution as well as his "stalwart" character. The search for legitimacy requires, *in addition to the recruitment of profession, the recruitment of similar interest groups*, such as parliament members, government officials and business elites. *Failure to secure the support of profession and other key elites has costs* in the form of potential criticism as well as opposition. According to Ishay (1987), finding the right partners or allies for the struggle and avoiding conflict with other groups are essential for the entrepreneur's success.

### Raising Financial Resources

Recruitment of the necessary professional and other constituencies requires massive financial resources. The entrepreneur, however, has to take into account the input of the businessman. Advertising and marketing the entrepreneur's ideas and hiring public-relations professionals, lobbyists and advertisers, are very costly. Therefore, joining forces with businesspeople is one of the political entrepreneur's preferred strategies.

Olson (1965) discusses the role of a by-product supplement as an additional channel for fundraising and recruiting political support. In this scenario, the entrepreneur uses a specific by-product to gain the cooperation of group members. The group members receive the by-product if they cooperate. For example, a performance of a famous artist in a political demonstration attracts the audience. This reward is meant to overcome the problems of free riders and of collective action.

Once the entrepreneur has secured the needed funds, he can begin recruiting broader public support, necessary to upgrade his or her chances to win the support of politicians for his idea. The greater the public support attracted by the entrepreneur, the more readily will policy-makers accept his solutions to the crisis because they will be viewed as reflecting the electorate's desires and needs.[46]

### Strategies for Recruiting Public Support

In democratic governments, public support must be recruited if attempts at formal institutional change are to be effective. Political entrepreneurs must therefore be open to adopting different recruitment strategies, each attuned to the individual character of each population segment. These strategies are, of course, geared to achieving what we have set as their ultimate goals: change in policy rules (a less costly objective) or a change of political rules (a more costly objective). As mentioned earlier, according to the literature, *the entrepreneur is expected to choose the less costly objective—promoting policy change—rather than the more costly objective of systemic transformation.* Entrepreneurs may sometimes be forced to initiate changes in political rules as a step toward realizing their goals, but their ultimate intention remains the change of policy rules. Figure 2.5 illustrates how political entrepreneur employ strategies to garner public support.

### The Media

Few would question the role of the media in molding public opinion and activating collective action, in motivating passive spectators to become active combatants. The media not only records the public's desire for change, it also keeps the social problem at the forefront of public attention. To be successful in transmitting their agenda, political entrepreneurs must learn to manipulate as well as to work with the

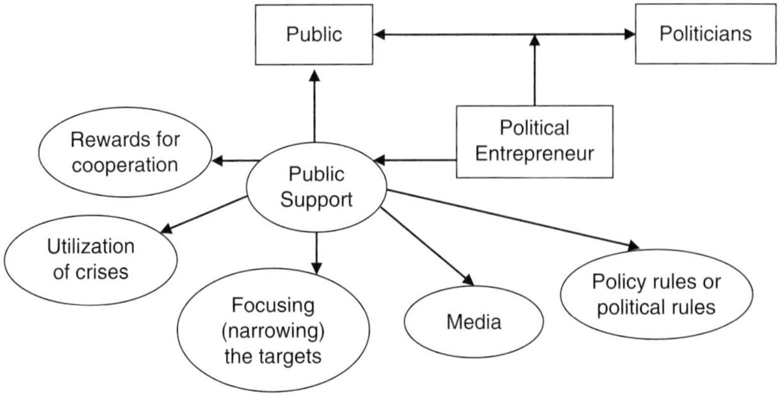


**Figure 2.5** The Political Entrepreneur and Public Support Recruitment Strategies

media.[47] Timing, which is crucial for these functions to be fulfilled, is determined by a series of factors.[48]

Focusing (Narrowing) the Targets

One important factor involves attracting the public's attention to the entrepreneur's objective, thus, during the initial stage of the campaign, a broader target is chosen so as to attract the broadest range of opinion. However, a broader target is hard to achieve since it needs a lot of support and efforts in overcoming political and cultural barriers. More often in the final stage a less costly preferred strategy is to redefine the target as a more feasible one, for example, moving from electoral change to voters' threshold (required to win a seat). It is worth noting that subtle types of persuasion are more successful when public opinion is diffuse. Blurring of differences between preferences creates an easy atmosphere[49] for political entrepreneurs to promote institutional changes.

Utilization of Crises

The entrepreneurs must be adept at using externally caused crises to project their views among the public. Consider terrorist bombings or other disasters; the public usually sees these events as indicating that the security measures currently in place are inadequate to protect them. The ensuing crisis of faith in the system leads to a decline in public trust, a situation that political entrepreneurs can take advantage of at low cost to them even though it holds out the prospect of great political rewards. At the same time, political entrepreneurs must be prepared to confront criticism coming from politicians or journalists regarding their exposure of the problem, which is framed as exacerbating public anxiety.

### Incentives for Cooperation

In order to encourage collective action on an issue, the entrepreneur must enlist the cooperation of group members, even those who may be "along just for the ride."[50] To accomplish this goal, entrepreneurs use a series of incentives—such as hiring popular bands to perform during political gatherings—to secure first their attention and then their cooperation.[51] Among the tools in the political entrepreneur's arsenal at this stage are distributions of books and soccer tickets and legal or other counseling.

In this section we have dealt mainly with the recruitment of public support. In the next, we examine the implementation of these practices when dealing with political decision makers.

## *Level 2: Entrepreneurs, Interest Groups and Political Decisionmakers*

Here we analyze the activities of political entrepreneurs when interacting with interest groups and political policy-makers. One key issue of concern is the contrast in time frame between lobbyists and legislative members, with the latter's perspectives falling within a shorter time frame than that of the former. Another is the need for cooperation between political entrepreneurs outside the system and those within it. Illustrations will be taken from the Israeli context. We will look at a number of central players such as heads of blocs, political parties and chairmen of parliamentary committees (especially the Constitution, Law and Legislation Committees) that play a central role in the design and change of formal rules.

### The Political Time Frame: Short-term Considerations

When playing any political game or analyzing any political process, the players' time frame acts as a significant variable for understanding the interactions between political entrepreneurs, interest groups and politicians (like other decisionmakers). Politicians generally operate under election-date constraints; they therefore entertain primarily short-term considerations.[52] The public, however, works within a longer time frame because it needs time to formulate a clear mental picture of the problem and the solution offered by the entrepreneur. During this interim, other players, especially politicians, will attempt to create a smoke screen around the problem in order to promote their own short-term interests in the guise of solutions.

Political Entrepreneurs

The practice of political entrepreneurship is similar to that of lobbyists, individuals who represent political interest groups. To promote their agendas in the corridors of the parliament as elsewhere, lobbyists keep themselves informed about the current status of issues relevant to employers. The effectiveness of their activity depends upon a well-planned strategy, determined well in advance of its execution and often involving some more-or-less provocative action designed to gain public attention and news coverage. Like lobbyists, political entrepreneurs cultivate strong relationships with the press. Again like lobbyists, political entrepreneurs' success depends on their being up-to-date about everything pertaining to their change objectives. This requires them to maintain a network of contacts with the media to obtain confidential information but also to encourage news coverage of incidents beneficial to their cause.[53]

Political entrepreneurs use tactics similar to those employed by lobbyists to enhance their chances of success while cementing loyalties and past friendships.[54] They appeal directly to members of parliament and institutional administrators and representatives, present appeals and petitions to the courts, and organization demonstrations and strikes.[55] Political entrepreneurs positioned outside the formal structure of the government also cooperate with lobbyists, who work within legislative corridors. Cooperation between them is almost natural, as they often share a profession and, in many cases, common interests[56] as well as strategies, including forging relationships with politicians and other policy-makers for the purpose of increasing their mentors' electoral capital.[57]

In the following discussion on Level 3, we explore how the model demonstrates the phase where the political entrepreneur accomplishes his or her goal: the passage of a formal institutional change proposal in parliament. This same model is later applied to our cases. Here, we continue to use the Israeli case for illustrative purposes.

### *Level 3: Political Entrepreneurs and Legislative Bodies*

After political entrepreneurs have gathered sufficient public support and lobbied politicians to the point where they are ready to translate the entrepreneurs' agenda into legislative proposals comes the stage of actual passage of the change-oriented law. All procedural rule reforms, if they require legislative backing for their implementation in the form of law, must pass through a series of steps, including review by parliamentary committees. Each of these bodies has its own interests, meaning that to gain passage, a proposal must comply with the political needs of the majority of politicians making up these committees and forums. Structural limitations as well as coalitional considerations therefore force the political entrepreneur to act in sometimes contradictory ways in order to pass all these hurdles.[58]

This setup exposes the entrepreneur to major political players (faction or bloc leaders in party institutions and chairmen of parliamentary committees) determining legislative conduct and, more importantly, agendas. They represent the procedural and structural barriers that interfere with the entrepreneur's achieve change objectives.[59] For instance, a committee chairman has a pivotal role in determining the committee agendas or which proposal is discussed first and how much.[60] Thus, if a chairman is interested in the entrepreneur's proposal, it has a better chance of being approved in the committee and, eventually, in parliament. Political entrepreneurs therefore direct much of their pressure tactics at committee chairmen. If the entrepreneurs are successful, their proposal's progress toward passage may be easier. If not, the entrepreneur will be forced to use the other resources to which he has access in order to overcome their opposition.

Turning to the executive branch, presidents and prime ministers are the main players in their respective political systems because of their political status as well as veto rights.[61] Political parties are also important players here as well as in the legislative arena, especially in party systems where small-group party members elect the members of the parliament. In this case the political entrepreneurs will try to influence this group in order to gain the support of the parliament members.[62]

Given the structural and objective conditions contributing to political players' short-term considerations, we should expect that any solution translated into a legislative proposal will constitute a compromise.[63]

I now turn to an analysis of the place of the bureaucratic players in the political entrepreneur's sphere of activity as a change agent.

### *Level 4: Bureaucratic Activity as a Function of Structural and Cultural Constraints*

Because of their unique interests, including protecting themselves from being targets in formal institutional change programs, bureaucratic players place special types of obstacles before the political entrepreneur. In the context of procedural (and sometimes political) rule-making, this conflict involves the state workers on the one hand and the Supreme Court on the other.

Major players in the bureaucracy related to the presentation of procedural rules are the legal advisors and secretaries of the administrative agencies who usually authorize the various legal proposals for presentation to the parliament.[64]

Israel's election system reforms affected mainly the electoral impact of various groups in the population; the reforms were not meant to affect the authority of officials working in the public administration. However, were a legislative proposal to be raised with the intent of decentralizing administrative authority for the benefit of outside interests, bureaucrats would strongly oppose. Such a reform would, obviously, undermine the reason for being for the administrators and their agencies within the structure of democratic government.

Social choice theory proposes a variety of models that maintain that the interactions between politicians and the bureaucrats who implement policy are subject to built-in conflict.[65] A political entrepreneur needs to understand the balance and relations between these two players as if he wishes to gain their support for his political change.

In a pioneering study, Niskanen (1971) found that bureaucrats are motivated first and foremost by the desire to maximize their office's budget as a way of increasing their power and indirectly maximizing the rewards they receive. Niskanen also claims that, in some cases, bureaucrats indeed achieve this end. Other studies show that the situation is more complex because politicians adopt a variety of strategies to control bureaucrats.[66] Given this inherent conflict, which often results in bending public policy in favor of one of these structural interests, harm is inflicted on society.[67]

With respect to the Israeli reform—the subject of this book—the Supreme Court does appear to have played a significant part in the process. The judicial branch in Israel has the status of first among equals relative to the other branches of government. Thus, for example, it enjoys a substantial degree of independence from political influence. Judges on the Supreme Court are appointed by the Judicial Selection Committee, composed of representatives from all three branches of government, ensuring a professional and apolitical selection process. The Israeli Supreme Court serves a wide variety of functions. First of all, it is the highest court of appeals in the Israeli legal system. Furthermore, it is the first venue in which disputes between individuals and the State are heard. This second role has caused the Supreme Court to be viewed by the general public as the watchdog over the rule of law and the champion in the fight against corruption and the protection of human and civil rights. To reduce the heavy burden of fulfilling this role, a reform has been enacted in which cases brought by individuals against the state will now be heard first by lower courts.

This Israeli reform materialized in the creation of the institutional, normative political culture during the 1980s and especially the 1990s in which the Supreme Court had a central place in Israel's public life.[68] Elevation of the Supreme Court to a position higher than the legislative branch increased the political system's nongovernability and indirectly exacerbated the policy crises that led in turn to the application of the specific strategies employed by political entrepreneurs.[69]

## 2.3 The Book's Contributions to the Field

Israel repeatedly goes through a process of pondering the prospects of reform as a solution to its social and political ills. Most reforms do not reach the level of implementation; they are usually nipped in the bud by negligence or newer reform proposals. The theoretical and empirical examination of the reform process is especially important in Israel nowadays because, according to scholars and citizens, Israel lacks the appropriate political culture and suffers from nongovernability to a level that may pose a real threat to its stability.[70]

The book adopts hypotheses and concepts taken from the institutional literature to develop a procedural model for the analysis of formal political rule change in a democratic system. The analysis stresses the role of political entrepreneurs in interactions with the factors most influential for such reforms to be implemented in governmental institutions.

The research literature lacks empirical studies meant to investigate the stability of change in light of structural and social factors, including the players' time frames.[71] We attempt to fill this gap by extending current understandings in two areas. We explain how the actions taken by various players lead to formal institutional change, by means of a theoretical as well as empirical analysis.

When analyzing the design of formal institutional change, we adopt concepts taken from social choice theory. The resulting model is unique in that it describes a process that combines structural, cultural and individual factors in the study of institutional changes. The model allows us to locate the structural factors causing the deviation from the preferred change strategy applied by individuals, a direction of analysis never before applied in this context.

Another innovation is the approach applied, in which we employ institutions as dependent variables, contrary to the social choice tradition that stresses the role of institutions as explanatory variables, linking knowledge gaps and expectations. The studies that do treat institutions as explained variables usually focus on informal institutions, established as a result of a creative behavior by entrepreneurs and imitated by individuals. After an experiential learning process, norms and rules arise.[72] We adopt a process-dependent learning rationale but apply it to explain formal institutional change.[73]

The model also stresses the salience of political entrepreneurs as creators of the conditions sufficient for political rule design. This perspective is relatively new within the framework of social choice theory, which generally begins with the way in which policy regulations realize public policy in different policy domains as well as affect the players' behavior. Contrary to such studies, we pay less attention to the types of formal institutional rules changes than to how they are adopted.[74]

The majority of studies dealing with changes in the rules of the game focus on policy rule change within the framework of political rules or political rule changes.[75] Unlike these studies, we do focus on the process preceding the actual rule changes. When doing so, we tackle the issue of when a political entrepreneur prefers a policy change within the framework of the political rules of the game to a policy change of these rules.

Most entrepreneurship studies deal with economic and social rather than political entrepreneurship. Social entrepreneurship studies show how social-cultural processes lead to the emergence of an entrepreneur and how his or her social influence molds society.[76] Social entrepreneurship studies usually do not stress the strategies and actions taken by entrepreneurs in order to promote formal institutional change.

Alternatively, the literature on economic entrepreneurship deals usually with the various aspects of the entrepreneur's personality, focusing on his behavior and appearance. This literature also discusses environmental factors that affect the success or failure of entrepreneurial behavior.[77] As opposed to these studies, which deal mainly with private-sector organizations and products, political entrepreneurship studies deal mainly with the public sector and its outputs. This distinction affects the factors explored in the process of political rule design. The political entrepreneurship literature has rarely emphasized these factors, focusing as it has on the involvement of entrepreneurs as lobbyists.[78] Here, we use arguments taken from the general entrepreneurship literature and apply them to the entire political entrepreneurship process. This approach contributes to the elaboration of the political entrepreneur's behavior throughout the different phases of political entrepreneurship: defining the social problem, proposing a formal institutional change as a solution, establishing an interest group, formulating a strategy and acquiring the means for raising the public's consciousness about the problem, promoting the institutional change proposal among legislators and, finally, examining the behavior of the political players in parliament.

This book also contributes to the empirical analysis of formal institutional rule change by comparing change attempts in Israel's political system with those in three other countries, New Zealand, Argentina and Italy, for the purposes of testing its hypotheses regarding the stability of institutional rule reform. Historically, the literature dealing with electoral reforms in Israel has stressed the 1992 reform and somewhat neglected its revocation in 2001.[79] This book attempts to redress that imbalance.

The research on institutional change in Israel stresses the social conditions that make the situation ripe for such endeavors. This literature highlights transformations in the normative and sociocultural environment,[80] characterized by a shift away from a collective toward an individualistic,[81] liberal ethos realized in economic privatization, the rise of civil society,[82] the relaxation of centralized market constraints and the increasing appearance of legal and electoral trends placing the political leader, rather than the political party, at the center of political action.[83] Other factors that will be considered are the activities of interest groups, social crises, political stagnation and political utilitarianism,[84] the considerations of new parties and politicians, and the conflict between the desire to maximize one's re-election chances and the implementation of long-term solutions to difficult problems.[85] Furthermore, by examining the issue of stability as well as the relationship between the sociocultural environment and the stability of institutional change, the book takes up where earlier studies have left off.

Regarding the actions of individuals, Diskin and Diskin (1988) claim that there is an imbalance between electoral reform proposals and the interests of those proposing the reforms. Yehezkel Dror (1996) describes the irrational presuppositions of those who promoted the Direct Elections Law in Israel. This book will examine the motives of the various entrepreneurs and players who are a part of the institutional change design.

By proposing an explanatory model that links the factors creating the social environment with variables that explain the stability of institutional change, it provides policy-makers with insights that might help them plan their own policy-implementation programs. This practical aspect of the book should not be undervalued, considering the number of societies facing heavy institutional obstacles to reform.

# CHAPTER THREE

# *Political Entrepreneurs and Institutional Change: The Case of Basic Law: The Government (1992)*

## 3.1 Introduction

In this chapter we describe one instance of change in a *formal political rule* as it unfolded in Israel, a state embracing a democratic political system. The political rule in question, passed on March 18, 1992, revised the procedure for selecting the prime minister; its content thus entails a fundamental institutional change. Commonly known as the "Direct Elections Law" (its formal title is *Basic Law: The Government (1992)—Direct Elections for the Prime Minister*), it incorporates two types of rules, *aggregation rules* and *authority rules*. The first type of rule defines the decision function used to translate preferences into results, whereas the second type delineates the actions that holders of different socio-political positions are allowed to take. In the case at hand, the institutional change redefined the political discourse as well as the balance of power between the various players.[1] We begin with a summary of its main features.

Unlike countries such as the United States and Canada that have coherent constitutional documents, Israel does not have a formal constitution. However, over the years, a system of basic laws has been enacted, designed to address specific constitutional issues. At some point in the future, they may be compiled into a complete constitutional document. The statutes that constitute the legislation entitled Basic Law: Human Dignity and Liberty, passed in 1995, are recognized as having constitutional status that takes precedence over regular law in Israeli judicial interpretation.[2] The recognition of the Basic Laws as having constitutional status was dubbed the "constitutional revolution."[3] Thus, Israel now has constitutional norms that override normal statutes and provide the legal basis according to which the Supreme Court interprets Israeli legal provisions and conducts judicial review of primary legislation. The basic laws that have had the most significant impact are Basic Law: Human Dignity and Liberty and Basic Law: Freedom of Occupation.

Similar to other states ruled by parliamentary regimes, prior to the law's passage, Israel's prime minister was not elected but chosen on the basis of his or her capacity to construct a government from among the newly (re-)elected members of the Knesset, by their party affiliations. Common practice—although not always realized—dictated that the prime minister come from the party garnering the largest number of votes in the last Knesset elections. The electorate therefore had no direct say over who would head its government:

*Basic Law: The Government*

Paragraph 5. Composition and Fitness

(a) The government is composed of the prime minister and other ministers.
(b) The prime minister is a Knesset member; ministers not belonging to the Knesset may be chosen. Ministers are to be Israeli citizens and residents. If a person named a minister holds a position that prevents him from running for the Knesset, he is required to leave that position before becoming a minister. However, a person who is a judge or an officer in the Israeli army must resign his position at least 100 days before entering the office of minister.

Paragraph 14. The Prime Minister and the Assembling of the Government

(a) A Knesset member who managed to assemble a government will be the prime minister and lead the government

Direct election of the prime minister therefore represented an institutional change—in the sense of a revision in the public's assumptions of how the prime minister was to be selected and to whom he/she would be accountable—as well as a procedural change.[4]

Prior to enactment of the Direct Elections Law, the prime minister was appointed by Israel's president on the basis of his or her ability to construct a government.[5] What the law did was transfer appointment power to the electorate, which meant bypassing political parties and politicians:

*Basic Law: The Government*

Paragraph 3. Source of Authority and the Government Panel

(a) The government panel includes the prime minister and members of parliament appointed to the position of minister.
(b) The prime minister achieves his position by means of general, state, direct, equal and secret elections, according to Basic Law: The Knesset and Basic Law: The Government.

Such a reassignment of authority clearly contains the potential to harm the interests of some of the politicians seeking or holding office; as expected, their response was often opposition to the reform. Indeed, consideration of the outcome of the proposed shift in power to the prime minister makes one wonder why any politician or legislator would agree to a law that could eventually curb his or her own political power. The relevant question is, then, what variables can explain the unique behavior of the players regarding a basic institutional change?

Treatment of this question obliges us to undertake a broader analysis entailing an investigation of the players' actions in societal, structural and political contexts. Therefore, the broad theoretical question to be examined in this chapter is why and under what conditions can basic formal institutional change of the political system take place? How are the character and design of such a change determined? Furthermore, what variables explain the stability of the change once introduced?

In the following section we describe the aforementioned case in greater detail and employ it to explain the model's parameters. We then review the same case from the perspectives of the strategies employed by various players in designing the law in question. We will demonstrate that the design of political rules—in addition to their stability—rests on a combination of two variables: on the one hand, *the level of political-economic stability*; on the other, the type of *political culture* characterizing a given society, observed in its democratic norms. These variables allow us to construct a two-variable scale for purposes of analysis and measurement of the structural conditions that affect considerations of time and behavior and, as such, explain the change's stability. For instance, Israel is characterized by the type of systemic centralization that causes *political-economic instability*. These structural conditions force decision-makers to act according to short-term considerations. In addition, the political culture is characterized by an *instrumental approach to democratic norms*. When translated into the terms of procedural democracy, this situation reinforces attention to the short-term considerations that explain which institutional changes are to be introduced into the system of democratic rules and, it follows, their impact on political life. In such an environment, we can expect institutional changes to be frequent and unstable.

These structural and cultural conditions, which can also be considered as the constraints and incentives promoting the behavior of different political players, led to the two-staged development of the Direct Elections Law.

In the first stage, feelings about the need for change developed and with it, the appearance of political entrepreneurs.

In the second stage, the character and design of this basic formal institutional change evolved in response to the actions of players such as politicians, bureaucrats and interest groups, each of which utilized the emerging feelings about change for their own benefit.

### *3.1.1 Case Description*

Amendment of Basic Law: The Government in 1992 capped a series of attempts initiated by various groups and individuals over the years to "reform" the electoral system and the complex of laws that function in place of a formal constitution. It is difficult to pinpoint the exact beginning of this process, especially if one wishes to clarify the roles of the political entrepreneurs who influenced the results. One might choose the year 1985, when Professor Uriel Reichmann, one of Israel's foremost constitutional scholars, established the "Constitution for Israel" movement. A more appropriate date might be still earlier, in the 1970s, when Reichmann first met Professor Amnon Rubinstein, another eminent constitutional scholar, political activist and future Minister of Education. Rubinstein, who was Reichmann's teacher at Tel-Aviv University's School of Law at the time, encouraged his protégé to obtain his doctorate in the United States (University of Chicago).

When Reichmann returned to Israel in 1975, he joined Rubinstein as a member in the Shinui political movement. Another key date was 1983, when Rubinstein, by now a sitting Member of the Knesset, filed a human rights law proposal that failed, as usual, due to opposition from the religious faction in the Knesset.

Partly in response to the demise of Rubinstein's proposal, Reichmann established the "Public Constitution Committee in Israel" (PCC) in 1985, whose goal it was to campaign for the introduction of a constitution. After formulating the draft, the PCC tried to rally support for its proposal through the media and public protests. In 1988, a convention was held with the participation of many artists and well-known personalities. Its three-fold goal to pass a constitutional change to the electoral system and allow direct election of the prime minister reflected the desire of the PCC to solve the problem of nongovernability, but, more than that, to ensure the target as a more feasible one.

That same year, the PCC began its collaboration with a group of Knesset members from other parties; its goal was passage of a bill to reform the electoral system. Participants in this effort included Ehud Olmert (Likud), David Libai (Alignment, Israel Labor Party), David Magen (Likud), Uriel Lynn (Likud, Liberals) and Ovadia Eli (Likud). The proposal passed its first reading in the Knesset, but failed in the second and third readings.[6]

As a result of these actions, a Knesset committee headed by Gad Yaacobi (Labor) was established to examine the possibility of revising the system. The committee, which worked on the idea for about a year, presented its recommendations in 1989, mainly to change the electoral system to a regional one. During its deliberations, the committee reviewed Reichmann's suggestions along with comments prepared by Dan Eliezer (the Jerusalem Center for Public Affairs), who had cooperated with the Israeli Constitution Movement, and Arik Carmon (one of the founders of the Israel Democracy Institute), a long-time opponent of Reichmann and his views. At the end Prime Minister Yitzhak Shamir (Likud) chose not to continue with the Yaacobi' recommendation.

In 1990, after Yitzhak Shamir was forced to reconstitute the government in the wake of a no-confidence vote, four Knesset members—Amnon Rubinstein (Shinui), Uriel Lynn (Likud, Liberals), David Libai (Labor) and Yoash Tsiddon (Tzomet)—filed four separate proposals advocating direct election of the prime minister. Later that same year, the four merged their separate proposals into one. This coordinated proposal eventually became law in 1992, two days before the end of the Twelfth Knesset, by a vote of 55 to 32.

A brief scan of the political parties represented by the proponents of the Direct Elections Law can lead us to conclude that the law expressed the political mainstream's belief in the urgency of reform. Here, however, we are interested in how this need was perceived and then spread by an elite group of legal scholars to the general public. Stated in terms of our model, our questions focus on how these political entrepreneurs designed and sold institutional change to the electorate. We begin (Section 3.5) by returning to that part of our model dealing with the interaction between political entrepreneurs, interest group members and the public. When doing so, we discuss how political entrepreneurs attempt to control others, particularly politicians and political decision-makers, through the distribution of their accumulated "electoral capital." We also point out the difficulties faced when the entrepreneurs attempt to persuade the public to take collective action for the purpose of influencing elected officials in a party-based electoral system. Attempts to overcome this difficulty lie at the heart of the next part (3.6), which analyzes the political entrepreneur's behavior within the framework of interest group activity, specifically, the provision of information on public preferences, relationships with other groups and strategies chosen to influence political leaders. The conclusion (3.7) of this chapter deals with the interactions between legislators, the political figures directly responsible for introducing formal institutional change.

## 3.2 Public Awareness of Political Rule Change as a Necessary Condition for Initiation of Institutional Design Change

Since the 1970s, the centralized structure of Israel's political and economic arenas has made effective functioning increasingly problematic, to the point of nongovernability. Initially, attempts were made to overcome flaws democratically, through protests and exit strategies. When these approaches failed, the public created alternative forms of political participation, such as the establishment of illegal settlements in the occupied territories ("de facto attitude"), meant to supply the missing goods and services by working around instead of through the system. In the process, the public came to the realization that the existing political rules needed reform. However, economic and political instability coupled with democratic procedural norms shifted the players' focus to short-term, immediate steps or to perceive institutional change, incorrectly, as a solution to economic and political crises. As a result, the institutional change introduced in 1992 was unstable. Alternative politics, together with political and economic instability, conspired to make the institutional change untenable.

## *The Rise of Alternative Politics*

The 1980s were characterized by strong tension between society and government. This process began in the early 1970s, only to gather momentum as Israelis began to demand better goods and services from the government. As the public realized how incapable the government was of delivering these goods and services, it also realized that there was a need for a change in the political rules.[7] The public's attitude toward change was not articulated directly; instead, it adopted behavior patterns that circumvented the existing institutional system. Such behavior indicated its readiness for institutional change. This is the point at which political entrepreneurs appeared to define the problem and the solution—introduction of a political rule change. The roots of this perception were, however, planted about half a decade earlier.

Since the 1967 Six Day War, Israeli society has experienced considerable foment.[8] According to Eisenstadt, the post-war period was characterized by the rise of what was then considered "extremist" political groups and organizations such as Gush Emunim, Matzpen, and the Black Panthers, each expressing its own critique of government policy. At the same time, the strength of the established political party leadership weakened at the rise of various commissions of inquiry such as the Agranat Commission[9] and the Kahan Commission.[10] According to Dror (1989), delegation of political power to investigative commissions reflected the tendency exhibited by Israeli politicians to avoid personal responsibility and decision-making in addition to government paralysis. This situation was exacerbated in the period after the 1973 Yom Kippur War, when the public lost confidence in the ability of Israel's institutions and leadership to cope with a wide range of domestic and international problems.[11] Waves of protest reflected the loss of faith in civil government and the military,[12] in addition to the broadening of gaps between ethnic groups and between the religious and secular citizens. In Nisbet's (1966) view, most Israelis found this situation untenable and thus began collective action to rectify it. Charges of corruption in the government, the political parties and the Histadrut[13] leadership did little to assuage the discontent. Tensions were so high that a financial infraction by Prime Minister Yitzchak Rabin's wife led to his resignation.[14]

The public's response to this nongovernability was initially channeled into attempts to formulate public policy through the existing rules. Public dissatisfaction reached a peak in 1977, when the Labor party, which had ruled Israel since independence, was replaced by the Likud party. However, the government bureaucracy, peopled primarily by supports of Mapai, prevented any real reform. Thus, despite the change in the heads of government, no meaningful change penetrated the government's implementation capacities.[15]

Another approach to policy reform involved appeals addressed to Israel's High Court of Justice.[16] The appeals, at first presented in a trickle, reflected the changing attitudes, with the public realization that the existing set of rules needed revision.[17]

Growing public awareness of ethnic and cultural gaps, suppressed during the 1950s and 1960s, coincided with the weakened control exercised by political leaders over their centralized parties.[18] The public chose to adopt an alternative behavior in the form of engaging in illegal practices in order to acquire the goods and services they wanted.[19] An alternative activity spread into other areas of life as well; by the 1980s, a black market flourished, the introduction of cable television pirate stations sprang up, while gray markets in education and health care proliferated. During this same period, political activities such as Gush Emunim succeeded in encouraging Jewish settlements through creating a new reality by establishing facts on the ground. This mode of behavior influenced later interest groups and political entrepreneurs to adopt this same strategy.[20]

Over time, the public grew more desperate about its inability to influence the government. The awareness of the need for an institutional change grew not only in the leftist parties such as Shinui, Ratz and parts of the Alignment-Maarach. In parallel, other circles, especially the religious ones (Gush Emunim, Kiriat Arba settlers and some members of Techia) began to feel that they represented a law that answered to a higher authority than the national law.[21]

## *Political Instability*

Another pivotal sign of a change in public attitudes was the weakening of the major political parties as institutions,[22] observed in the increase of local lists in municipal elections.[23] These signs reflect the political instability and loss of party control, which increased over time and was one of the factors that reinforced political instability and the priority of short-term considerations.

The political science literature divides the meaningful changes in the political party system into three periods.[24] In the early days of its existence, Israel's party system functioned with one dominant party at its center. During this period, Mapai (Land of Israel Workers' Party) and its successors (the Alignment (HaMaarach) and Labor (HaAvoda) were at the center of all coalition governments. During the second period, which began with the Likud's victory in the 1977 elections, the partisan system became more competitive, with power swinging between Labor and the Likud together with the small parties identified with them. This was the period when unified governments came into being, reflecting electoral equity. During the third period, the direct election of the prime minister was introduced. This period saw increasing bipartisan splits in the Knesset, accompanied by a rise in sectoral politics and the diametric decline in the attractiveness of the larger parties. Together, these last trends reflect the height of political instability. The number of parties competing for Knesset seats grew, reaching a peak of 33 in 1992. In the 1996 elections, 20 lists competed and in 1999, 31 lists competed. Growth in the number of parties seeking election occurred despite the 1992 rise of the Knesset entry criterion, from 1 percent to 1.5 percent.[25]

Since 1981, when both parties garnered about a million and a half votes, with only 10,405 votes separating them, the contest between the Likud and the Alignment (Labor and Mapam) has been close. From that point on, however, Labor has been losing votes.

This trend toward the multiplicity of parties and electoral dominance is especially significant when the total number of voters is examined. Between 1969 and 1988, total eligibility to vote increased by approximately 900,000 votes. The difference in the number of votes received by Labor in 1988 (685,363) and 1969 (632,035) was only 53,000 votes, while the number of votes for the Likud rose from 338,948 in 1969 to 709,305 in 1988, an addition of 370,000.[26]

In the 1990s, electoral competition did not decline, but the power of the two largest parties continued to weaken, so that their combined power declined below the level enjoyed during the years of the state's infancy. By 1999, the weight of the two parties in the Knesset had declined further. The combined number of seats secured was similar to the number that a large party secured in seven out of the ten elections held between 1949 and 1981. In the 1999 elections, One Israel (Yisrael Achat which included Gesher and Meimad)[27] secured only 26 seats, representing 670,484 votes (20.3 percent of all votes cast). The Likud fell to 19 seats, with the number of its voters declining to 468,103 (14.1 percent). In the special election for the prime minister held in 2001, low voter turnout was especially low: 62.3 percent compared to 78.7 percent in 1999 and similar percentages in the previous elections.[28] This unusually low voter turnout clearly reflected the deepening collective action, issue and political alienation among the public.

These changes in the party distribution are clearly reflected in the political instability measures used by Arian, Nachmias and Amir (2002). The split measure,[29] the effective party-numbers measure[30] and the centralization measure (Hirshman, 1945) all support the conclusions reached by Arian, Nachmias and Amir (2002: 107). Table 3.1 presents Rae's split-measure results, obtained Arian, Nachmias and Amir (2002: 109).

The Rae measure demonstrates the split between parties in the parliament. It is calculated by subtracting the squared percentage of the sum of votes cast for each party from the value 1.0. The values of this measure can range from 0 to 1. If only one party is represented in parliament, the value of the measure would be zero (no split). The greater the number of parties in the parliament, the closer the value of the measure is to one. Table 3.1, which shows the results for the years 1949 to

**Table 3.1** Rae's Split Measure 1949–1999

| *The Measure's Value* | *Knesset* | *Year* |
|---|---|---|
| 0.788 | 1 | 1949 |
| 0.792 | 2 | 1951 |
| 0.832 | 3 | 1955 |
| 0.797 | 4 | 1959 |
| 0.814 | 5 | 1961 |
| 0.788 | 6 | 1965 |
| 0.702 | 7 | 1969 |
| 0.701 | 8 | 1974 |
| 0.707 | 9 | 1977 |
| 0.680 | 10 | 1981 |
| 0.740 | 11 | 1984 |
| 0.770 | 12 | 1988 |
| 0.772 | 13 | 1992 |
| 0.820 | 14 | 1996 |
| 0.884 | 15 | 1999 |

*Source*: Arian A., D. Nachmias, and R. Amir (2002) *Governability and Executive Authority in Israel*, Jerusalem: Israeli Institute of Democracy, p. 107. [Hebrew]

1999, indicates the increasing splintering of the Knesset by party, with the highest value shown for 1999 (0.884).

The measure of centralization complements the Rae measure. Its values range between 0 and 1 as well. If the parliament has only one party represented in it, the value of the measure would be one. The lower the measure's value, the smaller the size of the parties in parliament.

The measure of the effective party number signifies the hypothetical number of equal-sized parties that might have similar influence on the split in the political system. The measure equals the sum (in percentages) of the seats each party has in a particular session of parliament. In most election campaigns, the effective number of the parties ranges from −1 to +1 in relation to the number of parties that won a tenth of the seats in the parliament. The value of the effective party number between the year 1949 and 1999 is represented in Table 3.2.

The findings shown in the table reflect an increasing trend toward political instability. As Arian, Nachmias and Amir (2002:110) note:

> The Knesset was split since its first days . . . in the year 1949, the split level was already relatively high (0.79), and there were approximately five effective parties. The greater the split became and the higher the number of effective parties, the more complex the job of putting together a coalition became and the less the chance of coalitional stability.

And so, from 1969 on, the findings show that the effective number of parties had been decreasing, with the centralization of the party system increasing. From 1969 on, a shift has occurred from a dominant party to a competitive party system. By the 1996 elections, the centralization measure had dropped to 0.18, while the effective party number went up to 5.61. In 1999, the effective party number continued its ascent to an unprecedented 8.68. The figure resulted from a highly complex process of coalition formation as well as declining coalitional stability, with the two trends confirming the public's perception of political instability.

From 1977 on, negotiations over government appointments and budgetary allocations have become more complex and grating. At first, the larger parties responded to coalition demands and enlarged the number of ministerial offices open to political appointees. Even though the Amendment (1992) to the Basic Law: Government, limiting the number of ministers to 18 (including the prime minister) was passed, the law was again amended to increase the number of ministers after Ehud Barak's election in 1999 due to difficulties in forming a coalition.

**Table 3.2** Effective Party Number and Centralization Measures, 1949–1999*

| *Centralization Measure* | *Knesset* | *Effective Party Number* | *Year* |
|---|---|---|---|
| 0.211 | 1 | 4.73 | 1949 |
| 0.207 | 2 | 4.83 | 1951 |
| 0.167 | 3 | 5.99 | 1955 |
| 0.203 | 4 | 4.92 | 1959 |
| 0.158 | 5 | 5.37 | 1961 |
| 0.211 | 6 | 4.72 | 1965 |
| 0.279 | 7 | 3.58 | 1969 |
| 0.298 | 8 | 3.35 | 1974 |
| 0.229 | 9 | 4.36 | 1977 |
| 0.320 | 10 | 3.13 | 1981 |
| 0.259 | 11 | 3.86 | 1984 |
| 0.228 | 12 | 4.38 | 1988 |
| 0.227 | 13 | 4.39 | 1992 |
| 0.178 | 14 | 5.61 | 1996 |
| 0.115 | 15 | 8.68 | 1999 |

*Source*: Arian A., D. Nachmias, and R. Amir (2002) *Governability and Executive Authority in Israel*, Jerusalem: Israeli Institute of Democracy, p. 109. [Hebrew]

Ehud Barak (Israel Achat) had 24 ministers. This trend accelerated when Ariel Sharon (Likud) took office in 2001—he had 30 ministers.

## *Economic Ineffectiveness*

Israel has gone through many periods of economic instability. Unemployment has oscillated from 17 percent in the State's first years to 2.5 percent–3 percent in the 1970s and back to 11 percent in the early 1990s.[31]

The effects of intensifying privatization and declining real wages were expressed mainly in the wages of uneducated and unskilled workers. Between 1980 and 1997, wages of these workers—which at first constituted 70 percent of the average wage—declined to 55 percent of the average wage. The wages of workers having eight or fewer years of education declined during the same period from 74 percent of the average wage to 59 percent.[32]

The percentage of government mortgages[33] granted, which are available only to selected segments of the population, also declined, from 38 percent of all mortgages taken by home buyers in 1994 to 25 percent in 1999. According to Swirsky and Connor, the decline reflects the inability of the government mortgage system to provide meaningful assistance. The result is reflected in the declining rate of home ownership in the lowest decile of the population, which decreased from 52.2 percent in 1987 to 43.3 percent in 1992 and to 24.2 percent in 1997. The ownership rate of the second lowest decile decreased from 58.0 percent in 1987 to 55.6 percent in 1992 and to 53.8 percent in 1997.[34]

Between 1992 and 1999, the cost of health care increased for all of Israel's families, at the same time that the number of families at the poverty level rose, as Table 3.3 indicates.

We should note that the poverty line in Israel is defined as income below 50 percent of the median wage.[35]

Transformation of the order of preferences occurred gradually. By 1985, the ineffectiveness of the national unified government[36] strengthened the public's feelings that the country had come to a dead end. This was the second year of the Likud-Alignment (*HaMaarach*) government, headed by Shimon Peres (*HaMaarach*). A series of economic, security, and foreign policy crises, such as the Israeli Defense Forces's (IDF)

**Table 3.3** Poverty Incidence among Families, Prior to National Security and Tax Payments, 1979–1998 (in Percentages)

| *Families (%)* | *Year* |
|---|---|
| 27.9 | 1979 |
| 28.1 | 1980 |
| 28.8 | 1981 |
| 29.8 | 1982 |
| 29.5 | 1983 |
| 30.7 | 1984 |
| 31.3 | 1985 |
| 32.6 | 1988 |
| 33.0 | 1989 |
| 34.3 | 1990 |
| 35.1 | 1991 |
| 34.7 | 1992 |
| 34.6 | 1993 |
| 34.2 | 1994 |
| 33.8 | 1995 |
| 34.3 | 1996 |
| 33.2 | 1997 |
| 34.1 | 1998 |

*Source*: Swirski, S. and E. Konor-Attias (2000) Israel: *A Social Report*, Tel Aviv: Adva Center, p. 15. [Hebrew]

withdrawal from Lebanon and the failed negotiations with Jordan and the Palestinians, combined with contentiousness surrounding the funds to be allocated to the religious sector, threatened to put an end to the government. The crises were initiated not only by politicians from opposition parties but also from within the coalition itself due to the latter's dissatisfaction with the government's activity and other coalition partners.[37] Public awareness of the unity government's paralysis spread,[38] causing them to seek a solution.[39] The time was right for the emergence of political entrepreneurs.

## 3.3 Political Entrepreneurs

Who were these political entrepreneurs? Some came from within the political system. A small group of politicians, including Professor Amnon Rubinstein, a professor of constitutional law who had served in the Knesset since 1977, formed the Shinui party (*shinui* in Hebrew means "change"). Others came from outside the system, such as Professor Uriel Reichmann, Rubinstein's former student, who was then serving as dean of the Tel-Aviv University's School of Law. Rubinstein and Reichmann understood the public's dissatisfaction and defined the problem as the paralysis inherent in coalition governments that prevented them from implementing policies that would satisfy the demands of all the different groups in society.[40] The solution proposed by these entrepreneurs was formulation of a constitution that would include an electoral system designed to ensure that the government would not be subject to pressures from small parties. A number of factors defined the context and contributed to the emergence of the political entrepreneurs:

1. Political values
2. Public visibility: The quest for power and the desire to maximize personal prestige
3. Professional and political affiliations
4. Past experience and learning
5. Identification and utilization of crises as well as changing public beliefs and preferences.

### *Political Values*

The entrepreneur's ethical stance reflects his political perception, which affects the way that he defines social problems and their solutions as well as the strategy he adopts to achieve his goals.[41] Those who, like Reichmann, came from outside the system favored the adoption of democratic values and economic interdependence, whereas those from within the system, like Amnon Rubinstein, David Libai, Uriel Lynn and Yoash Tsiddon, did not present themselves as political activists with respect to political institutional change. Instead, despite their rhetoric, they employed the dimensions of ethics and ideology to shape their own images and maximize their chances of re-election.

Amnon Rubinstein, born in Israel in 1931, studied law and economics at the Hebrew University in Jerusalem. He received his doctorate in law from the London School of Economics and later became the first dean of the Tel-Aviv University School of Law.[42] In his writings, he frequently expressed his vision of Israel as a liberal, egalitarian state functioning in accordance with universal norms, a free-market economy, respect for human rights and the search for peace.[43]

Uriel Reichmann, born in 1942, was also a native Israeli. He served as an officer in a paratrooper unit and studied law at the Hebrew University in Jerusalem. While studying for his PhD in law at the University of Chicago, Reichmann became influenced by the idea of a free market-economy, which later spurred his antimonopoly activities. After finishing his studies, he returned to Israel to serve as chairman of Shinui, the party founded by Rubinstein, among others.[44] Reichmann was very active in Shinui and Dash;[45] he strongly supported civil rights, limitations on government's intervention in the economy and the governing of Israel on the basis of universal norms that enforced the accountability to the public of elected officials as well as the public administration.[46]

David Libai, born in Tel-Aviv in 1934, also studied law at the University of Chicago, where he specialized in comparative and criminal law. Upon his return to Israel he joined the Faculty of Law at Tel-Aviv University. After the 1977 turnover (or *maapach*), when the Likud gained control of the government for the first time in history, Libai joined the Labor party and entered politics. He continued to work as a lawyer, served as the head of the Israel Bar Association and taught at Tel-Aviv University's School of Law. Libai belonged to the Peres camp for many years.

Uriel (Asulin) Lynn was born in 1935. He earned his BA in law from the Hebrew University in Jerusalem and his MA at the University of California, Berkeley. Lynn immediately entered into private practice in addition to his activities in the Liberal Party, beginning in the mid 1970s. This powerful centrist party was committed to the Zionist ideal, liberalism, a free economy, reduction of government intervention in the economy and, importantly, the need for a written constitution. The

Liberal Party joined the government, in coalition with the Likud, in 1977; by 1988, it had been absorbed into the Likud.[47]

Yoash (Chato) Tsiddon, born in Romania in 1926, immigrated to Israel at the age of 15, and studied mathematics and physics at the Technion. Tsiddon served in the Palmach, was a messenger for the Hagana in Cyprus and served in the fledgling Israeli Air Force. In 1967 he was discharged with the rank of colonel; he then busied himself with educational and industrial projects. In 1988, he was elected to the Knesset as a member of the right-wing Tzomet party, which espoused the right of the Jewish people to the entire ancient Land of Israel, democratic government, reduction of economic dependence on external factors, and the promotion of social and educational initiatives. When Tsiddon became politically active, he did not see himself as a career politician. Indeed, his ethical image was an important determinant of his behavior.[48]

## *Public Visibility*

According to the literature, a political entrepreneur is defined as a rational decision-maker who tries to alter the political situation by changing policy or the political rules of the game. His activity is motivated, among other things, by the desire to maximize his personal power and prestige on the public-political level.[49] Public visibility, as political entrepreneurs have long known, increases the chances of politicians being elected but also of entrepreneurs being effective. Our five "heroes" had clearly understood this lesson early in their careers.[50]

Amnon Rubinstein viewed himself as more than an academic. He also felt the need to perform some public service. His visibility and influence among the wider public increased after he was invited to host a televised interview program called *Boomerang*.[51] In the eyes of most young people, he represented the new, enlightened Israeli, educated and worldly. Reichmann had similar characteristics, including the capacity to arouse enthusiasm. In order to promote his social agenda, Reichmann started a magazine, *The Line of Law*, dealing with social and legal issues, which attracted contributors such as two former government legal counsels, Itzhak Zamir and Aharon Barak. David Libai initiated his public activities at the same time that he began his political career. Uriel Lynn, who also eventually sat in the Knesset as a member of the Liberal-Likud Party, had a long history of mixing public service with private practice. Yoash Tsiddon as well had long mixed political ideology with private projects.

### *The Entrepreneur's Professional and Political Affiliations*

Professional and political affiliations clearly influence one's success in the political realm. Rubinstein, Libai, Reichmann and Lynn all belonged to the legal profession and were educated in Israel's prime law schools as well as abroad. The liberal atmosphere of these institutions, especially at the Hebrew University of Jerusalem, was influenced by two main factors: its teachers and students, but also the liberal rulings of Supreme Court justices such as Shimon Agranat, Moshe Zilberg, Haim Cohen and Joel Zusmann.

### *Past Experience and Learning*

The case of the direct election of the Prime Minister Law represents the culmination of processes that began soon after Israel's establishment. Over the years, various attempts had been made to introduce a formal institutional change in the shape of a written constitution. The initiatives took a variety of forms: submission of a constitution to the Knesset as drafted by Prof. Binyamin Aktzin, the granting of limited constitutional authority to the Declaration of Independence, the granting of constitutional status to select basic laws and the formulation of a bill of rights. Several versions of a bill of rights were presented by Professor Yitzhak Klinghoffer, who served during the Fifth, Sixth and Seventh Knessets as a member of the Liberal Party, and later by Judge Dr. Binyamin HaLevi, during the Seventh and Eighth Knessets, when sitting as a member of the Herut Party and in the Ninth Knesset as a member of the Dash Party. All of these initiatives failed. Another avenue explored was the attempt to change the electoral system,[52] which failed as well.

The social-choice literature stresses past experience as the factor that shapes the considerations of political entrepreneurs when choosing their strategies for action.[53] Amnon Rubinstein's experience is a case in point. Beginning in 1974, when he founded Shinui, Rubinstein, and later Reichmann, went through a learning process. They could not help but notice the legislative success enjoyed by various interest groups in the 1980s such as the religious lobby and the agriculture lobby.[54]

### *Identification and Utilization of Crises, Changing Public Beliefs and Preferences*

One of the major skills required by a political entrepreneur is the ability to identify a crisis that results from changes in public beliefs and preferences and to use this information for his own purposes.[55] In 1974, after the Yom Kippur War, Rubinstein, already a public opinion leader, identified the Israeli public's readiness to change the format of Israeli governance. Rubinstein sensed the public's growing impatience and distress as its leaders and institutions exhibited their inability to cope with central domestic and international issues.[56] Rubinstein has openly stated that in order to promote his interests, he had to take advantage of the social crisis.

On the 17th of February, Mordechai [Virshubski] and myself went to Jerusalem to participate in the demonstration of thousands opposite the office of Mrs. Meir [Golda] as a token of support for Motti Ashkenazi's demand that Moshe Dayan resign. While returning from Jerusalem, Mordechai and I agreed that the demonstration had proven that, despite the elections for the Eighth Knesset, there was not only a need to establish a new political movement, but that there was also a chance that it would gain broad public support.[57]

Rubinstein defined the problem, in terms of Spector & Kitsuse (1987) as one in which a society does not conform to universal norms of behavior. The solution to this problem was the creation of a constitution that would make Israel a nation where all its people would act according to universal behavioral norms.[58] Rubinstein adopted a strategy meant to turn a social problem into a policy problem that might, in turn, provoke a desire for change throughout the political-bureaucratic system.[59] His initial intention was not, therefore, to change political rules but the substance of political decisions. It appears that Rubinstein had gone through a learning process around 1985 and had chosen to seek political power. As Rubinstein writes:

> I, myself, saw the change—even in the poor, hard and most depressing days—as the beginning of a process that would help bring us to power. The first phase was to hold on and enter the next Knesset with meaningful force . . . .[60]

Indeed, in 1977, when Dash was established after Professor Yigal Yadin said that he was ready to take part in political life, Rubinstein himself was elected to the Knesset. Yadin had become the center of attraction for a number of political factions, including Shinui headed by Rubinstein and the Free Center Party headed by Shmuel Tamir.[61] Rubinstein was apparently able to take advantage of the political prestige characterizing political entrepreneurs: "The survival of Shinui turned the matter into a personal one. Our pride would not let us fail.

The fall of Shinui would have been interpreted by me as a personal blow."[62]

A similar pattern is evident in Reichmann's behavior as well. In the mid 1980s, Reichmann, an academic, detected an openness to government reform within the Israeli public.[63] In Nisbet's (1966: 96) terms, Reichmann recognized that an intolerable social situation required rectification by means of collective action. Reichmann's fallout with Rubinstein and his training as a lawyer explain his strategy, which was to maximize his own power relative to that of his fellow lawyers and Shinui party members.

A crisis was thus in the making.[64] There was a lack, albeit temporary, of fit between the value system (the ideal) and the social system (the real), between expectations and reality. The timing of this crisis made it possible for social movements to employ the chaos as an opportunity to offer their individual solutions.

This period was indeed characterized by social, economic and state crises. In June 1985, the tension between Alliance and the Likud (rightist party), as members in a coalition government, had intensified over the entry into negotiations with the Palestinians. This friction led the Alliance to seek an arrangement with the religious parties. In exchange for their support, the Alliance promised to grant the religious MKs the freedom to vote on the issue of who may be considered a Jew according to their conscience as opposed to party dictates. At that point, Shinui renewed its call for the dissolution of the national unity government on the grounds that it had been reprehensibly slow in implementing economic decisions.[65] The economic crisis and erupting violence along the border became the major issues on the public agenda.[66] The newspapers published petitions for a reduction of violence and terrorism, preservation of human dignity and equality for all citizens, and the priority of the rule of law.[67] In response, Dr. Baruch Bracha from Tel-Aviv University's School of Law published an article warning against the unacceptable practices of government authorities and the future of Israel's constitutional regime.[68] A similar critical stand was taken by Reichmann, when he voluntarily defended the government's legal counsel, Yitzhak Zamir. Zamir had ordered a police investigation of the behavior of senior General Security Service (the *Shabak*) officers during the seizure of the 300 line bus (April 12, 1984) and the subsequent killing of one of the terrorists despite the government's objections. Reichmann wrote:

> The primary role of the legal counsel is to safeguard the legality of the government's activity. Therefore, he is given independence,

> and on certain occasions he is obliged to face down the government. The legal counsel's authority should be keenly guarded. In a state without a constitution and without proper separation between legislative and executive authority, it is essential that we safeguard the institutions that constitute the main guarantors of our freedom: the Supreme Court and the government's legal counsel.[69]

What Reichmann and Rubenstein before him had done was, quite simply, take advantage of a series of political and social crises to project their own program for institutional change—however they had originally perceived it—into the public sphere in a manner that utilized their personal prestige and public dismay to their own advantage.

## 3.4 The Players' Dependence on Structural and Cultural Limitations

With the appearance of Uriel Reichmann and a small group of political entrepreneurs located outside the official government system, the idea of a constitution as *the* solution to Israel's social problems began to be promoted to a wider audience, with the group using public protests against the government to further its cause. Given these initial conditions, the character of the institutional change was shaped during complex interactions between a large number of players, each of whom was trying to maximize his or her interests. More accurately, the initial phases of the change process can be analyzed as a series of decisions. Thus, in 1988, a group of Knesset members—Ehud Olmert, David Libai, David Magen, Uriel Lynn and Ovadia Eli—proposed a bill designed to reform the electoral system by electing 60 Knesset members through a national proportional voting system and another 60 according to a local-majority system. In March 1990, four Knesset members—Lynn, Libai, Tsiddon and Rubinstein—filed four private legislative proposals for the direct election of the prime minister. The proposals called for the prime minister's election through general, national, secret and equal elections. Later that year, the four propositions were merged into one; in 1992, the proposal was accepted after passing the third reading in the Knesset. On any occasion of the formal redistribution of power—in this case from the parties and the nation's president to the voters—questions must be raised as to why leading political players would give up their power, particularly when other players wished to bring about a change potentially harmful to their interests.

In response to this query, we now examine how the character and design of a basic, formal institutional change is determined on the three interactive levels indicated in the suggested model.

## 3.5 Level 1: Entrepreneurs—Group—Public

This chapter section analyzes political entrepreneurs' behavior in relation to their reference group and to the general public. The first part analyzes entrepreneurs' motivations for attempting to influence politicians, and we also examine the roles of public products, collective action, information, social crises and the desire to maximize one's chances of (re-)election play in the process. Afterward, we discuss the initial resources to be recruited in any campaign for institutional change. We likewise examine the entrepreneur's reference group, profession and public support recruitment strategy, which vary by the specific goal: policy rule change or political system or regime change. We also describe use of the media for resource recruitment and the rewards to be exchanged for public support.

### *Motivation: Pressure and Influences*

According to the procedural model presented in chapter two politicians, once elected, have the formal authority to introduce political rules or rule changes via legislation. Interactions are therefore required between the politician—or decision-maker—and the voters. As part of this interaction, the public demands public goods, and the politicians respond by satisfying these demands, an action that increases their chances of being (re-)elected. This process lies at the heart of the entrepreneurs' motivation to focus their actions on policy-making politicians.

We continue to draw upon the events leading to the passage of the law establishing direct election of Israel's prime minister to illustrate and support these arguments. The different strategies used are discussed later.

### *Public Products, Collective Action, Information, Salience and Election*

The different stages in the process and design of the Direct Elections Law—the proposition to change the elections system adopted in 1988, the filing of four private legal proposals for the Direct Elections Law, their merger into one proposition in 1990 and passage of the proposition in 1992—together constitute national decisions that, according to our model, represent one type of *"public product"* that each citizen may enjoy without necessarily participating in its production. This subjective cost-benefit function arouses the motivation to become a "free rider," that is, someone who can benefit from a product without being involved in its production and, as a consequence, none of the players gets involved with the others.[70] The result is a shortage of the public good, on the one hand, and a lack of interest in creating public pressure (collective action) in order to change the situation. Entrepreneurial and interest group activity is an exception to the idea of free riding. These groups, like Rubinstein and his associates in Shinui (1974), Reichmann's A Constitution for Israel movement (1986) and others (e.g., Avi Kadish's movement for the government reform) managed to overcome the collective action problem by recruiting the public's participation. Formation of such groups constitutes an important stage in the design of public policy as well as political rule change.

According to the proposed model, the ways in which interest groups exert influence reflect the informational approach to the study of interest group—politician interaction with respect to public-policy determination. In situations of nongovernability and the lack of public-policy response to social problems, these groups demand amelioration of the situation. By doing so, they provide politicians with information regarding the preferences of various sectors.[71] However, this information is received by politicians irrespective of whether they promote policies fitting the positions taken by the interest group.

It follows, then, that the mutual goal of political entrepreneurs and interest groups is to *influence* decision-making *politicians*. The actions of the disparate interest groups and community leaders attempting to change Israel's election system are a case in point. Reviewed schematically, the need for change was identified by the political entrepreneurs Rubinstein, Lynn, Libai and Tsiddon, who identified this demand as appropriate to their interests of maximizing public salience regarding political nongovernability and instability. The campaign they waged, together with the public salience, also maximized their chances of being (re-)elected to the Knesset.

Close inspection of the proceeding indicates that during all phases of the Direct Elections Law's design, solutions provided by political entrepreneurs were those adopted. Sitting and potential Knesset members accepted solutions that might further their public salience in such a way as to increase their chances of (re-)election. We define this component here as *electoral capital*. That is, all assets (image, real resources, and group support) that can be utilized to influence voting outcomes can be considered electoral capital. It follows that winning public support for a policy advocated, such as constitutional change, including a change in the electoral system, can sometimes be translated into electoral capital. In the late 1980s but especially the early 1990s, the solution proposed by the said entrepreneurs—institutional rule change as a means to solving the social problem caused by paralyzing centralization and nongovernability—constituted a major portion of their electoral capital.

These events comply with the conclusions reached by Kitsuse and Spector (1973) regarding the entrepreneur's need to define social problems effectively.[72] According to Kitsuse and Spector, as well as Nisbet, any effective definition process contains two main stages. During the first stage, *the entrepreneur, who defines the problem, transmits his message to society*, explaining that the existing situation is dysfunctional and intolerable; by doing so, the entrepreneur threatens the system. This goal is accomplished by raising the public's awareness of the issue to the point where it becomes a public preoccupation.[73] During the second stage, *the entrepreneur proposes a solution to the situation*. He suggests alternatives to the policy that created or encouraged the problem's development in order to alter public perceptions of the situation's inevitability.

It might certainly be claimed that by pointing to enactment of a constitution (which would inherently include electoral system change) as a possible solution, the political entrepreneurs in the Israeli case openly drew attention, for the first time, to the electoral capital these specific politician-legislators had chosen to exploit in order to maximize their chances of being (re-)elected. In George *Tsebelis*'s (1990) words, the individual interests of the politicians at various stages—such as Olmert, Libai, Magen, Lynn and Eli in 1988, or Rubinstein, Libai, Tsiddon and Lynn from 1990 on—explain the paradox of filing a proposition that seemingly constitutes a self-destructive redistribution of power.

Going further, the structure of bureaucratic-political centralization had led to the nongovernability and economic instability which had led, in turn, to the priority of short-term considerations. Such considerations led to the construction of national unity governments on the one hand and struggles, such as those between Shimon Peres and Yitzhak Shamir, regarding the religious parties on the other. Short-term electoral considerations were at the heart of the proposals presented in 1988 and also from 1990 on, despite the reluctance of their proponents to claim that the respective proposal could be passed.[74] Thus, while governability and stability were the players' declared goals, their true goals, due to their *short-term electoral horizons, were increasing their electability in addition to their (non)partisan and public prestige.*[75] The last two aims would be fulfilled if they were able to promote institutional change that would nonetheless require continuing work, thus keeping them in the limelight. Even more so, their prestige was fed by the seemingly bipartisan nature of the formal change proposed, as opposed to the partisan politics waged by Peres (Labor-Avoda) and Shamir (Likud).[76]

Irrespective of the strength of our claim that politicians, by definition, aspire to maximize prestige and chances of (re-)election with the help of electoral capital, realization of these objectives is subject to structural and cultural conditions and constraints. The more internalized the democratic norms in a given society, the greater are the possibilities that the proposed institutional change will be shaped by long-term considerations because voters in such a society expect politicians to act from within this perspective.

## *Summary*

Up to this point, we have dealt with the rationale lying at the heart of the interaction between politicians and the voters: The public endorses policies that determine political rules and, in exchange, politicians provide the policies that maximize their chances of being (re-)elected. This rationale affects political entrepreneurs' motive to focus their activities on policy-making politicians. In conducting this analysis, we applied the theory of public goods and referred to the collective action problem to be overcome by entrepreneurs and interest groups. We pointed out the importance of the information supplied by interest groups to politicians regarding public preferences. We now turn to a discussion of the initial recruitment of resources needed to gain public support and influence politicians.

## *Resource Recruitment: The Group, the Profession and Funds*

Political entrepreneurs, like entrepreneurs in other spheres, are faced with the necessity of recruiting resources during the first phase of their activity. This holds true whether the entrepreneur belongs to the political system or comes from outside it. Political entrepreneurs determine what is needed based on the level of public involvement in the process. For instance, when attempting to pass the Law for the Direct Election of the Prime Minister, the entire public's involvement was needed;

hence, a greater amount of resources was required in comparison with the law's revocation in 2001, as we shall see in the next chapter. Here we focus on the relationship between the entrepreneur and his or her group while stressing recruitment of profession support and funds, as noted in chapter two.

### *The Entrepreneur and the Group*

Social movements can be created and sustained only if their founding entrepreneurs can reach the public. This relationship is more complex than first thought because an entrepreneur's role is characterized by *a divergence of interests between himself or herself and group members.*[77] This divergence is rooted in the structure characterized by both the players *Entrepreneurs are defined as people who can coordinate a group's members, start an organization, recruit resources and pressure the government* to provide the public goods desired by the group. Entrepreneurs enjoy power, prestige and political careers, whereas group members enjoy the personal and collective benefit that the entrepreneur provides.

Entrepreneurs tend to exhibit significant organizational skills, verbal and technical skills, dominant personalities and access to the media and government officials. Reichmann, for example, as Dean of the School of Law at Tel-Aviv University, had established the "Constitution for Israel" movement. Despite representing the group's positions, he had to overcome the problem of their collective nonresponsiveness. Reichmann did so by employing his power as a dean to provide a financial incentive for inducing them to formulate a constitution: covering the cost of trips abroad for some researchers.[78]

Entrepreneurship is not a linear process, given to easy identification of its phases, whether in stagnation or even at the conclusing phase. An abrupt shift may occur especially when the crisis that led to the initial activity subsides.[79] At this point, entrepreneurs must reappraise the situation by examining the gap between the desired and actual situation on a number of levels. On the level of entrepreneur-group member relations, *they have to revitalize their relationship with the group and be attentive to the covert attitudes of free riding.* They should also be especially attentive to adjusting the desired policy to a level satisfactory to meet group members' demands (Jones, 1978) in order to give the impression that they are not providing poorer results than anticipated.[80] Indeed, in order to meet the expectations of the group the entrepreneurs themselves have created, they have to revamp the struggle and replace the original (e.g., passage of a constitution) with other, "cheaper" goals. Thus, beginning in early 1987, after adjusting their sights, Reichmann and his colleagues presented more focused propositions, such as changing the electoral system to a regional-proportional mix as well as introducing direct elections for the Prime Minister as a more focused goal. This signaled to their group of supporters that there was a good chance of succeeding in a "cheaper" goal rather than passing a complete constitution for Israel. At a meeting held on January 16, 1988, the leaders of the Constitution for Israel movement agreed to tackle electoral reform as their first objective when the Eleventh Knesset convened.[81]

When entrepreneurs activate marketing strategies de-emphasizing or ignoring group learning and internalization, the outcome of their efforts may be loss of collective identity among group members and, in turn, departure of activists (Axelrod, 1984).

This marketing approach characterized Reichmann's pattern of operation and, as predicted, his campaign followed the model. After Reichmann managed to organize a massive public demonstration, held in Tel-Aviv's main square, Malchey Israel, on January 16, 1988, he frequently turned to the media to transmit his message, which succeeded in constructing the initial collective awareness prerequisite to political mobilization on a mass scale.[82] Yet, a collective identity with respect to the group and its mission was not sufficiently inculcated at that time. According to Yael Ishai (1987), interest groups unsuccessful in creating a strong collective identity are bound to fail. The Knesset's 1988 failure to further the electoral reform proposed by Olmert and his colleagues in the Constitution, Law and Justice Committee thus represented a crisis for the thousands of Constitution for Israel supporters. They expressed their disappointment by leaving the movement, which dried up the flow of contributions necessary to support extended activity.[83]

How a group is put together relates directly to the character of the social problem and its solution as defined by the entrepreneur. The entrepreneur must maximize his legitimacy among the public to ensure that the solution proposed is credible and acceptable. Regarding the case in question, the strategy applied by the Constitution for Israel Movement was rooted in the personality and prestige of its chief entrepreneur, Uriel Reichmann. The group he attracted to steer the movement included members of the elite who identified with Reichmann even if they did not hold political office. These included a businessman and the founder of Israel Aircraft Industries Al Schwimmer, the political consultant Arye Rotenberg, the professor of marketing *Dov Pekelman,*

Jacob (Shpick) Shapira, the film producer Yossi Yasur and two distinguished law professors, Ariel Rosen-Tzvi and Baruch Bracha.

Taken together, the members of this group fit Olson's (1965) definition of a "*privileged group*," composed of individuals willing to bear the costs of a societal action irrespective of the contributions of the other individuals also interested in that action's outcomes. The character of their activity is essentially political, regardless of the arena in which they function on a daily basis. In other words, their activity affects the allocation of social values, which they attempt to accomplish by utilizing the media as a mechanism for influencing public opinion and raising public awareness about the issues at hand. According to Olson, a privileged group's uniqueness is its low cost, that is, fewer resources are needed to sustain the group than those required for construction of a mass movement. Indeed, as Bechor (1996) mentions, the group's meetings were highly focused and initially held in Reichmann's office at Tel-Aviv University.

Another recruiting strategy available to political entrepreneurs goes by the name of *group reduction*.[84] This strategy is based on the idea that the collective action problem diminishes as the group becomes smaller. In small groups, relationships between group members affect the scope and strength of the benefits received by each. Such a dynamic may encourage the cohesion of group members and thus ensure that the entire group's interests are furthered. Application of this logic can be seen in the campaigns launched by members of the Constitution for Israel steering committee. What they did was appeal to residents of diverse locations via advertisements in which they specified the special benefits the residents of the particular locations might enjoy from the reform. Thus regionalizing the issue creates group reduction. For instance, Tel-Aviv–Yaffo residents were promised they would enjoy the new electoral system[85] while residents of the Upper Galilee were promised that their special interests would be promoted if they elected Knesset members from their region.[86] Electoral reform was chosen as the subject for intense activity because work on the idea, done by Yaacobi's Knesset committee, had been recently publicized so the issue was fresh in the mind of the public. In fact, however, this effort was part of the overall plan to move from formulation of a constitution to a "cheaper" goal of direct elections of the Prime Minister.[87]

### *Professional Recruitment*

Professional recruitment is related to the idea of maximizing public support for a proposed solution. Accordingly, Reichmann *chose several well-known legal experts to write the constitution*. These included Ariel Rozen-Zvi, Baruch Bracha, Avigdor Klagsbald, Amos Shapira and Joshua Porat among others.[88]

The paradox lies in Reichmann's decision to formulate a totally new constitution. It remains unclear as to why he did not build on previous proposals, such as that written by Prof. Binyamin Aktzin in 1962. One would expect an entrepreneur to prefer the "least expensive" way to maximize his or her objective. According to Bechor (1996:26), Reichmann's decision to write the constitution was melded with his desire to influence the Israeli public from his position as dean of Tel-Aviv University's law school. Still, this does not adequately explain why he abstained from incorporating previous propositions.

It appears that Rubinstein's 1983 failure to obtain passage of his proposed bill of rights had taught Reichmann that the broadest collective action possible was to be included as an element in the definition of any political objective. The rationale behind his discarding previous proposals may have been linked to his desire to use a totally original constitution to galvanize the public in the "*hope that public discussion would lead to the development of a new path for the State of Israel.*"[89] Moreover, Reichmann's first goal was to unify the group. Adoption of existing material requires less professional input, a "savings" that would have been reflected in reduced support from his professional colleagues.[90]

During this stage, Reichmann chose to recruit support from *other groups* as well, including Knesset members, businessmen and members of the academic and social elite. From the entrepreneur's point of view, recruiting support from existing groups constitutes one method to maximize resources. For instance, Reichmann and his associates attempted to recruit the "Aviv group," which included Knesset members (Meir Sheetrit, David Magen), businessmen (e.g., Aharon Dovrat, Eli Papushado, Al Schwimmer, etc.) and academics (e.g., Dr. Arik Carmon), who also wished to change the electoral system. The attempt, however, failed. The leader of the Aviv group, Carmon, disagreed with Reichmann (who was his brother-in-law) about the content of the proposed institutional change,[91] making it impossible for Reichmann to recruit support from other members of this professional community.

Reichmann then turned to community leaders to garner support. A group of heads of local government was formed. In 1975, the municipal electoral system underwent major reform and mayors were elected through direct elections. Based on that, Reichmann recruited them in favor of a reform of direct elections in the central government as well. Bechor (1996:109) writes that the Constitution for Israel committee members thought that community leaders might be interested in a structural reform that would intensify the relationship between voters and elected officials and thus strengthen the status of local government. A number of these local politicians, including Teddy Kollek, the mayor of Jerusalem, Shlomo Lahat, the mayor of Tel-Aviv, and Prosper Azran, the mayor Kiryat Shemona, were among those attending the kick-off meeting in Tel-Aviv on January 16, 1988.

Reichmann remained only partially successful in recruiting professional support, a problem that would have incurred significant costs later on. As mentioned, Reichmann chose to recruit professionals in order to minimize possible criticism against the alleged reform. However, the factions excluded from his supporters constituted a potential source of criticism. The main struggle was between lawyers and political scientists[92] and between legal scholars from Tel-Aviv University and those from the Hebrew University of Jerusalem.[93]

Promoting an idea requires funding. Few persons in the public sphere have sufficient private resources to enable them to defer from raising funds from outside sources. That is the reason why businessmen belong to the favored group targeted by political entrepreneurs in need of funding. In our case, the Constitution for Israel committee, with money raised from Abraham Lev, a wealthy businessman from Petach Tikva, was able to print booklets containing the constitution for distribution to the public. Funds were likewise sought from abroad. Donations raised by Jewish volunteers in Canada and the United States were channeled to the committee through the New Israel Fund. According to the Fund's reports, it transferred to the movement $169,000 in 1988, $180,000 in 1989, $275,000 in 1990, $414,000 in 1991, $245,000 in 1992 and $85,000 in 1993. Other organizations, such as the Meyerhoff Fund in Baltimore, Maryland, sent money to the committee at the behest of members such as Binyamin Netanyahu and Yitzchak Rabin.[94]

### *Summary*

In this section, we analyzed the political entrepreneur's actions prior to his or her recruitment of funds. The method for seeking contributions is related to the type of public involved in the process. We also examined the relationship between the entrepreneur and his group, with a special emphasis on his recruitment of funds and professional support. In the next section, we examine the different strategies of recruiting the public's support after initial resources have been secured.

## *Strategies for Recruiting Public Support: Policy versus Political Rule Change, the Media, Focusing (Narrowing) the Targets, Utilization of Crises, Reinforcements*

In this section, we examine the different strategies entrepreneurs use to recruit public support. These strategies are derived primarily from their objectives: whether to introduce changes in policy (within the system) or in political rules (system change). With that in mind, entrepreneurs will use the media, destination focusing, crises and reinforcements as they deem necessary.

### *Objective: Policy versus Political Rule Change*

According to the collective action literature, entrepreneurs are predisposed to choosing the least costly objective for political change—promotion of policy change rather than system change. Thus, when pondering his course of action, Reichmann could choose one of two options: to continue promoting institutional change by focusing on electoral change or to shift to the behavior stipulated in the existing rules, in this case, running for the Knesset. However, against the model's predictions, Reichmann chose the more costly route of electoral change instead of running for the Knesset, despite the fact that he lacked the necessary resources and that the public agenda had changed, an event that ushered in a period of decreased public support. The question therefore becomes, why did he make this choice?

The intensive external lobby caused the members of the movement's steering committee to ponder whether it might be preferable to join the political system and struggle from within. In other words, would it be more productive to run for the Knesset as a party that favored adoption of a constitution? A survey invited by Reichmann found that a new movement-based party could earn the support of 36.8 percent of the public, with 41 percent opposed to the idea of a constitution and over 22 percent having no opinion on the matter.

After consulting numerous professionals, Reichmann gathered the steering committee members at the Dan Hotel in Tel-Aviv. Arye Rotenberg (Kesher Barel advertising agency), Moshe Teomim (Gitam agency) and Yossi Yasur headed the electoral campaign. Rotenberg and Yasur opposed the notion of direct competition in the political sphere. They were already obligated to the Labor Party and had no intention of becoming full-time politicians. Al Schwimmer, as a close friend of Shimon Peres (Labor Party), also vetoed the notion. With his closest supporters objecting to the tactic of forming a political party and running in the elections strategy, Reichmann found that the costs of his campaign had risen beyond his capacity. He was therefore forced to yield to his colleagues and choose the option of external collective action.[95] In other words, although Reichmann's first choice was to run for a Knesset seat as predicted by the literature, his choice of the second option, collective action, resulted from the structural constraints within his privileged group.

### *The Media*

A major tool employed by political entrepreneurs is the media. They use it to influence groups, shape public opinion and highlight the issues of interest to them (Doron, 1986). And so, from the very start, members of the Constitution for Israel movement placed numerous advertisements in the daily press and on buses, held interviews, wrote articles and held conferences, all of which were widely covered by the media.[96] Rotenberg managed to persuade the publishers of *Haaretz* and other local dailies to provide him with advertising free of charge. He promised that if the movement eventually collected sufficient funds, it would repay them. One major role of the ads was to appeal to the public to join the struggle and donate money.

Another issue related to the use of media is that of *timing, which is crucial* for placing an issue at the forefront of the public's awareness. For instance, in 1987, public opinion polls began to indicate that Shimon Peres, Chairman of the Labor Party and leader of the Alignment, was losing his popularity relative to Yitzhak Shamir, the sitting prime minister.[97] This led to a series of political crises reflected in Peres's attempts to convene an international peace conference as well as his threats to dissolve the unity government and call for elections.[98] These events led Amnon Rubinstein (Shinui) to withdraw from the government. In a letter to Shamir, he pointed out the reasons for his departure:

> A complete rejection of Peres' peace initiative...such a humiliating and intolerable state of mutual paralysis...that turns...the government into a laughing stock....[99]

These and other crises shaped the public's feeling that "the government and the Knesset cannot take a stand on principals...the legal system fills that gap,"[100] and that "this is a state that has not been ruled in the recent years...and the blunders have no address...there is a deliberate lack of desire to make decisions. The fear of a political stalemate preoccupies Labor and the Likud . . . ."[101]

A solution that began to be bandied about was "*change in the electoral system.*"[102] A number of other groups began to act in parallel with the Constitution for Israel movement. These included the Aviv group as well as a group of parliamentarians, led by two Knesset members, Mordechai Virshubski and Gad Yaacobi, who submitted a legislative proposal for electoral change: from proportional elections to regional elections. These events prompted Reichmann to turn to the media in order to portray himself as the initiator of the latest demand for a written constitution in the public's eye.[103]

### *Focusing (Narrowing) the Targets*

Another strategy available to political entrepreneurs is to narrow the struggle's destination. This strategy is usually employed in the more advanced stages of collective action, because at *the first stage, the strategy for recruiting public support involves choosing a general destination* that coincides with the broadest range of public opinion. Reichmann chose such a destination in 1985 when he established the Constitution for Israel committee to promote the general idea of an Israeli constitution. His purpose was to galvanize public opinion and cause a wave of collective action while "*hoping that from the public discussion, a new path would develop for the State of Israel.*"[104]

We should note that additional elements may explain Reichmann's choice to promote the general idea of an Israeli constitution, outside the parliament. Events since the 1970s have shown that outside interest groups in Israel as elsewhere can successfully advance legislative policies that work in their favor. Well-organized interest groups have therefore accumulated a great deal of power. For example, the *Yad LeAchim* organization influenced a revision in the laws covering the behavior of missionaries, consumer organizations have influenced passage of consumer protection laws. Agricultural settlement movements managed to persuade the Ministry of Agriculture and the Ministry of Finance to cancel the millions of dollars of debt they owed to the Ministry of Agriculture, which had provided them with government-backed loans.[105] The familiar model of influencing legislation by being elected to the Knesset had been supplanted by the effective lobbying of powerful pressure groups.

Another explanation could be that Reichmann's experience with Rubinstein had taught him that choosing a general destination is more productive for recruiting the support of the electorate than a specific one.

At the same time, Rubinstein's Shinui party underwent an internal political crisis when it decided to join a government coalition that included the religious parties, with Ariel Sharon (a rightist and militarist) as Minister of Commerce and Industry.[106]

*A similar strategy was adopted by Reichmann after the so-called "dirty trick" crisis.* Accelerating popular discontent with crisis-prone Israel's governance system had, by this time, produced three avenues for public protest: Reichmann's Constitution for Israel movement, Avi Kadish's movement—he started his hunger strike on March 27, 1990, and the community leaders' movement that became active at the end of March 1990. All three avenues called for electoral change as a solution to the problem of nongovernability. On April 7, 1990, the steering committee of Reichmann's Constitution for Israel movement planned a major demonstration in Malchey Israel square, featuring the above three groups gathered together under a banner reading "Down with Corruption." This initial unification of resources continued in newspaper ads for the purpose of pressuring the Knesset to pass Reichmann's proposal. One ad placed on the eve of the Knesset vote read: "Tomorrow, Monday, May 28, 1990, we shall know who votes for and who against direct election of the prime minister."[107]

Evidence that the steering committee had found a solution sufficiently general to appeal to all types of players can be observed from the size of the rally; nearly 250,000 people participated in the demonstration in Malchey Israel square.[108] That three public protest groups had combined resources was a fairly rare event in Israel's political culture. The solution entailed focused on changing a crucial segment of the electoral system—which was to choose the prime minister. Later, the support of other interest groups was recruited, such as handicapped veterans and outspoken community leaders. In effect, Reichmann and his colleagues had established: "An umbrella group . . . for all the protest organizations demanding a change in the political system."[109]

After rallying public opinion, the next step entrepreneurs must take is choosing a strategy that will sustain public support and group member expectations within the framework of the resources at their disposal. Focusing (narrowing) the target of the struggle is just such a strategy. More often in the final stage a less costly preferred strategy is to redefine the target as a more feasible one. The history of the formulation and passage of the Direct Election Law illustrates how this strategy worked in the Israeli political environment.

In 1983, when Rubinstein sat in the Knesset as a member of Shinui, he resubmitted Hans Klinghoffer's original draft legislation regarding Basic Law: Human Rights, for a preliminary reading in the Knesset. The proposal's availability eliminated the need for him to invest significant resources in the preparation of a new draft. The shift in objective *from passage of a constitution to passage of one basic law* meant the narrowing of an objective due to resource constraints.

Still another example is the process begun after the meeting where Reichmann first presented his movement's demand that the current session of the Knesset pass *three laws: one pertaining to human rights, one instituting direct election of the prime minister, and one revising the Knesset elections system* (November 12, 1988). *Each law thus focused on a specific segment of Israel's political institutions without demanding* thoroughgoing institutional change.[110] As the process continued, a further episode of destination focusing took place. Reichmann and the steering committee decided to drop electoral system change, which was reframed as part of a gradual solution, to *focusing on the destination of direct elections of the prime minister.* This change in destination came about at low cost to Reichmann as an entrepreneur. It also better fitted the core of the sociopolitical crisis—the need to select the prime minister in a more transparent way, free of the political manipulation intrinsic to Israel's parliamentary governance system.

## *Utilization of Crises*

According to the model, political entrepreneurs prefer long-lasting crises because the longer the crises remain high on the public agenda—which in today's world also invites intense media exposure—the greater the opportunities to leverage those crises into a framework for keeping their own ideas before the public. The fundamental claim made here is that entrepreneurs translate social crises into policy problems for which they can propose a solution. This proposal is then transformed into electoral capital which may (or may not) be accepted by different players; in some circumstances, that solution can take the form of an institutional change. According to the model, utilizing crises to promote salience is a low-cost strategy for obtaining high benefits in terms of salience.[111]

Political crises facilitate this process by *exposing the problematic nature of the existing social order* at very low cost to political entrepreneurs.[112] Revelation of poor institutional functioning can constitute a crisis from the point of view of the political system as a result of the subsequent decline in public faith in its government. But from the political entrepreneur's perspective, that same crisis lends credibility to his or her interpretations of its source and thus resolution.[113]

This state of affairs makes it easier—and less costly—to resolve the "collective action problem." But what constitutes a crisis? In the following, we demonstrate the change in the public's crisis-resolution preferences, generally reflected in "semi-exit" behavior. This behavior reflects the public's preference for finding policies proposed by external policy-makers or, in other words, for solutions originating outside the existing system of political rules. For now, we shall deal with crises that would have reached catastrophic magnitudes if a solution had not been found in time.

We now return to 1983, when Rubinstein, now a Knesset member (Shinui), decided to resubmit Klinghoffer's legislative proposal for a Basic Law: Human Rights, for a preliminary reading. His timing is explained by the structural conditions that reflected public dissatisfaction with the conduct of Israel's government during the Shlom HaGalil operation in 1982.[114] Rubinstein effectively utilized this crisis by being the first one to identify it and apply it to achieving his own purposes.

Similar considerations came into the play in the summer of 1988, when Reichmann decided to turn to the media to publicize his ideas regarding reform of the electoral system and again in November 4, 1988, during a previously mentioned gathering at Tel-Aviv University's School of Law and the protest at Malchey Yisrael Square.[115] The session's timing was designed to maximize Reichmann's leverage just prior to the 1988 elections, when the parties and factions were preparing their campaigns.[116]

Timing also played a role in March 1990, when Rubinstein, Libai, Lynn and Tsiddon filed their respective legislative proposals demanding direct election of the prime minister. What drove submission of the propositions was the political crisis incited by the "dirty trick"[117] scandal (March 1990), initiated by Shimon Peres, who was then in the throes of his attempts to form a narrow coalition government composed of left-wing and religious parties. Peres's aim was to establish a Labor government, which he would head, including the religious parties as its coalition partners. The event initiating this process was Shamir's denouncement of the political peace process. In March, 1990, Labor handed the Likud an ultimatum—to accept the US Secretary of State James Baker's proposal and let Palestinian representatives from abroad and East Jerusalem participate in the negotiations between Israel and the Palestinians, to be conducted in Cairo. Once Shamir refused, Labor, together with Shas, held a vote of no confidence. On March 15, the national unity government fell, with 60 Knesset members voting for and 55 against its dispersion (Shas's five Knesset members did not attend).[118] Newspapers wrote about the religious legislation Peres had promised would be passed, which caused a public uproar.[119] That is, during coalition bargaining, Knesset members had often displayed a tendency to desert their parties in order to help a rival faction based on offers of ministerial positions. This phenomenon increased the public's anger still further.[120] The crisis, whose structural roots lay in Israel's parliamentary system of government, became a golden opportunity for promoting electoral system reform as the demanded solution to the crisis.[121]

At the same time, new players joined the fray, increasing the sense of crisis. Avi Kadish and Shahar Ben Meir (Reichmann's student), initiated a hunger strike near the Knesset. Sensing the public's mood, the media played up the story.[122] In a few days, thousands of citizens gathered around the Knesset and the two strikers became national heroes. Taking advantage of the protest's electoral potential, numerous prominent community leaders joined the steering committee and organized a major demonstration.[123]

*However, the positive effects of the problem's exposure may invite some negative consequences.* For instance, due to the public's interest in the behavior of Knesset members, the media and the press gave extensive coverage to Knesset sessions. A poll conducted by the Teleseker Institute in March 1990 found that 67 percent of the public supported the idea of a constitution. The exposure led to criticism from journalists,[124] Academia[125] and politicians, such as the Minister of Justice Abraham Sharir (who later became a major participant in the scandal), Likud, and Yossi Sarid, Ratz, the Movement for Civil Rights and Peace, and the religious parties, all of whom had been indifferent to electoral reform prior to the scandal.[126] The religious parties were especially vehement in their protest because they feared the religious freedom a constitution would grant.

The literature states that when a social crisis subsides, the change initiative weakens.[127] And this is what happened: On April 26, 1990, Peres informed the president of his inability to assemble a government and Yitzhak Shamir, together with 38 Knesset members, began attempts to establish a government to be headed by Shamir. Two retired Knesset members from the Likud Party, Yitzhak Moday and the same Avraham Sharir, returned to back Shamir's government. Knesset member Efraim Gur left Labor to join the Likud. Three far-right factions—Techia, Tzomet and Moledet—with seven seats and the Mafdal with five seats;

Shas with five seats, including the Minister of Absorption Yitzhak Peretz, who retired from Shas, joined as well, as did Degel HaTorah with two seats and Eliezer Mizrahi (Agudat Israel).

On June 11, the government proposed by Yitzhak Shamir (Likud) received 62 votes for and 57 against. With the approval of the government, the waves of protest subsided. As the journalist Zvi Gilat wrote: "Thus, after inciting the entire nation against it, the system celebrates its victory."[128] That is, once the internal institutional crisis was resolved by means of mechanisms—political rules—peculiar to that institution, the public tends to lose interest in reform, a response that paves the way for future crises originating in the same structural malady.

*As the crisis subsided, Reichmann was forced to begin a waiting period* in anticipation of the next crisis. He would not have to wait long. Months after Shamir's government was installed (June 1990), several minor crises erupted, reflecting the system's nongovernability with respect to issues related to religion and the state,[129] negotiations with the Palestinians and coalition structure.[130] These crises continued until late 1991, when new elections were scheduled for June 1992. These issues, resonating through the media, made fertile soil for the Constitution for Israel steering committee members to renew their struggle.

## *Techniques for Attracting the Public*

The interaction between the political entrepreneur and his or her group members or the general public is based on a built-in conflict[131] due to the presence of "free riders" as well as the "collective action problem." This forces entrepreneurs to use incentives coming from other spheres of life (secondary products) to keep them interested and active.[132] One highly efficient secondary product is entertainment. And so, to spark public interest, the Constitution for Israel steering committee solicited the participation of well-known singers to perform at the demonstration held in Malchey Israel Square on January 16, 1988. The artists selected, including, Shalom Chanoch, Shlomo Gronich, Corinne Alal, Chaim Moshe and Ariel Zilber, were trusted pop stars. Their presence conferred legitimacy and a measure of trendiness to the movement.

## *Summary*

In order to recruit public support, entrepreneurs apply many tactics and techniques. Their choice depends, first and foremost, on the decision as to whether the objective is a change of policy or of political rules. In the preceding, we surveyed practices such as utilization of the media, destination focusing, crisis utilization and incentives. The next section examines how these practices are directed at politicians.

## 3.6 Level 2: Entrepreneurs—Interest Groups—Politicians

This section analyzes the activities of political entrepreneurs within the framework of interest groups and political relations. Here, the main tool in the entrepreneur's arsenal is lobbying, that is, the application of strategies that address Knesset members' short-term interests for the purpose of convincing them to make the "right" decision. In the following, our analysis focuses on cooperation between outside and parliamentary entrepreneurs in reference to implementation of the Direct Elections Law.

### *Politicians' Time Perception: Short-Term Considerations*

Short-term considerations, the major variables shaping interactions between entrepreneurs, interest groups and politicians, certainly came into play during the struggle to pass the law providing for the direct election of the prime minister. Thus, in 1988, with elections for the Twelfth Knesset drawing closer, Ehud Olmert (Likud), David Libai (Alignment, Israel Labor Party) and others decided to maximize their chances for re-election and enhance their prestige by proposing a bill that called for a change in the electoral system towards regional-proportional elections.[133] During that summer, Labor decided not to vote for reform, which had been supported by the Knesset's Constitution, Law and Justice Committee. The reason for this refusal was the proximity of the elections. Peres (Alignment-Labor) and Shamir (Likud) were preoccupied with the upcoming elections and therefore reluctant to undermine the interests of those small parties that were expected to constitute the decisive force as to who would construct the future coalition government.[134] Dan Margalit, a leading political journalist, noted that Labor would not vote on the reform due to an "understanding between Labor and the Mafdal that Labor would not approve the proposition despite its platform's obligation to do so. The Mafdal urged that Labor relinquish reform in return for support by the religious parties regarding the separation of elections for the Knesset from local elections."[135]

Shamir's reasons for acting as he did were a bit more complicated. He was anxious to increase the Likud's prestige by supporting a proposition regarding the "who is a Jew" issue,[136] submitted by the religious parties.[137] In order not to be perceived as overtly pro-religious, as demanded by his party's coalitional agreements with the religious factions, support for electoral reform was necessary. In order to disentangle himself from this vice of contradictory interests, he allowed his party's members to vote freely, "according to their conscience," during the first call of the election system change proposition. This declared freedom to vote made it possible to pass the proposition in the first call. All Labor Knesset members voted for the proposition, while the Likud's voices were divided, with Ratz voting for the proposition while Mapam, Techia and all of the religious parties voting against. Sixteen Knesset members chose to absent themselves during the voting. With the end of the voting, a commotion rose: Yitzhak Peretz (Shas) claimed that the Likud had not fulfilled its promise of rejecting the proposition. Shamir had, in effect, taken advantage of the first call vote to overcome the coalition barriers placed by the religious parties. *Haaretz* reporters later wrote that "after voting on the elections system change, the prime minister [Shamir] had said that the religious parties had nothing to worry about: the proposition would be killed in the Constitution, Law and Justice Committee."[138]

Time also explains the interesting interaction between Reichmann and Rubinstein, the two main political entrepreneurs in our story. One would expect them to cooperate on the basis of their professional bonds, ideological views and shared experience. However, throughout the period, while Reichmann promoted his goals of passing a constitution and changing the electoral system, Rubinstein refrained from active involvement. Why? The answer is timing: with elections in the offing, it was not to Rubinstein's interest to support dramatic institutional change. It was Rubinstein, after all, and not Reichmann, who now sat in the Knesset and was concerned about re-election. Furthermore, Reichmann's more vocal anti-religious party stance would have harmed Rubinstein's desire to appeal to centrists were they to be seen as active partners in the initiative.[139]

Similarly, Rubinstein indicates by the above that he does not approve of Reichmann's destination focus on the electoral system. The concentrated activity of the Constitution for Israel movement against the religious parties was damaging its ability to link itself to the political center. In the current context in which Ratz (a leftist secular party) had already taken steps toward electoral reform, any expected benefit from taking a similar stand was small when compared to criticizing the security situation.[140]

Another explanation for the lack of cooperation lies at Rubinstein's understanding of the intra-parliamentary legislative processes. Past experience had taught him to prefer the tactic of narrowing targets and using proposals of laws (the second filing of Klinghoffer's proposition regarding Basic Law: Human Rights, June 1982) to the one Reichmann chose to apply a broader target such as a Constitution for Israel. Rubinstein had learned that the tactic of "procedural alacrity"—a strategy that entails taking advantage of parliamentary procedures to promote an idea swiftly—to minimize resistance, especially from the larger groups, was more effective. Commenting on Rubinstein's 1990 proposal to limit the participation in political parties of state employees, journalist Zvi *Zrahya* from *Haaretz* noted that: "Knesset member Rubinstein asked me not to publish this before the elections, so as not to raise a commotion. 'Let me pass this proposal before the larger parties thwart my attempt,' he had asked. Tactically speaking, Rubinstein was correct. However, publicly speaking, the proposal should be freely and openly debated."[141]

Returning to Shamir's reason for letting Likud members vote freely in March 1992, the atmosphere was charged with campaign tensions and Shamir was attempting to maximize the Likud's chances of winning the election. Polls had shown that the public viewed electoral reform as the solution it Israel's nongovernability. The time was perfect for keeping all the groups promoting change within the public eye. Taking advantage of public preferences, Labor introduced reform into its platform to take advantage of the idea's electoral capital, which locked the party into this position. Concurrently, the Likud's internal instability, with various factions challenging Shamir's leadership, strengthened Labor's popularity. Three days before the end of the Knesset session, Shamir allowed Likud Knesset members to vote freely as a ploy to increase his party's chances in the competition with Labor, which had adopted the idea of open primaries and recently elected Yitzhak Rabin as its chairman (February 1992).[142]

Timing becomes most critical, obviously, when legislation or decision-making is related to elections. Maximizing one's chances of being elected is paramount among the factors considered by all politicians, even after an institutional change has transpired.[143] An examination of the voting patterns of some Knesset members during the second and third readings of the direct election for Prime Minister Bill allows us to readily observe the related effects. The law passed with a majority of 55 to 32, on the third reading on March 18, 1992. Quite noticeable was the deliberate absence of some Knesset members who, we may surmise, assumed that such a step would reap the benefits necessary to increase their chances of being elected. These included Yitzhak Shamir, who had opposed the law from the beginning but chose to absent himself rather than vote counter to public opinion. Similarly, Ehud Olmert, even though he was among those who proposed the law, was absent, because its passage would have decreased his chances against Netanyahu, his chief competitor for the Likud's leadership. A similar argument explains the position of the Likud's Moshe Arens, Yitzhak Moday and Roni Milo, as opposed to that of Netanyahu[144] and Tzachi Hanegbi, one of Netanyahu's supporters. Yitzchak Rabin (Labor), who the public preferred to Shamir and to his main contender, Peres, also chose to be absent as a means to maintain his centrist position, similar to that of Shamir. This tactic nonetheless did not prove useful at the time: Shamir and the Likud lost the 1992 elections.

## *Summary*

A politician—as well as any political entrepreneur and interest group—is influenced in behavior by his time perspective. Thus, the major criterion deciding politicians' choice of strategies is maximization of their chances of being (re-)elected, an inherently short-term goal. In the next section, we discuss lobbying as the prominent activity of the political entrepreneur.

## *Lobbying Against the Knesset Members*

The practice of political entrepreneurship resembles that of political pressure groups: both are attempts to influence Knesset members who belong to the Knesset committees meeting on issues of concern to them. In addition, the effectiveness of lobbying often depends on planning different activities in order to obtain media attention and coverage. A major portion of the political entrepreneur's time is devoted to cultivating intensive relationships with the media; akin to the activity of a public relations office or spokesperson. Within this framework of persuasion, lobbyists compete with fellow spokesmen from government offices and private interests in feeding information to the media that may affect the public's daily agenda.[145]

Yael Ishai draws a distinction between two types of groups: those interested in limited problems and those who try to change the world. According to Ishai, the more a group tends toward the second type—and the broader its objective—the greater the probability that it will use pressure tactics in order to achieve its goal. Ishai's research has indicated that "this does not mean that the groups that do not use pressure, do not have a broad public impact, but that applying pressure is not the prominent characteristic in the activity of the public organizations in Israel."[146] In the following, we demonstrate that in the case of the Direct Elections Law, pressure tactics came to characterize the Constitution for Israel steering committee's activities; including use of national-level and personal threats. This approach might be explained by the movement's internal structure: nongovernability (political and economic instability) as well as alternative political culture. Such conditions support short-term considerations as well as the use of pressure to maximize short-term results, actions that promote institutional instability.

For instance, in 1990, the four MKs who filed the proposal for the direct election of the prime minister decided, together with Reichmann and the Constitution for Israel steering committee members, to address the public by means of a press conference to be held (September 11, 1990) prior to the proposition's being filed with the Knesset Constitution, Justice and Law Committee. The shared proposal evoked favorable[147] as well as negative reactions. Opponents to the proposal were represented by Dr. Arik Carmon, Head of the Israel Democracy Institute.

One could characterize Constitution for Israel steering committee members as a political pressure group, Knesset lobbyists who met with Knesset members and pressured them. The Knesset is the forum in which changes in law are legislated, made legal. Knesset members are therefore the obvious targets in which to invest resources. A marketing campaign was therefore launched by the committee, with Knesset members who supported the proposal lauded in newspaper advertisements while those who opposed it criticized in the same way. By means of advertising and articles published in all the major newspapers, the committee would expose politicians' positions[148] and pressure those who hesitated[149] and encouraged others.[150]

As lobbyists in the Knesset, external entrepreneurs cooperate with internal, parliamentary entrepreneurs. This cooperation emerges from shared professional identity, as in the case of Reichmann and Rubinstein, who shared the same liberal approach to the legal profession, as well as positions in public service. The two had worked together in the same political parties and later struggled to introduce support for institutions of higher education other than universities into the government budget. By shifting the struggle's focus to electoral system from passage of a constitution, Reichmann wanted to preserve his public status and meet his reference group's expectations, both at the same time. His program came to match the interests of a group of politicians led by Olmert and Libai.

Cooperation can be explained by *identity of interests* too. For instance, in 1988, what tied the members of the group of politicians led by Olmert and Libai was more than professional. The respective link was opportunism or, an opportunity to practice political entrepreneurship. Each saw a change in the electoral system as providing them with the electoral capital that they could use to promote their private interests, which included elevated prestige and re-election. The attraction of filing the respective proposal was its responsiveness to the public dissatisfaction[151] that had been furthered by the announcement of early elections.[152]

Another instance of cooperation among political entrepreneurs took place on October 16, 1990, when the Knesset approved the request made by the Constitution, Law and Justice Committee to merge four change propositions. This agreement marked the beginning of shared parliamentary and public activity to promote the Direct Election Law, beginning with recruiting funds abroad and ending with lobbying Knesset members.[153]

An interesting incident of cooperation between external entrepreneurs took place between Constitution for Israel members, the Jerusalem Center for Public Affairs led by Professor Dan Elazar, the government reform movement led by Avi Kadish, the Citizens who Care movement and the United States and Canada Immigrants Union. They coordinated their activities on three fronts: (1) the public front, to apply pressure on legislators; (2) the media front, to shape public opinion and increase pressure on legislators, and (3) the partisan-parliamentary front, with direct contacts established with the four Knesset members who had filed the aforementioned proposed legislation.[154]

*Lobbying is not unidimensional; the practices it adopts are rationally chosen for their efficiency in pressuring* policy-makers and politicians. The ability to do so—and the action patterns chosen to achieve a lobbyist's goals—is the product of the structure of the political sphere and its institutions.[155] Reichmann in particular used a variety of strategies to further his goals. These included:

1. Taking advantage of the Knesset's visitors' gallery.
2. Taking advantage of a majority presence in the Knesset to promote a legislative proposal.
3. Applying "procedural alacrity."
4. Recruiting other parties as resources to exploit structural conditions.

5. Focusing on specific Knesset members with the intent of increase their chances of being re-elected.
6. Taking advantage of confusion during decision-making.

In the following, we detail these strategies.

1. *Taking advantage of the Knesset's visitors' gallery.* On June 7, 1988, when the first reading of the proposed legislation changing the electoral system was conducted, only 30 Knesset members were present. Eliezer Kulas (Likud), chair of the Knesset Constitution, Law and Justice Committee, who supported the proposition, tried to create a holiday atmosphere. He therefore seated most of the members of the Likud's liberal factions in extra chairs in the special visitors' balcony. However, it remained almost empty. Amos Ben Vered later wrote that the empty gallery signified "the public's indifference toward Professor Uriel Reichmann's invitation for a mass presence in the Knesset at the time the proposition was being submitted."[156] As the discussion proceeded, Chairman Kulas understood that the bill would not pass, so, at the last moment, he postponed the vote (for a detailed account of the central role played by Kulas as the committee chairman, see the next section).

2. *Taking advantage of a majority presence in the Knesset to promote a legislative proposal.* In 1988, as the Knesset was nearing the end of its term, the Constitution for Israel steering committee members decided to apply pressure on Knesset members, especially Eliezer Kulas, Chair of the Constitution, Law and Justice Committee chairman, a supporter of the proposal, who had the power and position to promote the bill.[157] Kulas set the debate for June 14, 1988, because he knew that the two largest parties would congregate their members for a debate on the touchy subject of "who is a Jew"; he thought that this would be an appropriate moment to submit the proposal because a majority (61) of Knesset members would be present. There would be no discussion during this session, with voting taking place immediately after the proposal's announcement. As a result of this ploy, the proposal to change the electoral system was passed by a majority of 69 (for) against 37 (opposed) Knesset members.

3. *"Procedural alacrity,"* a strategy that entails taking advantage of parliamentary procedures to promote an idea swiftly. In doing so, the entrepreneur masks his or her real motives either by promoting ambiguous (reached through compromise) proposals that will not upset his

or her potential opponents, or by using parliament's breaks to rush through laws. Another rationale for applying "procedural alacrity" is the opportunity it provides to benefit from changes in the structural conditions that previously had frustrated the processes.

For instance, in 1988, just before the Knesset dispersed prior to the upcoming elections, Reichmann attempted to foster a settlement between the *Likud* and the *Alignment-Labor* so that the proposal for mixed regional-proportional elections could be approved by the Knesset Constitution, Law and Justice Committee, necessary before it being presented for its second and third Knesset readings. Eliezer Kulas, chair of the Constitution, Law and Justice Committee, who had lost in the Liberal Party's internal elections, "had nothing to lose" by furthering the law's passage;[158] so, on July 26, 1988, Kulas convened the committee's members in an attempt to reach a compromise formulation, expecting the law to be pass a few days before the Knesset dispersed. While the Constitution, Law and Justice Committee members were discussing the law's particulars, Kulas received a telephone call from Prime Minister Shamir, who instructed him to table the voting on the proposition and postpone the whole thing until the next Knesset was formed in the wake of election results. Shamir wanted to retain the support of the religious parties because they could tip the electoral scales in favor of the Likud as opposed to the *Alignment-Labor.*[159] This, indeed, is exactly what happened.

"Procedural alacrity" is especially useful when trying to take advantage of transformations in those structural conditions that had formerly been available for blocking entrepreneurs. When these conditions change, the entrepreneurs can use this timing to promote their proposals. Such an event took place on March 19, 1990, during coalition negotiations with the ultra-Orthodox parties, which generally opposed the idea of direct elections. Dan Meridor (*Likud*), Minister of Justice, had opposed the electoral reform proposals filed by Libai, Tsiddon, Lynn and Rubinstein on the basis of government's appointment of a special bipartisan committee (headed by Gad Yaacobi) to investigate the matter.[160] However, contrary to expectations, the propositions passed the preliminary reading despite the government's opposition. Two months later, on May 28, 1990, after the Constitution, Law and Justice Committee's confirmation, four proposals were filed for the first reading in the Knesset. After their acceptance by the majority, Reichmann and his steering committee published an advertisement praising the four Knesset members.[161]

The success of Reichmann and his steering committee was attributed to their having taken advantage of the weakening power of the major party leaders, Shamir (*Likud*) and Peres (*Alignment-Labor*), both of whom were facing internal party opposition. The Likud had started negotiations to replace Shamir just while he was in the midst of assembling a government.[162] Peres's chicanery (the "dirty trick" incident) and Labor's failure in the 1988 elections had led to a renewed struggle for the party's leadership between Peres and Rabin, including a call for Peres to resign.[163] Public protest against a demonstration planned by Reichmann's Constitution for Israel steering committee was also a factor, it being scheduled during the voting for the four alleged proposals and presented as an opportunity to vent public frustrations with government. Shamir's request to unite the original four proposals into one,[164] timed as it was after the successful first reading of the proposed law, led to further procrastination,[165] which in turn aroused additional protest.[166]

4. *Recruiting other parties as resources to exploit structural conditions* that obligate party leaders to make value decisions. Entrepreneurs make use of this tactic to apply pressure on party and faction leaders. On the other hand, they also use the rules of the game that promote small parties, especially those that play a central role in the legislative process.[167] For instance, in 1990, Rubinstein (*Shinui*) and Tsiddon (*Tzomet*) decided to recruit their parties to promote their reform proposals, which were readily achieved. *Tzomet* even sent an ultimatum to Prime Minister Shamir, threatening him that it would leave the government if he did not raise the bill for a second reading before November 20, 1990. *Tzomet* also reminded Shamir that the right to vote freely had been granted to coalition partners in return for their agreement to join the government. The parties sought to keep the issue alive in anticipation of the possibility of early elections.

Since Israeli politics are managed through national parties running national lists of candidates, they have far greater influence on the public than that of any lone Knesset member, even if he does belong to their party.[168] Moreover, parties in the Israeli system have the power to influence individual Knesset members. Therefore, the individual candidates face relative weakness as well as lack of specific accountability of the MK once elected because his loyalty is to the party and not the voter. The need to establish a coalition turns the parties into powerful political players. For example, to achieve coalition after the "Dirty Trick" (March 1990), the Likud accepted Agudat Israel's suggestion of joining the coalition—and thus strengthening the Likud's ability to control legislation—in return for its submitting four sectoral bills for Knesset approval, each placing bans on significant aspects of public behavior: the sale of pork, abortion, offensive advertisements, and public transport on the Sabbath.[169] The *Likud* accepted these terms but also promised to remove electoral reform from the Knesset's agenda.[170]

The Likud's acceptance of the religious parties' terms placed the former at odds with the platforms of its other coalition partners, Tzomet and Shinui, which were obliged to take an opposite stand. This stand was chosen not for ideological reasons but because it was viewed as maximizing these parties' chances of re-election, especially since the public was beginning to feel that the government had shifted radically toward the right by acquiescing to the religious bloc's demands,[171] which might work to their benefit in the upcoming elections. This situation also served as a stage on which different groups could put their parties' platforms on the public agenda.[172] During the ensuing coalition juggling, other Knesset members saw the opportunity to force the government to consider other matters as well.[173]

5. *Focusing on specific Knesset members with the intent of increasing their chances of being re-elected.* Since early 1991, the Reichmann political lobby had been focusing on Likud members. By taking such actions, the four political entrepreneurs (i.e., Rubinstein, etc.) were trying to maximize their chances of having their bill passed on the second and third readings. Although many Likud members supported the proposal, the possibility still existed that Shamir might impose party or coalitional discipline. This possibility increased the centrality of the prime minister in their efforts. Reichmann and his colleagues attempted to influence Shamir through his party's Knesset members.[174] Thousands of postcards were sent to Likud members, and newspaper advertisements were placed naming those Likud activists who would no longer vote for the party.

An additional tactic was to publish the results of public opinion polls given the pending elections. The results of one poll[175] indicated that 78.9 percent of the respondents supported direct election of the prime minister. With such public backing, the Constitution for Israel steering committee hinted that it would compete as a political party. The committee members, although of left-center orientation, argued that their method ensured the Likud's electoral success because the majority of Orthodox Jews would vote for a *Likud* candidate.[176] This argument convinced many of the Likud members.

However, Shamir opposed the idea, stating that in the wake of the Gulf War (August 1990–February 1991) and preparations for the Madrid peace conference, the country must have a united government. For him, this was not a time for changes. Similar claims had been made against the formulation of a constitution by all previous Israeli prime ministers, including David Ben Gurion and Menahem Begin. Peres changed his mind about the proposition after gauging his own chances of becoming prime minister. Therefore, he now supported only the idea. Peres's reversals, like those of other candidates then and later, directly reflected how they perceived support of reform and affected their political futures. Throughout these events, the political entrepreneurs ensured a steady stream of polls in order to "help" them make their decisions.

6. *Taking advantage of confusion during decision-making.* A tactic meant to disorient decision-makers may work to the benefit of political entrepreneurs, especially if fatigue comes to characterize the players. Consider, for instance, the voting on the proposal for a Direct Election Law, held January 7, 1992. Due to the numerous disagreements, the Knesset's Chair Dov Shilanksi (Likud) divided the proposals into individual paragraphs, to be discussed one at a time. The debate was very lengthy and took its toll in terms of fatigue. Eli Dayan (Alignment-Labor) demanded that the vote be called, declaring that: "we are neither prisoners nor hostages. Release us!"[177] In the confusion about the main issues and members' exhaustion, mistakes were made in the voting.[178]

Another characteristic of endless debate is the increase in disputes. This contentiousness can also be manipulated for the entrepreneur's benefit. For instance, during the aforementioned debate, Knesset members periodically left the chamber, passed notes to one another, screamed and protested about the results of the votes. Avraham Verdiger (*Agudat Israel*) voted twice on paragraph 3 (direct election of the prime minister). Due to his error, the results were a tie (57 to 57) and the paragraph was rejected. When Haim Ramon (*Alignment-Labor*) discovered what had happened, he objected, but Shilanski would not end the voting. At 5:00 a.m., Knesset members would mumble "for" or "against" in a state of grogginess, and the Direct Election Law was finally passed with the majority of 57 MKs against 56 MKs. However Lynn as the chair of the Constitution Law and Justice Committee demanded the return of the law back to the committee for further discussions since the final result was different from the proposition.[179] This situation reflects the chaos in the decision-making process characterized by short-term considerations.

This conclusion fits explanations of institutional change provided by Kenneth Arrow (1963) and William Riker (1980), who noted that in the background of every reform lie the conflicting preferences of many people. We claim that political and economic instability as well as procedural democratic norms impact on these preferences; together, they drive short-term interests to the fore. The consequent institutional change will aggravate the instability and thus be of short duration.

In conclusion, this section demonstrates the strategies used by political entrepreneurs to lobby political decision-makers. Entrepreneurs manipulate the media, cooperate with some of the Knesset members and take advantage of other people's states of mind. All of the strategies are applied according to the structural conditions characterizing the government. In the next section, we discuss what happens when a legislative proposal, as electoral capital, reaches the doorstep of the legislators in the form of a draft law.

## 3.7 Level 3: Political Entrepreneurs and Legislative Bodies

According to our model of political entrepreneurship (see chapter two), after a politician has made a decision, chosen a preferred policy and dealt with bureaucratic constraints, his or her legislative proposal must be approved by a legislative body. Members of that body—in this case Knesset members—usually have a range of interests, meaning that for a proposal to be passed and made into law, the policies of the individual legislator must fit the majority's preferences. To unravel how this web of interests is constructed, we now turn to analyzing the actions of politicians in parliament as well as their interactions with outside political entrepreneurs. The main parameters to be analyzed are:

- Central factors: prime ministers, party institutions, the chair of parliament's committee for constitutional matters (in this case, the Knesset Constitution, Justice and Law Committee)
- Ideology, profession and experience
- The type of compromise (sincere or strategic) reached between the objective and the subjective aspects of the reform proposal

### *Central Factors: Prime Ministers, Party Institutions and the Chair of the Knesset's Constitution, Justice and Law Committee*

Three factors shape the process of institutional change design: the power of party leaders, party institutions, and the status of the chair, the Knesset's Constitution, Justice and Law Committee. As noted earlier, their power results from their position in the political structures and institutions available to entrepreneurs for use in achieving their sought-for political outcomes.[180] We provide several examples to illustrate how political entrepreneurs employ these entities.

### *Prime Ministers as Focal Players*

Prime ministers are the chief political players in Israel. Their power derives from the political rules of the game that control the decision-making process.[181]

One might claim that the prime minister's—or party leader's—centrality in the public policy design process consists of two factors. The first one is the prime minister's structurally defined ability to demand discipline from his party members. Alternatively, if party members are free to vote as they please, a greater variety of policy ideas may be produced. The second factor is the prime minister's own attitude toward a given law. It should be noted that his attitude in turn depends on factors such as his or her status within the party, as coalition leader, and in the public's estimation. These parameters are interconnected and influence one another. Clearly, if the prime minister enjoys a strong degree of power, his attitude regarding the law will affect the attitudes of other politicians.

Until 1992, Yitzhak Shamir (*Likud*) and Shimon Peres (*Alignment-Labor*) wielded a great deal of power in their respective parties; this allowed them to navigate the process of institutional change and around partisan institutions. After 1992, their individual power declined. Polls reflected the return of Rabin's power as well as that of the revitalized Labor party. This situation induced both party leaders to promote the Direct Election Law.

The story of the formulation of the law requiring direct election of the prime minister also indicates instances where entrepreneurial efforts failed because their interests did not fit those of the sitting prime minister or party leaders. For instance, in 1988, Shimon Peres (*Alignment-Labor*) and Yitzhak Shamir (*Likud*), as party leaders, were busy preparing for the upcoming elections for the Twelfth Knesset. To avoid an image of acting against the interests of the smaller parties that have historically been pivotal in constructing Israel's coalition governments,[182] the two prevented the second and third votes (or readings) on electoral reform (which already passed the first vote) in the Eleventh Knesset.

In recognition of the party leaders' votes as central players, political entrepreneurs always include them at some point in their strategic planning. Over the history of the Constitution for Israel movement and the other reform proposals, we see that the political entrepreneurs had learned from their lessons about the importance of party leaders and so began to invest their resources in that direction. At the beginning of March 1988, when Knesset members Olmert, Libai, Magen, Lynn and Ovadia Eli (Likud) filed their proposal regarding electoral system change, the Constitution for Israel steering committee paid for a sizeable advertisement calling on the public to influence the party leaders:

> ...precisely today, due to the political crisis, we may have a chance to change something. *Write today to your party leader* [emphasis added—A.M.] saying that you support the proposition and demand that he and his party also support the electoral system change. We still have hope, but we do not have much time. (Signed) The Constitutional for Israel Committee.
>
> You can take part in an historical moment. Join the Constitution for Israel Committee.[183]

This direct appeal to the public was the response to the discovery that Shamir, as prime minister, was the main force behind the opposition to the proposal. The movement's leaders had met with Shamir several times but each time the meeting yielded no results. Shamir saw no value in promoting an electoral change that might threaten his position. The steering committee members thus continued their crusade by going directly to the public through articles published in the press[184] and by demonstrating outside the prime minister's house.

Viewed from the perspective of the sitting government, institutional (electoral) reform is clearly threatening. Party and faction leaders therefore also employ a variety of opposition tactics that must be considered in order to understand the process of institutional change. The main strategy by the leadership is committee formation. For instance, Shamir and Peres together thus established the Yaacobi Committee to examine Israel's governmental system. The Yaacobi Committee was designed to end in deadlock. As far as Shamir and Peres were concerned, the committee was merely a way to deal with public dissatisfaction.[185]

*What, then, are the factors influencing a prime minister's decisions? Although a prime minister's* centrality is determined by his or her place in the political structure, the political rules of the game affecting their electoral possibilities narrow their interests in action to short-term considerations, attuned to surviving, at minimum through the current term of office. Therefore, whenever structural conditions ensure the stability of the position, the cost of a prime minister's agreeing to a change of political rules exceeds its benefits. Even though a change in structure may alter the prime minister's considerations, this chance is not worth taking.

Haim Assa, a political strategist during Yitzhak Rabin's tenure (1992–1994), explains that "the preservation of political power is the first and foremost consideration of every prime minister."[186] Assa therefore maintains that if polls show that the public supports a law, the prime minister would support it to retain or enhance his electoral capital (consider passage of the 1994 National Health Insurance Law). This explanation sheds light on Shamir's behavior as well. For instance, it explains Shamir's agreement to allow free voting by his party's Knesset members in 1992, a release that led to passage of the Direct Election Law for Prime Minister. In the waning days of the Twelfth Knesset, with the upcoming elections on everyone's mind, polls revealed the public's preference for electoral reform, as if it was a major formula for curing the nation's sociopolitical ills. Such attitudes led the Israel Labor party to enter reform into its electoral capital column. Passage of the reform legislation effectively committed the Israel Labor party to take this position despite the fact that its support was primarily rhetorical, made for campaign purposes. Internal divisiveness in the Likud over the reform strengthened the Israel Labor party in the public's eyes. Shamir's release of Likud Knesset members from party discipline was therefore meant to enhance his status as a "democrat" and "reformer" before the voters.[187]

Maximization of electoral chances also explains Rabin's agreement to support the Direct Election Law as well, despite the fact that Israel Labor party was against allowing the law to pass during the current Knesset term. The Israel Labor party essentially attempted to co-opt the law by claiming that if it won, it would pass the law demanding direct election of the prime minister. The polls, however, indicated the public's impatience with such a delay.[188] Moreover, Rabin feared that if the Constitution for Israel Movement decided to participate in the elections as a separate list, Israel Labor's chances of winning would decline. In a meeting between Rabin and Uriel Reichmann held prior to the elections, the latter threatened to run that if the law was not passed in the current Knesset term. Rabin, of course, asked Reichmann not to do so.[189]

In these circumstances, as the chances that a political rule change will be accepted improve, the probability that change will be utilized as electoral capital also improve. Thus, when Shamir let his party's Knesset members vote freely in 1992, Knesset members from other parties began to jump on the pro-reform bandwagon, with everyone intent on making passage of the law its own electoral capital. Such considerations led Knesset members ranging from the Mafdal (a religious Zionist party) and the Likud to Mordechai Virshubski (*Meretz*)[190] to support the law. Their support nonetheless was qualified, depending on whether a number of conditions were fulfilled: (1) the law would come into effect during the next Knesset term; and (2) the Knesset could express its displeasure with a prime minister by means of a no-confidence vote that required a majority of only 61 Knesset members for acceptance. The law's promoters accepted these conditions, understanding that these conditions were requisite to pass the law.

### *Parties and Party Institutions*

The parties and their institutions in Israel constitute a structural factor able to promote political rules despite the decline in their power since the 1970s (Korn, 1998). Thus, in 1989, following the Yaacobi Committee's release of its recommendations regarding electoral reform, the parties faced the need to affirm their acceptance of the proposals within their institutions. *Alignment-Labor*, led by Peres, approved them the next day. Contrary to Shamir, Peres saw approval as a way to acquire public credibility as well as a lever for shaping an agenda that excluded rotation (note: Labor was then part of the national unity). From an internal, institutional perspective, he also wanted to silence the group of critical Knesset members, led by Libai. Turning to the *Likud*, Shamir, through Moshe Arens, the party's chair, appointed a three-man committee (Haim Corfo, Michael Dekel and Mordechai Ben-Porat) to reexamine the proposal as a ploy to postpone implementation of the approval process.[191]

Another instance took place in 1990. After the "dirty trick" incident, the Constitution for Israel steering committee met with four Knesset members—Rubinstein, Lynn, Tsiddon and Libai—to further direct election of the prime minister. For its campaign to be effective, the major parties and their institutions were to be recruited. Alignment-Labor, whose public image had been tainted by the "dirty trick,"[192] decided to support the Constitution for Israel proposal.[193] Alternatively, Shamir preferred to retain the existing system that had allowed him to rule, especially after having signed an agreement with Agudat Israel not to support the proposed system.[194]

In this battle for legitimacy and public support, Uriel Reichmann delivered to the Knesset (December 11, 1991) the movement's financial reports for the years 1988–1989 (the reports did not include the names of contributors). In 1989, the steering committee filed an appeal to the HCJ against the Minister of Finance and the Income Tax Commissioner, requesting recognition of the movement as a nonprofit association and contributions as tax-deductible. The sitting judges were Aharon Barak, Dov Levin and Gavriel Bach. The unanimous ruling, written by Barak, dismissed the appeal and determined that the organization's main purpose was to force the Knesset to accept constitutional change, an objective missing from its list of goals. The HCJ also ruled that the Minister of Finance's decision was not unreasonable and that politically oriented NGOs would not be entitled to tax relief.[195]

The centrality of the parties and their institutions in designing the proposal for direct election of the prime minister meant that political entrepreneurs had to be prepared to overcome party opposition and persuade party members to support the process. This meant shifting the sphere of activity to inside the parties.

To illustrate, in 1991, Reichmann's steering committee members understood that in order to pass their proposal for direct election of the prime minister, they had to focus on Likud members, especially on Prime Minister Shamir. One way to achieve this goal was to put pressure on the Likud's Central Committee, which could then pressure Shamir. The committee established a common headquarters with Likud activists and published advertisements in which David Magen, a Likud Knesset member, encouraged Central Committee members to join him in making history. These efforts were to no avail, especially after Shamir's intensive negative campaign, led by Corfo. However, the law's supporters, led by Magen and Netanyahu, understood the Central Committee's support of Shamir's stance did not obligate all Likud members.[196]

On June 9, 1991, after Corfo's declaration that the bill might harm the *Likud*, the small *Tzomet* party threatened to leave Shamir's coalition government if the party continued its antagonism to the proposal. It is worthy of note here that in November 1990, Tzomet had filed an ultimatum demanding the law's acceptance, but did nothing to realize its threat. This time, after the Likud's Central Committee voted against the proposal, Tzomet leaders Rafael Eitan and Yoash Tsiddon chose to leave the coalition. They claimed that the party discipline imposed on Likud members regarding a vote on the proposal had led to their decision. Shamir tried, unsuccessfully, to prevent their leaving, claiming that the Central Committee's decision did not obligate all *Likud* members. Yet, *Tzomet's* decision may have been more related to the short-term perception of the politicians and the upcoming elections in 1992 than the substance of the law. By leaving the coalition, *Tzomet* felt it could increase its credibility—hence, its electoral capital—with the public.[197]

### *The Chairman of the Constitution, Law and Justice Committee*

All democracies have legal and structural barriers that make it difficult for players outside the parliamentary system to achieve their goals.[198] One of the most important of these barriers in Israel is the Knesset's Constitution, Justice and Law Committee, which must approve every legislative proposal.

The committee's chair there, as in similar committees common to this governance regime, has considered power due to his or her role regarding construction of the committee's agenda.[199] If the committee's chair is interested in promoting a specific proposal, the entrepreneurs' chances of success increase, and vice versa. The readiness of entrepreneurs to cooperate with the committee chair therefore plays a key role in a proposal's passage. This was certainly true with respect to direct election of the prime minister because, from the point of view of the model, the committee's pivotal position made its chair a prime target for the steering committee's persuasion attempts.

For instance, on May 10, 1988, Eli Kulas (*Likud-Liberals*), the Constitution Committee's chair during the Eleventh Knesset, made a decision that increased the chances of passing the Olmert, Libai, Magen, Lynn and Eli proposal. Indeed, Kulas decided to approve submission of the Yaacobi Committee's compromise proposal for a first call reading in the Knesset.[200] Kulas himself was acting as an inside entrepreneur. His ideological affinity for the Constitution for Israel movement enables him to support the Olmert-Libai proposal. His backing was, however, rooted in the hope that it would increase his chances of being re-elected by promoting a law that would reduce the centralized power held by the Likud chairman, Shamir.

Another incident involved the actions taken by Uriel Lynn, the Constitution Committee chair during the Twelfth Knesset. Lynn, together with Rubinstein, Libai and Tsiddon, had tried to promote the Direct Election Law with all the means at his disposal. For instance, the debate on the proposal's second and third readings was set for late at night on January 2, 1991. Shamir imposed party discipline on Likud Knesset members. At that point, after about a hundred dissentions with the law were filed, leading Uriel Lynn used his structural power to delay the voting under the reasonable assumption that the proposal would not pass.

In a related event, Lynn delayed voting on the proposal by stating: "This is not the law we intended to bring before you."[201] Due to the possibility that the suggested amendments could alter the law completely, Lynn asked (January 2, 1992) for the committee's agreement to bring the revised proposal once more before the committee for added discussion. His anticipated scenario indeed materialized.

Parliamentary *committee chairs are also political players, motivated by their desire to maximize their chances of re-election.*[202] This observation best explains, as we have indicated, the behavior adopted by Eli Kulas in 1988 while serving as chair of the Knesset's Constitution, Justice and Law Committee. Despite the criticism of the proposed reform, he set discussion of the legislation for June 7, 1988. Opinions differed as to the possible success of this move. Dan Margalit, a leading political reporter, surveyed opinions regarding the chair's move:

> The majority should support the proposition, yet there is doubt whether they will be able to bring 61 supporters to the assembly...the Alignment-Labor will support the change in the electoral system, although some of its members are not in favor of the change. The Likud's leadership let its members vote freely on the proposition. The assessment was that only ten Knesset members will vote for the new election system.[203]

The situation created a quandary for Kulas. During the period in question, elections were held (June 23, 1988) in the Liberal party for the purpose of naming its Knesset candidates, to run as part of the Likud list. Forty individuals were competing for seven to eight vacancies, excluding Yitzhak Moday, Moshe Nissim and Avraham Sharir, whose places on the list had already been confirmed.[204] Kulas's place remains unsure.[205] Could promotion of the proposal under these circumstances—i.e., against Shamir's position—support Kulas's chances of re-election? Yet, it seems that considerations other than electoral led Kulas to act as he did. At the head of his priorities, it appears, was the national interest and a reform that might influence the future of Israeli society. If he supported the legislation, his prestige would increase considerably, an important asset for his post-Knesset career.

What this part of our discussion has demonstrated is that prime ministers, factions, parties and their institutions, as well as parliamentary committees and their chairs all play central roles in the passage of a formal institutional change. Political entrepreneurs must be prepared to deal with objections from any and all of these actors if they want to succeed. Moreover, election considerations do not always motivate politicians. Sometimes, issues of prestige, capital to be exploited in later phases of the politician's career, are more important. We can therefore now turn to an analysis of the ideology, profession and the experience that shape parliamentary behavior.

### *Ideology, Profession and Experience*

Ideology, one's profession and personal experience may all explain politicians' considerations in whole or in part, often depending on how they interact with other behavioral parameters.

With respect to the proposal for the direct election of Israel's prime minister, its substance emerged from a liberal political ideology. However, its long-term ideological component was diluted by short-term considerations, which weakened it. Ultimately, the proposal was used as electoral capital in a short-term electoral power struggle. In addition, the value of political stability eventually melded with the ideological struggle surrounding the establishment of a Palestinian state. In this context, a *Likud* Knesset member, unwilling to allow the Arab sector to use its voters to influence election outcomes, would vote against the Direct Election Law. Such a consideration might verily influence the right-wing position of those who opposed the law, Similarly, a Liberal Party Knesset member, who had no chance of (re-)election as a member of the Likud list, might vote for the law to improve his or her image in the eyes of extra-parliamentary communities such as his professional colleagues, lawyers, etc.

A professional relationship between different players, i.e., the legal profession might also explain their behavior. For instance, on October 7, 1991, Uriel Lynn, as chair of the Constitution, Law and Justice Committee, brought the proposed Direct Election Law to its second and third calls. This was done with the agreement of the Constitution for Israel steering committee and in defiance of Shamir's antagonism. The Knesset's Chairman, Dov Shilansky (*Likud*) would not set a date for the voting on the law proposition. Shilansky's noncooperation was political, based on legal precedents and procedures. When the ads condemning Shilansky[206] did not have the desired effect, the committee members and a few Knesset members filed an appeal to force Shilansky to set the time for the second and third calls. The attorney general of the period, Dorit Beinish, talked Shilansky (who was a lawyer by profession) into bringing the proposition before the Knesset in order to preclude the clash of authorities between the HCJ and the Knesset. As a result, the petitioners cancelled the lawsuit.[207]

### *Strategy and Sincerity Considerations*

Strategy and sincerity considerations easily blend with maximization of the chances for re-election and ideological considerations. We mentioned them together because they operate in tandem and simultaneously. Separation of the two without mentioning the structural and cultural conditions that shape a player's other considerations creates a certain dichotomy. For instance, there are cases where a politician uses ideology strategically, to enhance his or her public image. In essence, ideology is a factor that maximizes the politician's chances of being elected because it is so integral a part of one's public image. This means that electoral objectives are not always the crucial interest shaping a politician's stance (see the above regarding Eli Kulas's behavior). We therefore maintain that a political entrepreneur has to take the entirety of structural and cultural conditions into account when mapping his interactions with a politician.

The tension between sincerity and strategy reflects the built-in tension between objective policies that maximize social benefit and subjective policies that reflect the decision-maker's personal interests.[208] From the point of view of society, a policy that combines objective and subjective considerations is not the preferred alternative. Such a policy does not maximize benefits to society nor does it adequately reflect the decision-maker's interests.[209] In the following example, we will analyze the compromises made in formulating the change in the electoral system of concern to us here.

Former Knesset member Yossi Beilin (*Alignment-Labor*) notes in an article from 1996 that: "The electional system reflects the power relations and the political interests of the period."[210] We claim that this explanation is insufficient. Political power relations express the extent to which a society has internalized democratic norms. The deeper/more superficial the internalization, the more likely it is that short-term considerations will play a role in political decision-making. Israel's political culture reflects internalization of exclusively procedural democratic norms. Therefore, one should expect short-term considerations to shape basic conditions and their changes.

March 18, 1992, was the closing day of the Twelfth Knesset. As noted before the Direct Election Law passed on a night-time vote on January 7, 1992. However, Lynn, the chair of the Constitution Law and Justice Committee of the Knesset, asked to return the law to the committee for another discussion since the final result of the law was different from the proposal. Three days before the end of the parliamentary session of the Twelfth Knesset, due to public and political pressures, Prime Minister Shamir chose to bring the law back for Knesset reading, thinking that passing the law would maximize his electoral capital. Although Shamir allowed free voting of the Likud MKs the struggle went on. Thus, on March 18, 1992, on the day of the vote on the Direct Election Law, Haim Corfo (Likud) proposed delaying implementation of the proposal—should it pass—until the next election of 1996. His suggestion was motivated by the hope that, should his proposal be accepted, the government would be able to delay the Knesset vote for another week, during which it could amend it.[211] Because March 18, 1992, was the closing day of the current Knesset session, the proposal could be buried. However, Corfo's suggestion failed. From the moment that Knesset members were granted the right to vote freely, the law passed with 55 MKs in favor, 32 against, 1 abstention and 32 absent. MKs began evaluating the parliamentary outcomes of the proposal's passage from their own perspectives: (1) Would the law be effective during the next Knesset term? 2) Was the Knesset expressing its lack of faith in the prime minister by passing the law with majority of only 61 Knesset members? (3) Would the prime minister accept the results? The law's promoters accepted these outcomes, based on the assumption that this was the only way to ensure a positive vote.

An ancillary clause added to the proposal's final formulation demanded that the Knesset endorse it, a stipulation absent from the original formulation. Yaacobi (*Alignment-Labor*) explains that this compromise was attached "due to the pressures exerted by small parties and Knesset members who disagreed with the law."[212] In a similar display of personal interests was the fear expressed by Zevulon Hammer (*Mafdal*) that a directly elected prime minister would be able to appoint someone else to Hammer's position despite his being his party's chair.[213]

But politicians are not the only players in this game to make compromises; proposal initiators must do so as well. Muli Peleg, executive director (1993–1995) of the Constitution for Israel movement writes that:

> Due to their desire to nullify criticism against their initiative calling for the direct election of the prime minister, the proposition's authors hastened their attempts to calm fears of [the election of-AM] a populist, omnipotent leader who would 'hold the state in his clutches.'...The reformulated legislation, Basic Law: The Government, passed in the Knesset during March 1992, thus creates an equilibrium between the Knesset and the government: Each has balanced the other...."[214]

The case of Dan Meridor then the Minister of Justice (*Likud*) provides an excellent example of what we call "copyright perspective of legislators" (meaning who will be the founding father of the law as a factor explaining preferences. Under certain circumstances, copyright perspective can lead to the maximization of re-election chances or prestige for future use. In a January 7, 1992, session, Dan Meridor chose to disagree with a long list of paragraphs contained in the proposed Direct Election Law. Given his opinions one would have expected Meridor to support the proposal. Ultimately, however, he chose to absent himself when the vote was taken. Later on, Meridor tried to explain his motivations: "[It's] not because I oppose them... but because they have no place in a basic law (Rather, in an ordinary law- A.M.)... with all due respect, this is exactly the [type of] legislation that should be presented as a basic law, which I hope to submit to the Knesset... but not now."[215] Such a position is consistent with his liberal image.

As opposed to Meridor, Uriel Lynn explained his position as follows: "I do not weigh the law according to the amount of personal damage it might cause, I believed in this law, I still believe in it. Any personal damage it could have caused me was already done."[216] The question is whether Lynn's activity meant to promote the law undermined his chances of being elected or made him look more liberal.[217]

Moreover, when the issue is major institutional change (political rule) not policy rule (within the existing political rules of game), politicians generally choose to act in a manner consistent with their public images. Such adherence obliges them to openly state their views because not doing so might damage their credibility and undermine their electoral potential. Therefore, Moshe Arens (*Likud*) opposed the law by calling it a hybrid between a parliamentary and a presidential system; Mordechai Virshubski (*Meretz*) opposed the entire bill, fearing it would induce anarchy; Benny Begin (*Likud*) treated it as an adventure; Aharon Abuhatssira (*Likud*) opposed the limitation set on the number of ministers (18); Shimon Shetreet (*Labor*) spoke about the fear of dictatorship, while Shulamit Aloni (*Meretz*) opposed the law's protection, and instead suggested the ordinary majority of MKs once one wishes to amend the law, fearing that the direct election law will turn out monstrous.

In conclusion, in this section we described the types of interactions maintained between political entrepreneurs and three of the most salient of parliamentary figures: leaders of parties, party institutions, and the chair of the Constitution, Justice and Law Committee. We noted that ideology, profession and experience contribute to our understanding of politicians' behavior and affect the compromise between the objective and the subjective perspectives of the legal proposal.

## 3.8 Summary

In this chapter, we traced the roles played by political entrepreneurs, outside and inside, in the process of introducing a formal institutional (political) rule change in a democratic political system. All of our illustrations have come from the case involving passage of the Direct Election Law regarding Israel's prime minister.

This change could easily undermine the interests of currently active politicians, most of whom did oppose the change. Therefore, the question arises, why would politicians and legislators interested in maximizing their benefits and power agree to a reform that could cause them to relinquish at least some political power? Moreover, how are we to explain the fact that despite the long-term considerations motivating the political entrepreneurs involved, they likewise acted in accordance with short-term considerations?

Adequate treatment of this question requires a comprehensive analysis that frames the actions of political players in social, political and structural contexts. Therefore, we here rephrase the question to: Why and under what conditions do basic formal institutional changes of the political system take place? What determines the character and design of a basic formal institutional change? And what are the factors determining the change's stability?

We responded in two stages. First, we offered a general explanation of the parameters involved; we then discussed the specific strategies applied by the players in formulating and submitting the proposal for legislation into law.

In the first stage, we examined why an institutional change takes place at all, stressing the development of feelings that such a change is due. We pointed out the economic and political centralization that, since the 1970s, had led Israel to achieve a state of extreme nongovernability, that is, the inability to provide public goods. First, there was an attempt to provide the missing goods through political participation patterns characteristic of democratic societies, such as protests and exit. However, in light of the centrality of the moribund political system as well as Israel's society's weak substantive democratic norms, participation gradually took on the characteristics—such as "quasi-exit (alternative) behavior"—of democracies in crisis. In other words, the public attempted to provide the missing goods itself by adopting behavior that worked around rather than through the existing system of rules. What we can describe as a learning process led to different groups understanding that the political rules of the game needed to be changed. However, the structural-cultural circumstances of each political player provoked each to focus on short-term considerations such as the maximization of personal interests or the use of an institutional change as bandages in the resolution of urgent economic, political and social crises. As a result, the institutional change initiated in 1992 was unstable and later in 2001 was canceled, as we will elaborate in the next chapter.

The beginning of the process saw the appearance of political entrepreneurs: Amnon Rubinstein and Uriel Reichmann, joined later by David Libai, Uriel Lynn and Yoash Tsiddon. These entrepreneurs identified the public distress, defined the social problem and pointed out a solution—a formal, written constitution—which, due to radicalness in the contemporary political context, brought in its wake the compromise proposal for the direct election of the prime minister.

The importance of political entrepreneurs lies in their ability to link public dissatisfaction with a proposed solution. We defined the proposed solution as electoral capital (image, real resources, group support), to be utilized during elections. We pointed out that entrepreneurs identify and employ electoral capital after assessing various structural and social conditions. By doing so, they actually translate the social problem into a policy problem, expressing but not creating public preferences.

We also examined the behavior of political entrepreneurs according to five parameters: political ideology, motivations of personal power and prestige maximization, political and professional affiliations, past experience and the learning process, identification and utilization of crises and changing public beliefs and preferences. These variables explain the strategies applied by the entrepreneur, the moment of his or her appearance, the specific definition of the social problem, the presentation of institutional change as a solution to the social problem and, finally, its translation into a policy problem.

During the second stage, we examined the ways in which the character and design of a basic formal institutional change—in this case, the proposal for the direct election of Israel's prime minister—is determined. The analysis stressed the activity of players such as politicians-bureaucrats, the public, and interest groups that use electoral capital to maximize their benefits while taking structural and cultural constraints into account. Four interactive levels were identified.

The first interaction dealt with the relationship between the political entrepreneur and his reference group, and the general public. In this analysis, we stressed the motivation that guided Reichmann, Rubinstein and others to pressure politicians who had the power to pass the legislation proposal. The second interaction dealt with the relationship between the political entrepreneur, interest groups and politicians. We stressed the approach used by the entrepreneur to recruit the support of politicians. Rather than seeking public support, the entrepreneur lobbied Knesset members while taking advantage of the politicians' short-term time perspective, all the while focusing on the central institutions (party and faction leaders, party institutions, and committee chairs) involved in the process. These interactions represented the main stage of entrepreneurial activity among politicians.

At this stage, we analyzed the interactions among politicians, primarily inside parliament (the Knesset). Each politician has his or her own interests; in order for them to accept a new idea, that idea has to fit the position taken by the majority of their peers. We focused on the main parameters relevant to achieving the entrepreneur's objective: politicians' time perspective, maximization of re-election chances, estimates of the proposal's chances by politicians, the prime minister's and the party leader's position, ideology, professional affiliation and experience. We pointed out that the design of an institutional change, as such, reflects compromises made to bridge the gap between the objective and the procedural sides of the proposed law.

As a result of this analysis, we found that officials (or bureaucrats) had relatively little influence on the outcome, especially political rule change. As in the case of the Direct Election Law, the crucial factor is the interaction between politicians and voters. Officials usually offer little resistance to such changes. There was one exception to this rule, however: the judges who sit in the Israeli High Court of Justice, which played an important role in the formulation and acceptance of the bill. The High Court's main contribution was in creating public opinion favoring the proposed law. We also pointed out that, since the 1980s, the High Court has provided a special venue as an alternative source or arbitrator of policy. Whatever the benefits of judicial oversight, within the Israeli context this role increased legislative nongovernability and contributed to the deepening crisis that prompted the appearance of political entrepreneurs.

## CHAPTER FOUR

# *Political Entrepreneurs and Institutional Change: Cancellation of the Direct Election of the Prime Minister*

## 4.1 Introduction

This chapter describes the formal revision of an institutional rule in the political system operating in a democracy. The empirical question examined in this chapter is: Why and under which conditions do basic institutional changes take place in a political system? What determines the character and design of such changes? What factors explain the change's stability? We shall use the law canceling the direct election of Israel's prime minister as a case study for the purpose of examining these questions in general and the various action strategies of specific players in particular.

On March 7, 2001, Israel passed a law canceling direct election of the prime minister in an attempt to introduce greater stability into its parliamentary system of government. The law, like many other institutional modifications, combined two rules, aggregation rules and authority rules. *Aggregation rules* redefine the decision functions that translate preferences into political outcomes. *Authority rules* define the system of actions that holders of different social and political roles are authorized to take. Such institutional change redefines the de facto framework in which the political discourse as well as the power relations between players are maintained.[1]

The argument demonstrated throughout this chapter pertains to political rule determination, formulation and stability. This process combines two variables: economic and political stability on the one hand, and society's attitudes toward democratic norms on the other. These variables enable construction of a bivariable scale for the analysis and measurement of the structural conditions that affect the players' short- and long-term considerations that explain the stability of institutional change. Israel, for instance, as a sociopolitical entity, is characterized by economic and political instability. Moreover, its political culture has come to be characterized by a fairly instrumental approach to democratic norms. Procedural democracy likewise encourages a short-term perspective regarding institutional changes. This combination of structural and cultural conditions has encouraged the dominance of short-term considerations in behavior in addition to changes in the country's political rules. Hence, changes are expected to be unstable and frequent.

According to the model that guides our analysis, structure and culture are essential for institutional change design. They constitute the system of constraints and rewards that affect behavior in the political sphere. Given these primary conditions, we will analyze the cancellation of the "Direct Election Law" in two phases. In the first phase, we will follow the development of the recognition that a political rule change was needed, one that reversed the previous reform. This is the situation that led to the appearance of political entrepreneurs. In the second phase, we examine what determined the character and design of the formal rule change. We highlight the activities of the players, including politicians, bureaucrats, the public, and interest groups, all of whom took advantage of the alleged rule change to maximize their rewards within the current structural and cultural constraints.

### *4.1.1 Case Study*

On March 7, 2001, Israel passed a law nullifying Basic Law: the Government, also known as the Direct Election Law of the Prime Minister. As specified in chapter three, in 1992, a group of Knesset members led by MK Amnon Rubinstein and outside entrepreneurs headed by Professor Uriel Reichmann succeeded in passing the Direct Election Law, whose implementation was postponed until the 1996 elections. During the 1996 elections, separate votes were cast for the Knesset and the prime minister's office for the first time in Israel's history. Two candidates ran for the office of Prime Minister—Binyamin Netanyahu (Likud) and Shimon Peres (Labor). Netanyahu won and served as prime minister for only three of the four years of his term.

However, although Netanyahu won the election for Prime Minister, Labor won the Knesset elections, beating the Likud-Gesher-Tzomet alliance, meaning Netanyahu had to rely on a coalition with the ultra-Orthodox parties, Shas and United Torah Judaism (whose social welfare policies flew in the face of his capitalistic outlook) in order to govern. In May 1999, Ehud Barak (One Israel-Israel Labor party, Meimad and Gesher) was elected prime minister. His term of office was cut short after two years. During his term several parties such as Meretz and United Torah Judaism quit the coalition after the Camp David 2000 Summit, which was meant to finally resolve the Israeli-Palestinian conflict, failed. The Haredi party, Shas, which had received an unprecedented 17 seats in the 120-seat Knesset, quit the coalition and Barak resigned. His resignation in 2001 was followed by the election of Arik Sharon (*Likud*) in a separate campaign, divorced from Knesset elections (in the former system, the two were to take place concurrently). In the beginning of Sharon's term in 2001, direct election of the prime minister was revoked. In 2003, elections were held according to the renewed system. The *Likud* received 40 mandates in that election, a sufficient number to allow it to construct a coalition.

It is difficult to pinpoint the exact beginning of the revocation process, especially if our interest is to be focused on the political entrepreneurs who affect the results. One might begin in June 1996, when Uzi Landau (*Likud*), Yossi Beilin and Moshe Shahal (both *Labor*) proposed a bill that would nullify the Direct Election Law. However, it would be more appropriate to look further back, to the 1980s, when Arik Carmon, a political outsider, and Yossi Beilin, a political insider, collaborated to undermine an original proposal calling for direct election of the prime minister, promoted by Reichmann and Rubinstein.

And so, on June 25, 1996, Uzi Landau, Yossi Beilin and Moshe Shahal proposed legislation that would revoke the Direct Election Law passed in 1992. Their proposal was defeated on November 14, 1996 by a majority of the government coalition members (50), joined by Haim Ramon, Uzi Baram and Hagai Meirom (all *Labor*), Yossi Sarid, Amnon Rubinstein and David (Dedi) Zucker ( all *Meretz*). In March 1997, The Association for Parliamentary Democracy was formed by Carmon and Beilin as public movement whose objective was revocation of the law. The movement made heavy use of the media and direct pressure on Knesset members.

On May 20, 1998, the legislation was reintroduced and brought before the Knesset. By now, the proposition had gained supporters: not only the Association for Parliamentary Democracy but also Shimon Peres, Moshe Arens (Likud) and Yitzhak Shamir (Likud). After a stormy

Knesset debate, the proposition was accepted and moved to the Knesset's Committee for the Constitution, Law and Justice in preparation for its first reading. After passing the first reading, the process came to a halt due to the 1999 elections and afterwards the Camp David 2000 Summit. It was not until March 7, 2001 that the Knesset finally revoked the Direct Election Law and restored the one-vote parliamentary system of government that operated until 1996, approving a reformed version of the original Basic Law: The Government.[2]

The current chapter, which focuses on the nullification process, is divided into sections according to the model's structural and cultural parameters. The first section will discuss the etiology or internalization of feeling that change in Israel's political rules is once again needed. The appearance of a political entrepreneur to drive achievement of this goal will be analyzed in the second section. The chapter's third section analyzes how the character and design of this rule change was the determined as reflected in the relevant Knesset and public debates. The third section is divided into three subsections, the first of which deals with the interaction between the political entrepreneur, his supporting group and the public. The second subsection analyzes the activities of political entrepreneurs with the interest groups that provide politicians with information regarding public preferences and other support, the entrepreneur's relationships with various groups and the strategy applied in view of the given structural and social conditions. The third subsection deals with interactions within the legislative decision-making body, in our case, the Knesset. Lastly, we provide a summary and conclusions.

## 4.2 The Public's Sense of the Need to Change Political Rules as a Necessary Condition for Initiating Institutional Change

In order for a change in political rules to take place, the public must first sense the need for change. In political systems, political entrepreneurs, identify the needs and preferences of the players and capitalize on them for their own benefit and for the promotion of the proposed institutional rule change.

In our test case, the institutional rule change that took place in 1992 did not promote either political or economic instability. The chronic political instability simply encouraged political players to amplify their short-term interests. As described previously, structural features such as growing judicialization, the emergence of the High Court of Justice as an alternative arena for governance, extreme government centralization, extreme nongovernability and increasingly alternative political behavior by pressure groups[3] served as the background reconsideration of the original reform.

Between 1992 and 1997, the public's attitude toward electoral reform had altered. This transformation had begun after Yitzhak Rabin's election as prime minister in 1992 and his ineffectiveness in this position, later followed by his assassination, Netanyahu's difficulties in putting together a coalition and his inability to rule, as well as the Knesset member activity with respect to postponement of the Direct Election Law's effective date. The public gradually learned that structural reform was insufficient to cure the system's ailments. Political entrepreneurs identified this feeling and judged the public's readiness for change.[4] The breakdown of the large party (or, more correctly, large faction) system, observed in the profusion of small, one-issue parties whose behavior and demands paralyzed the government, and the turn to alternative political arenas, contributed greatly to this change in public attitudes.

### *Political Instability and Increasingly Alternative Political Behavior*

The law providing for direct election of the prime minister was passed in 1992, but its implementation was postponed until 1996. The 1992 elections were conducted with the pending law in mind, which was presented as the sole solution to the current instability and nongovernability.[5] Rabin's government was installed in an atmosphere where the public felt that it had ushered in a new era of stable, effective governance.[6]

However, the existence of one-issue parties, with the attendant coalitional bargaining, exacerbated nongovernability. The coalition in place—Labor, with 44 Knesset members; *Meretz* with 12 Knesset members; *Shas* with six Knesset members, together with *Hadash* (Jewish and Arab left-wing party) and the *Arab Democratic Party*—decided to implement the *Labor–Meretz* idea of instituting a written constitution during the present (the Thirteenth) Knesset. The presence of *Meretz* (liberal, left-wing) and *Shas* (ultra-Orthodox, right-wing) in the same government was an inherent source of greater tension, which raised the question of whether the Rabin government could make any difficult decisions and remain intact.[7]

An external, situational factor contributing to government instability was the increasing incidence of terrorist acts on Israeli streets, which reached a peak in March 1993. Some of the political coalition partners, especially those on the right, linked the increase in terror to the Rabin government's readiness to modify its position on the Israeli-Palestinian negotiations. The government's short-term solution to terror was the imposition of a curfew in the occupied territories, along with border closings and the installation of a large number of military checkpoints on the major and minor roads leading from the territories into Israel. The consequences of these actions were very serious for the Palestinians and Israel: the livelihood of the tens of thousands of Palestinians working in Israel was harmed while the construction and other service industries in Israel came to a standstill.[8] During this period, tension along Israel's northern border rose due to Hezbollah's firing on Israeli towns in the area. Israel responded with a military operation code named "*Din Veheshbon*—Account and Reckoning" (Summer 1993). The high-level political advances made, such as the signing of the Oslo Accords and the Israel-PLO agreement (September 1993), simply motivated increasing frustration and violence on the part of everyday Palestinians.

The consequent government paralysis led to a sense that Israel's political system had come to a dead end, an impression that led to the search for alternative political arenas and a change in political behavior. Grassroots movements questioning Rabin's policy arose in the Golan, Judea and Samaria and Gaza. A movement called "The Third Way—*HaDerech Hashlishit*" (July 1994) was established, opposing any withdrawal from the Golan Heights. Its creation signaled Rabin's government that his supporters might not continue to back him. At the same time, the High Court of Justice began intervening in many aspects of daily life by encouraging the passage of laws such as the Basic Law: Human Dignity and Liberty (1992) and Basic Law: Freedom of Occupation (1992, 1994).[9]

Political entrepreneurs also took part in the shaping these feelings. The period 1992–1995 was characterized by recurrent attempts by outside and internal entrepreneurs to revise the Direct Election Law while other entrepreneurs tried to postpone the law's implementation until 2000. Political players in effect attempted to transform the Direct Election Law into their own private electoral capital, for use as needed.

The public mood was reflected in a far-reaching upset in the elections for the head of the Histadrut.[10] In 1994, Haim Ramon (the former Minister of Health and a member of Labor) established a faction called "New Life in the Histadrut" that received 46 percent of the votes as opposed to 33 percent for the Labor Party list. The results were shocking when remembering the Histadrut's decades-long association with

Labor. Ramon's triumph reflected the personalization of elections, the shift of political identity from parties to individual candidates. The election campaign focused on Ramon's personality and his plans for the future, which were sold as opposing the old "apparatus" or "system" led by his opponent, Haim Haberfeld.[11]

The personalization phenomenon was observed on a grander scale in the municipal elections, reflected in the increase in the number of nonpartisan local lists. The election campaigns focused on local candidates and made considerable use of the media to create an image of the candidates' independence from the party machines. This informal change in the rules of the game forced the party lists to emphasize their own candidates' history and administrative ability in turn.[12]

As competition shifted from the organizational to the individual level, it reinforced the continued weakening of the two largest parties, Labor and the Likud. Their joint power declined, accompanied by a sharp rise in party splits.[13] The 1996 election results, together with the flawed behavior of Netanyahu, the first prime minister chosen via direct elections, demonstrated to the public that direct election of the prime minister had increased divisions in the Knesset without shielding the prime minister from partisan pressure.[14]

Netanyahu's government was characterized by an inherent incapacity to govern; ongoing social crises—social and ethnic group divisions; economic problems; the status of the army and declining motivation to serve; religious-secular relations and the constitutional status of religion; the relationships between law, society and politics—as well as the identity issues of a changing society having to cope with a changing world reinforced the sense of chaos. The activities of a multiplying number of interest groups and political entrepreneurs came to color the political sphere.[15] Yet, political power remained concentrated in the hands of the executive, headed by the prime minister. The almost-irreversible centralization of the political system increased the public's sense of hopelessness.[16]

Such feelings were also expressed in Israel's business community. Business had generally supported the Labor Party and regarded the peace process as a factor favoring economic development. While Netanyahu was prime minister, the business community criticized his economic policy as well as the stagnant political process. Demands had been made that government expenditures be reduced by $7.2 billion; they were eventually reduced by only $4 billion. The slashing of the social welfare budget led to opposition by Knesset members who saw themselves as representing the social lobby (for instance, the Gesher faction).[17] In view of these events, the Histadrut announced a general strike, declaring that the rights of working men and women were being harmed.[18]

By 1997, the public understood that the Direct Election Law had failed to solve the problem of nongovernability. In the absence of administrative decentralization or improvements in service provision, the public sought substitute avenues to obtain the goods and services that the government had previously provided, often by means of alternative political organizations. The increase in the number of parties and the decrease in their size was a symptom of the malaise. The political instability described previously was reflected on every level of political behavior.

## *Economic Instability*

The economic sphere suffered from instability as well, as observed in the measurements described in chapter three: The unemployment rate, for instance, reached over 11 percent. Although it declined insignificantly at the end of the 1990s (eight to nine percent), it spiked again in 2001 with the collapse of the high-tech bubble, high-tech being one of Israel's major export industries. Figure 4.1 indicates the increase in unemployment between 1995 and 2001.

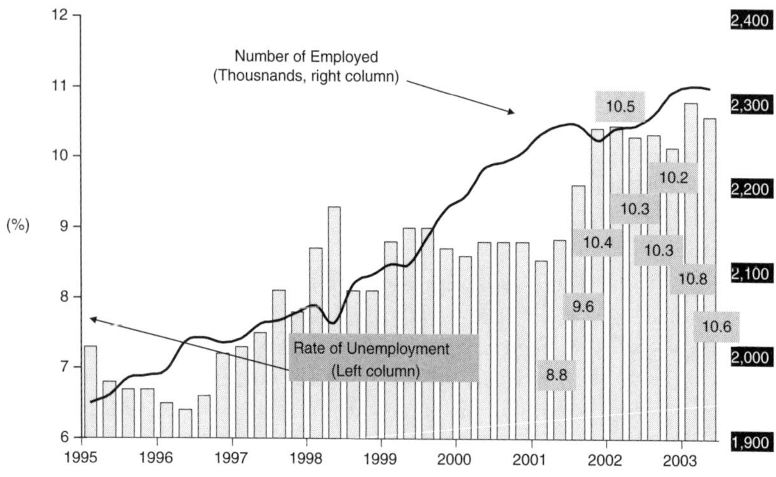


**Figure 4.1** Number Employed and Rate of Unemployment (Israel, 1995–2001).

*Source*: *Trend Report in the Israeli Economy*, Treasury Department, August 30, 2004.

By 1997, political entrepreneurs had sensed that the public was ready for a real change in the political system.[19] They utilized the situation as electoral capital to advance their agenda—revocation of the law instituting direct election of the prime minister. We now turn to a description of how political entrepreneurs identified the new public preferences and employed them for their own purposes.

## 4.3 The Political Entrepreneurs

Dissatisfaction with the government led a group of political entrepreneurs to intervene. Many will be recognized as among the political entrepreneurs acting against passage of the Direct Election Law in the 1980s and early 1990s. Some of them, like Yossi Beilin (*Labor*) and Uzi Landau (*Likud*), belonged to the inner circle of parliamentarians, while others, like Dr. Arye Carmon, president of the Israel Democracy Institute, came from outside official institutions. They went on to redefine the pervasive problem as one of governmental paralysis, the major repercussion of direct election of the prime minister. It was this political rule that was preventing the enactment of policies that would comply with public demands.[20]

As might be anticipated, the parameters that figured in the design and implementation of the solutions adopted by political entrepreneurs in 1997 were similar to those affecting political entrepreneurs during the previous change attempt:

1. Political values
2. The quest for power and the desire to maximize personal prestige
3. Professional and political affiliations
4. Past experience and learning
5. Identification and utilization of crises as well as changing public beliefs and preferences.

### *Political Values*

The entrepreneur's political values influence his definition of social problems, their solutions, and choice of the strategy considered most appropriate to reach his or her goal.[21] In Israel, political entrepreneurs found inside and outside the government generally profess democratic-liberal values and liberal attitudes toward the economy. Internal entrepreneurs rarely perceive themselves as "political go-getters," ready to trade in their ideologies to achieve their objectives. Consistency in their approaches maximizes their prestige, improves their chances of election and reinforces their positions outside the Knesset. For instance, in 1988, Moshe Shahal (Labor) resigned from the Knesset to return to the private sector. He established a thriving law practice and took part in much public activity outside the Knesset. Similarly, Yossi Beilin's electoral appeal rested on his prestige as a principled liberal and political pioneer. His values led him to resign from the Knesset in 1999 in order to take a ministerial position in Barak's government. Because there were no Knesset elections when Ariel Sharon ran for prime minister in 2001, Beilin was unable to reenter the Knesset. His personal prestige, however, helped keep him active in the public sphere outside the Knesset (he participated in the Geneva Convention of 2004 as one of the proponents of the Geneva Accords). He later withdrew from the Labor party to found "Yahad and the Democratic Choice" list[22] and eventually was elected to chair Meretz in 2004.

What similarities, if any, were shared by the various entrepreneurs? Despite belonging to rival political parties, inside politicians such as Yossi Beilin (*Labor*) and Uzi Landau (*Likud*) shared secular-liberal identities that determined their political value, in common with outside entrepreneurs such as Arik Carmon and Moshe Shahal. For that reason, short biographies of the four political entrepreneurs active in promoting revocation of the Direct Election Law can provide a taste of how political values converge with political entrepreneurship.

Dr. Yossi Beilin was born in 1948 in Tel Aviv. He studied Hebrew Literature and Political Science at Tel Aviv University, where he also completed his doctorate (in political science). Beilin first worked as a journalist for the left-wing *Davar*[23] newspaper and taught political science at Tel Aviv University. He began his political career as a spokesman for the Labor Party and as an assistant to Labor's chair, Shimon Peres. Beilin subsequently held several positions, including government secretary, Knesset member (*Labor*) and Deputy Minister of Foreign Affairs when Peres was serving as Minister of Foreign Affairs.[24] Beilin was consistently one of the leaders of the "dovish" faction in the Labor party. As early as the mid-1980s, he proposed establishment of a Palestinian state in Gaza as a first step in achieving a peace agreement that included Israel's withdrawal from all of the territories in question. He was one of the major initiators of the attempt to end the national unity government in March 1990, which he saw as a dead-end Government. As Deputy Minister of Foreign Affairs, he participated in the negotiations that led to the Oslo Agreement with the PLO (1993). After Rabin's assassination, Peres appointed Beilin to the position of Minister of Economics and Planning. While occupying this position, he negotiated the Beilin-Abu Mazen Agreement as well as the Beilin-(Michael) Eitan Agreement. In November 1995, he became a Minister without Portfolio in the Prime Minister's Office. From July 1996, he served as a member of the Knesset Constitution, Law and Justice Committee as well the Committee on the Status of Women. Time and again he expressed his political views in published works: "The State of Israel is a state of its citizens that acts according to universal norms, favoring adoption of human rights on one hand and political activity to ensure peace, on the other."[25]

Dr. Arye Carmon was born in 1943 in Jerusalem and received a B.A. in History and Philosophy and an M.A. in History from the Hebrew University of Jerusalem. He went on to earn a Ph.D. from the University of Wisconsin with a major in European History and a minor in Educational Policy Studies. Carmon began his public activity when the political system had reached a major level of instability, with no leading party (late 1980s). In his desire to introduce change, he joined the "Aviv" group, whose members came from the Knesset such as Meir Sheetrit (Likud) and Businessmen such as David Kulitz and Aharon Dovrat. The Aviv group called for electoral change in favor of personal direct elections. He and the group began to propose reform of the electoral system as a solution to the country's social problems. Carmon expressed his political views through this activity, envisioning a liberal, secular Israel that applies universalistic principles to create a stable government and cultural moderation.[26] Like Beilin, Carmon's values reflect the left wing of the liberal political spectrum.

The attorney Moshe (Morris) Shahal (Patel) was born in Baghdad in 1934. He immigrated to Israel in 1950. Before he studied law at Tel Aviv University, he earned a degree in economics, sociology and political science from the University of Haifa. Shahal became politically active during the Wadi Salib demonstrations in the late 1950s. Later, he took part in the Haifa Workers Council (1959–1971) and the Haifa City Council (1965–1969). He first served as a Knesset member (Labor) party in 1971. In the Knesset, he served on numerous committees, as Deputy Chair and Chair of the *Maarach* (Alignment) faction. By the end of the 1980s, he was competing for the leadership of the Labor party, calling it to adopt more dovish positions (Carmel, 2001: 1076). Although he failed in his attempt, Shahal remained one of Peres's closest associates, taking an active part in the parliamentary maneuvers that led to the early elections of the Eleventh Knesset and negotiations to establish a national unity government in 1984.[27] In 1984 he was appointed Minister of Energy and Infrastructure.[28] In 1992 Yitzhak Rabin later named him Minister of Communications and then Minister of Internal Security.[29] The following year, he again became Minister of Energy and Infrastructure[30] and later Minister of Internal Security. Throughout his career, both in the Knesset and as a private individual, Shahal worked to realize his political vision of Israel as a liberal and secular state. In this respect he is similar to other entrepreneurs.

Within our selection, Dr. Uzi Landau was the only political entrepreneur expressing right-wing political views. He was born in Haifa in 1943. He completed his undergraduate studies in industry and management at the Technion and went on to obtain a doctorate in engineering at the Massachusetts Institute of Technology. The son of Haim Landau, a former activist in the Etzel pre-state underground and of the Herut Movement, Uzi Landau was a member of the Betar youth movement and joined the Herut student organization when at the Technion. A close associate of his father, he was appointed Director-General of the Ministry of Transportation in 1981. He served as a Knesset member (*Herut*) in the Eleventh through the Fifteenth Knessets. While in the Knesset, he served as chair of several important committees, such as the Security and Foreign Affairs Committee and the Knesset Oversight Committee. In September 1993, he was elected to the chairmanship of the Likud faction in the Knesset. Although Landau consistently expressed a hawkish position with respect to international affairs,[31] he, like the other three political entrepreneurs, is a firm believer in a liberal-democratic political regime. He also has a reputation for integrity.

All of the entrepreneurs believed in the supremacy of the Knesset as opposed to the executive authority headed by the prime minister. That is why they cooperated in promoting the idea that the prime minister should be the leader of the faction that receives the majority of the votes in any Knesset election. The advantages of the former institutional structure were succinctly summarized by Yossi Beilin:

> This system ensures the ongoing existence of all the largest political movements, prevents splitting and reduces the political power of the smaller parties. If we add to this the German system—we might be able to create a healthier system for political activity in

Israel, with checks and balances, and the political movements will continue being the focus of national discussion.[32]

### *The Quest for Power and the Desire to Maximize Personal Prestige*

The literature views political entrepreneurs as rational individuals who try to alter political situations by changing policy or the rules of the political game. The motivations for their activity rest, among other things, on the desire to maximize their personal power and prestige; with respect to politicians, this means increasing their chances of being (re-)elected.[33]

One might assume that their prestige, together with their reputations for integrity, helped Beilin, Shahal and Landau maximize their chances of re-election at the time when nullification of the Direct Election Law was being debated. In a sense, they perceived themselves as candidates for the leadership of their parties (Carmel, 2001). Given their values and their histories, support of institutional reform, especially one that returned the parties to their former supremacy in the system, could obviously have been viewed as electoral capital for these three inside entrepreneurs.

Beilin and Shahal began their entrepreneurial activities as early as 1988. What linked the two was their relationship to Shimon Peres. This closeness may have influenced their decision to vote for the Direct Election Law in 1992. Yet, throughout the period 1992–1995, they attempted to postpone implementation of that law because they identified themselves with Peres during the latter's competition with Rabin.[34] The inconsistencies in their positions appeared after Rabin's assassination (November 4, 1995), when Peres replaced him as prime minister. Once in office, Peres opposed postponement of the Direct Election Law's implementation because, we may assume, the law now served his aspirations. Therefore, the question becomes why did Beilin and Shahal sustain their efforts to postpone the law's implementation? Uriel Lynn's[35] explanation—that Beilin's struggle sprang from his rivalry with Rabin—seems insufficient. So, were Beilin and Shahal acting sincerely, or was their behavior simply strategic?

We believe that answer probably combines the two. Strategically speaking, their own ambitions to accede to the post of party leader accord with their reluctance to be perceived as Peres's lackeys[36] by *Labor* party activists even more than the general public. Moreover, in Beilin's case, direct election of the prime minister was unlikely to improve his chances of re-election because, as a political dove, he would lose in any electoral confrontation against Rabin. Furthermore, the little experience with direct elections of the prime minister had shown that, at least in Israel, direct elections favored candidates taking positions on security that were close to the political center.

In Shahal's case, one might argue that the struggle to postpone implementation of the Direct Election Law helped him regain his prestige and compensate for his poor showing (twenty-fourth place in the Labor Party primaries for the Fourteenth Knesset).[37] Given this decline in his popularity, Shahal's opposition to implementation of the law after Peres had changed his own position implies less evaluative consistency and a more practical frame of mind. In 1998, Shahal left the Knesset for a law practice and public activity. Beilin left the Knesset as well, in 1999, although he held the position of minister in Barak's government. When Sharon was elected prime minister in 2001, Beilin changed the venue of his political activity to outside the Knesset.

A combination of honesty and strategic behavior might characterize Uzi Landau's political activity as well. He was chosen chair of the Likud's Executive Committee in 1993 and probably contemplated running for the Likud's leadership.[38] Landau has consistently voiced a decisively hawkish position, which led to many confrontations with Netanyahu. Postponement of the law's implementation might therefore have helped him prevent Netanyahu's election as prime minister. Direct elections would have maximized the chances of the very popular Netanyahu to be elected. Landau's position also agreed with the perception that postponement or cancellation of direct elections would reduce the impact of Arab votes. This rationale might also have motivated his absence from the voting on the Direct Elections Law in 1992.

Sincerity and strategy bonded in the case of Dr. Arik Carmon, the outside entrepreneur among the four. His political activity complies with the results of economic entrepreneurship studies indicating the motivation to maximize one's power. Carmon's ambitions were not, however, solely personal: effective extra-parliamentary activity would also maximize the power of the body he headed, the Israel Democracy Institute, as a means to further realization of its vision regarding the State of Israel.[39]

In conclusion, the behavior of these political entrepreneurs reflected a mix of integrity and strategy. These explanations complement the structural and social conditions of any period in which political entrepreneurs operate. This implies that the attempt to differentiate between them may be problematic. Carmon, Beilin, Shahal and Landau may have had some evidence that direct elections would seriously weaken Israel's political system (which indeed occurred at the end of the 1990s). However, this does not necessarily mean that their activity was totally devoid of personal interest, at least from the perspective of their prestige. Could it be that Beilin was left as a supportive Knesset for reasons other than his beliefs? Perhaps he had reasoned that because following his ideology to its logical conclusion had failed to gain him election to the Knesset or a prominent place in the Labor Party hierarchy, the same step would help him become chair of the "Shahar" (later incorporated with Meretz) movement. Beilin thus maximized his prestige in order to gain greater political salience.

### *Professional and Political Affiliations*

Beilin and Carmon were members of the social science academic community—Carmon being an historian and Beilin a political scientist. The profession considered most relevant to the politics of formal rule change in the 1980s was law, not political science. Beilin notes that "there is an interesting argument between the departments of political science in Israeli universities, most of which opposed the idea [of direct elections–A. M.] and the law departments, most of which supported it."[40] On the other hand, the fact that the idea of a constitution emerged at Tel Aviv University's School of Law irritated many from the social sciences who were not allowed to take part in the law professors' initiative. As the previous chapter has indicated, this legalist approach toward institutional reform proved ineffective. To assuage egos and utilize professional unity as a resource in their struggle, Carmon and his fellow entrepreneurs decided in 2001 to create an organization that would institutionalize this collegiality. That organization was the Israel Democracy Institute, to be formally headed by Arik Carmon.

The activities of political entrepreneurs perhaps best encapsulate the values that shape public activism as well as the tension arising between adherence to democratic values (including the goal of a stable government) and the promotion of personal interests. For instance, in 2001, while serving in the position of Chair, the Constitution, Law and Justice Committee, Amnon Rubinstein pushed for revoking of the Direct Election Law despite the fact that he actually disagreed with this position.[41] Similarly, Yossi Beilin gave up his seat as a Knesset member to serve as Minister of Justice in Ehud Barak's government even though he would have preferred to serve both as MK and Minister. Our claim here is that whenever entrepreneurs want to promote an institutional change on the basis of ideological considerations, current structural-cultural conditions often force them to shift their behavioral priorities to short-term goals. Their actions thus tend to reflect the effects of short-term considerations, observed in the strategy of procedural alacrity, for example, and in our case, promotion of an institutional rule change by means of strategies that play on politicians' desires to be re-elected. In an interview given shortly after the voting in 2001, Carmon sketched his horizon: "We have raised the bar, but there is still a long way to go. Additional changes are still required, but they should be done moderately."[42] Carmon's statement echoes that made by Reichmann in which he claimed that institutional change is only temporary.[43] It is a view that supports our contention that institutional changes take place within the context of short-term considerations and evidence instability.

## *Past Experience and Learning*

The case of Direct Election Law's nullification constitutes another stage in a development that dates back to the establishment of the State of Israel. In social choice theory, the history of that development represents past experience and events shaping the political entrepreneur's choice of action strategies.[44]

Carmon, Beilin, Shahal and Landau were involved in institutional rule change at the end of the 1980s and the beginning of the 1990s. The political system was then in a complex stasis. To prevent upsetting that careful balance, the Knesset was tempted into spending billions for partisan causes. According to Carmon:

> It started 12 years ago, the day the terrible idea of direct election of the prime minister arose. Even then, in 1988–1989, I tried to recruit opposition to its implementation. The first to join were a small group of academics, Prof. Emanuel Gutman [professor of political science Hebrew University- A.M] and Prof. Yitzhak Galnoor [professor of political science Hebrew University and former head of Israel's Civil Service Commission-AM]. Later on, two politicians who went with it all the way, Uzi Landau and Yossi Beilin, joined in as well. However, we failed. In July 1996, a bit after Netanyahu was elected prime minister, Moshe Arens [Likud], Ephraim Sneh [Labor], Prof. Naomi Chazan [Meretz], Yael Dayan [Meretz] and another you would never guess, Knesset member

> Moshe Gafni [United Torah Judaism- Yahadut HaTorah], joined us. Later on, Hadash (a Jewish and Arab party- A.M.) members, as well as Rehavam Ze'evi [Moledet—A nationalist right-wing party—A.M.] and Benyamin Elon [Moledet], joined in."[45]

The entrepreneurs' accumulated experience led them to the conclusion that in order to void the law, it was necessary to add outside to inside (parliamentary) resources. On the one hand, the strategy proved useful in 1992, when the Direct Election Law was accepted; on the other, Beilin, Shahal and Landau's attempts to promote such a proposal had failed during a preliminary vote in November 1996.[46] Therefore, the path chosen was extra-parliamentary activity. The entrepreneurs' knowledge and understanding of Israeli politics convinced them to focus their activity on parties rather than party leaders, combining public assemblies and public opinion polls. A detailed account follows.

### *Identification and Utilization of Crises as well as Changing Public Beliefs and Preferences*

For political entrepreneur, identification of possible crisis as well as changes in the public's beliefs and preferences are resources to be utilized to further their own goals.[47] Such a crisis situation appeared in 1996, at the beginning of Binyamin Netanyahu's government, as a result of a split in the Knesset and Netanyahu's dependency on partisan pressures, Netanyahu faced difficulties in establishing coalition since, according to the Basic Law: the government the number of Ministers was limited to 18. A similar situation reoccurred in March 1997, when Carmon identified a political opening revolving around the frequent crises regarding the Minister of Foreign Affairs, David Levy, who was constantly being undermined by Netanyahu's office as well as Netanyahu's damaged relationship with Ariel Sharon. The latter had met in public with Shimon Peres, intending further establishment of a national unity government (Korn & Shapira, 1997: 361). Additional ingredients were provided by Knesset members from the right and the left, led by Rubinstein (one of the Direct Elections Law initiators), who called for a return to the previous electoral system. The proposed legislation demanded that 61 Knesset members (instead of the 80 required in the Direct Election Law) could dismiss the prime minister without dissolving the whole Knesset.[48] Similar calls were raised in 2000, when Barak's government was coming to its premature end. The collapse of the negotiations in Camp David, the withdrawal of the National Religious Party-*Mafdal* and *Yisrael Beitenu*[49] from the coalition government, the frequent crises with Shas over budgeting their programs and Barak's announcement of a "civil" revolution,[50] reflected extreme nongovernability, with factions seeking to make gains before elections were called.[51]

We end our discussion here of the factors that explain the appearance of political entrepreneurs such as Arik Carmon, Yossi Beilin, Moshe Shahal and Uzi Landau. These entrepreneurs identified the dissatisfaction with Netanyahu's government in 1996 and proposed revocation of the Direct Election Law as its solution. This solution was perceived as electoral capital that could, under the correct conditions, be maximized for the purpose of re-election or, like Carmon, the increase in prestige and power.

We next describe precisely how this electoral capital was used by the different players. We shall explain why, despite the opposition of numerous important politicians during most of the process, the four entrepreneurs managed to amend Basic Law: The Government (Direct Election of the Prime Minister), and explain its final configuration.

## 4.4 The Players' Activity with Regard to Structural and Cultural Constraints

As noted earlier, public dissatisfaction in the mid 1990s led a large group of political entrepreneurs to suggest revoking the Direct Election Law. This group made able use of public discontent with the government. Given these initial conditions, the character of the institutional change was shaped by complex interactions among a wide variety of players, with each attempting to maximize his or her interests. In fact, the change process might verily be described as a continuum of decision-making. For instance, in 1996, Beilin, Landau and Shahal presented a parliamentary proposal to revoke the Direct Election Law. In March 1997, the Parliamentary Democracy Association was established for this very purpose. At each occasion, questions were raised as to why some players were willing to relinquish power and others were supporting changes that might harm their own interests.

In this section, we examine the character and design of this formal institutional rule change. This examination shall be conducted on the three interactive levels discussed in chapter two: Level 1 deals with the interaction between the political entrepreneur, his supporting group and the public; Level 2, deals with the activities of political entrepreneurs with the interest groups that provide politicians with information regarding public preferences and other support, the entrepreneur's relationships with various groups and the strategy applied in view of the given structural and social conditions; Level 3 deals with interactions within the Knesset—the Israeli legislative decision-making body.

## 4.5 Level 1: Entrepreneurs—Group—Public

### *Public Goods, Collective Action, Information and Getting Elected*

Each stage in the decision-making and design of the proposal to revoke the direct election of the prime minister constitutes a "public good" that can be enjoyed by anyone, regardless of his or her participation in its production. Such an outcome promotes "free riding" and explains the public's indifference to political rules. The literature calls this syndrome the collective action problem. Entrepreneurial and interest group activity contradicts the notion of "free riding." The group, including Beilin, Shahal, Landau and Carmon, together with the Parliamentary Democracy Association (PDA), managed to overcome the collective action problem and, following the model (chapter two), contributed to an important stage in public policy design.

The ways in which interest groups and politicians exert influence has been analyzed according to the information approach with respect to public policy determination. We maintain that a group's success also depends on the structural-cultural fit of its program as well as its ability to take advantage of conflicting situations while identifying with the interests of other players in the political system.

One might conclude from the above that the motivation of political entrepreneurs, like interest groups, is to influence policy-making politicians. These activities can come to present demands capable of influencing politicians interested in maximizing their chances of being (re)elected. Thus, the actions of the PDA might be perceived as expressions of public demands. In the present case, some confusion existed between parliamentary or inside entrepreneurs and outside entrepreneurs (as opposed to the original direct election proposal). In the latter, the committee led by Reichmann was clearly an outside entrepreneur, whereas Rubinstein and his associates were inside entrepreneurs. When it came to revoking the law, the PDA recruited inside and outside entrepreneurs. The PDA therefore reflects an increasingly common pattern observed in Israeli society during the 1980s, when paralyzing nongovernability together with procedural political culture gave rise to increasing quasi-exit behavior by politicians, thus, forcing people to favor short-term considerations over long-term ones.

An in-depth analysis of our case indicates that every participant in the campaign used the proposed revocation of direct election of the prime minister as electoral capital. In the beginning, the political entrepreneurs proffered this proposal as an attempt to solve a social problem they defined as the incapacity for governance. Doing so presented society with a definition of the status quo as dysfunctional, intolerable and threatening. In the second phase, the entrepreneurs presented a solution to the problem that they themselves had defined.

Despite the hope of improved governability and stability extended by the entrepreneurs, the politicians adopted unstable, short-term criteria to maximize their chances of being (re-)elected and increasing their prestige. They were forced to do so in response to Israel's political instability and procedural political culture. Their objective was to promote institutional change even while understanding that the specific reform was an incomplete and required amendment.[52] When democratic norms are deeply entrenched, the chances increase that an institutional change will be designed according to long-term considerations irrespective of politicians' desires for (re-)election.

To conclude, a political entrepreneur's interactions with the public are based on policy demands regarding political rules and the proposals for rules and their changes supplied by politicians maximizing their chances of being (re-)elected. This scenario lies at the base of the entrepreneurs' motivation to focus their attentions on policy-making politicians. From a theoretical perspective, public good theory and the collective action problem pertain to the barriers that entrepreneurs and interest groups have to overcome. They overcome these hurdles, at least in part, by providing information about public preferences to the politicians. In the next section we deal with the initial recruitment of the resources needed for political entrepreneurs to achieve their goals.

## *Initial Resource Recruitment: Recruitment of Groups, Professionals and Funds*

Whether he or she is positioned inside or outside the parliamentary system, the political entrepreneur must obtain resources before attempting to influence policy-making politicians. The nature of the recruitment depends on the entrepreneur's perception of the public's involvement in the process. For instance, to promote passage of the Direct Election Law, the social-political context required massive public involvement; tremendous resources were therefore needed. In contrast, the PDA's struggle to revoke the reform focused on more deep-seated structural and cultural conditions. These conditions reinforced the introduction of short-term considerations when making decisions. As these structural and cultural conditions were highly entrenched, the collective action problem deepened. In this section, we examine the relationship between the entrepreneur and his group, highlighting the recruitment of funds and professional support.

### *The Entrepreneur and His Reference Group*

In order to create the social movement that will support efforts to introduce new or revised formal institutional rules, political entrepreneurs must reach the public. Yet, the entrepreneurs' interests vary from those of the group's members.[53] The case of the Parliamentary Democracy Association (PDA) constitutes a clear example of an elite group that, although it did not require vast public support, operated in a structural-cultural situation that promoted short-term considerations and increased the collective action problem. The division in interests consequently created additional confusion.

Political entrepreneurs are defined as persons capable of coordinating individuals, establishing an organization, gathering resources and pressuring governments to implement sought-after policies (public goods). Entrepreneurs enjoy prestige as well as (occasionally) political careers; their group's members enjoy the personal and collective benefits they provide. Political entrepreneurs also have the time available for organizational activities, the requisite technical and verbal skills, the appropriate personality as well as access to the media and government officials. Arik Carmon made use of all of these skills as president of the PDA.

In the previous section, we noted that when a crisis subsides, entrepreneurs enter an interim phase, waiting for the next incident. During this phase, they reevaluate the gap between the desired and the existing realities on several levels. The literature indicates that on the entrepreneur-group member level, entrepreneurs are required to be attentive to their members as well as to the covert feelings of free riders. They must work diligently to provide the desired policy on a level satisfying the group's demands[54] so as to avoid the impression that they are giving less than anticipated.[55] In the case of the PDA, the gap between group-member and entrepreneur expectations was diffused.

The more the feeling within the public grew in favor of canceling the Direct Election Law, the gap reduced. Carmon's efforts to feed the relationship and bridge the gap (between group-member and entrepreneur expectations) could be expected to be fewer. In contrast, the gap between Reichmann's and his group's interests in the mid-1980s were quite distinct, making it necessary for him to narrow the target from constitutional change to "Direct Election Change."

As far as elite groups are concerned, internalization of values by its members allows the entrepreneur to use fewer resources and maintain a looser organization. This reduces the need for repeated interactions for the purpose of reinforcing the entrepreneur's message.[56] This description aptly fits Carmon's behavior, which required few resources and stressed marketing activities. In Reichmann's case, the great stress on the marketing side damaged the public's and the group's willingness to internalize the message that the crisis was acute and required public cooperation for its alleviation.

Group recruitment is conditioned by the social problem as defined by the entrepreneur as well as the solution. The entrepreneur's goal is to convince the public that his or her solution is reliable and acceptable. In the case of the PDA, the strategy adopted reflected the identities of its carefully selected founders: Shimon Peres (*Israel One*), the attorney and former government member Haim Zadok (identified with *Labor*), Yossi Beilin (*One Israel-Israel Achat*). Moshe Shahal, Abba Eban (identified with Labor), Itzhak Shamir (*Likud)*, Moshe Arens (*Likud*), Uzi Landau (Likud), Moshe Gafni (*United Torah Judaism*), Professor Naomi Chazan (*Meretz*) and Dr. Yossi Olmert (identified with *Likud*). The group's objective was to bring about revocation of the Direct Election of the Prime Minister Law. This was to be done by returning to a single voting ballot and the adoption of a constructive no-confidence vote (in other words, a no-confidence vote for a current government that ends its term is possible only by voting for an alternate government).[57]

The founders came from different parties and sectors, a tactic meant to lend legitimacy and trustworthiness to the notion that nullification of the Direct Election Law was the correct solution to the crisis. The group included personalities chosen to appeal to Israel's elite and middle class. It therefore fit Olson's (1965) definition of a "privileged group," that is, a group composed of individuals ready to bear the costs of social action regardless of the activities of others affected by the results of their actions. The character of their activity, regardless of the sphere in which they choose to act, is essentially political. In other words, their actions affect the allocation of social values and the practices adopted in consequence. The media cooperates in their efforts, helps them shape public opinion and brings issues to the public's attention. According to Olson, the group's uniqueness lies in the lower level of resources needed for its activities in contrast to other groups recruited from a broader social basis.

## *Recruitment of Professionals*

Recruitment of professionals is motivated by the desire to maximize public support as well as the belief in the proposed solution. Like Reichmann, Carmon also adopted a strategy in drafting the proposition to cancel the Direct Election Law. The work was done at the Israel Democracy Institute, a prestigious organization due to the reputations of its academic members, including Professor David Nachmias, Professor Asher Arian, Professor Mordechai Kremnitzer, Professor Ruth Gavison and Professor Yaron Ezrahi, among others. The institute initiated conferences dealing with the Direct Election Law and hosted visits from Knesset members. It published studies on the subject, such as those by Professor Michal Shamir and Dr. Itai Sened analyzing the partisan polarization resulting from implementation of direct elections.[58] These studies bolstered the struggle to revoke the law and offered a solution that was deemed reliable. This approach contrasts with a "cheaper" one (in terms of electoral capital), which entailed submitting a proposal to the Knesset, adopted by Beilin, Shahal and Landau.

To illustrate how Carmon's strategy worked, we describe the first meeting of the Israeli Democracy Institute's public council held in July 2000. Its subject was what form of government was most desirable for Israel. During the discussions, three models were proposed: presidential, direct elections, and parliamentary democracy.

> A number of people spoke about the disease of the direct elections system as well as the present state of the political system. Prof. Yaron Ezrahi, a senior member in the Israel Democracy Institute, maintains that the current political system 'does not create the legitimate political power capable of determining public policy and carrying it out... we have created negative democracy in Israel.' According to him, Israel today is closer to a state of deadlocked democracy. Prof. Zeev Segal, from the Public Policy

Program at Tel Aviv University, described the current state of the political system as follows: 'What we have in the existing model is tremendous power centered in small parties, high representation, the crushing of the larger parties and non-governability.

The conference concluded that:

Most of the participants agreed that the parliamentary model was preferable. Moreover, there was agreement not to return to the old parliamentary system but to make changes and introduce amendments in order to improve the stability of the political system. Prof. Ben-Tzion Zilberfarb of the Economics Department, Bar-Ilan University, maintained that a parliamentary system is best for coping with the social issues on the agenda: polarization, increasing social gaps, the secular-religious divide. Prof. Mordechai Kremnitzer, a senior member in the Israel Democracy Institute, claimed that 'the previous system was characterized by sickness, we should not look back with nostalgia... the old system was problematic and we should think of the rational, balanced and moderate changes we can make.' Prof. Amos Shapira of the School of Law, Tel Aviv University, noted that the model he prefers is an 'improved and renovated parliamentary system, including a lifting of the vote threshold as well as adoption of constructive no confidence measures.' The former government minister Yoram Aridor believed that the malady characterizing the former system has strengthened. Therefore, he claimed that there is need to go back to the old system with some modifications. Knesset member Moshe Arens proposed that the changes be incremental.[59]

The rationale for Carmon's actions was supported by additional researchers who had not joined the PDA. However, their contribution was in the formulation of the analysis that the Direct Election Law had failed to promote governability.[60] Thus, the organization was assisted by professional scholars—Professor Abraham Brichta, Professor Gideon Doron, Professor Yehezkel Dror, Professor Hanna Herzog, Dr. Moshe Maor, Dr. Itai Sened, and Dr. Boaz Shapira—in their struggle.

In addition to professionals, political entrepreneurs are also required to recruit business people because they are the major sources of financial support. Indeed, during the movement's first phase, Reichmann and his supporters recruited the initial resources to finance an office and staff as well as a part-time general manager. This position was given to Dr. Israel Peleg Former Director-General of the Ministry of Environmental Protection and Shimon Peres's close associate The funds were raised during an evening conducted by Eli Horovitz, the legendary founder of Teva Pharmaceuticals, at his own residence for the business community. The next phase was the search for contributions from abroad. The appeals program was targeted at Israelis who were involved in the global market (e.g., the manufacturer Dan Proper and the financier Eliezer Fishman) or at Jews known for their philanthropy in Israel, such as Lester Crow.[61] Without their contributions, the movement could not have hired the academic consultants nor conducted the public campaigning necessary for success.

In the next part, we examine the different strategies for recruiting public support.

### *Strategies for Recruiting Public Support: The Media, Utilization of Crises, Incentives*

The entrepreneur uses various techniques to recruit public support. Among the avenues available are the media, crises, and incentives, as detailed in chapter two. Their choice of specific tools to be employed depends first and foremost on the decision to change either policy rules or political rules. Although the literature states that entrepreneurs are expected to prefer policy (regulation) change (the less-expensive goal) over political rule, this did not quite happen in Israel, as we will show. To achieve their objective, the PDA's entrepreneurs made use of the media, crises, and incentives.

#### *The Media*

In contemporary society, the main tool in the entrepreneur's arsenal is the media, acknowledged as perhaps the best vehicle for influencing public opinion and placing an issue on the public agenda. Indeed, throughout 1997, media advertising was stressed by the PDA. Parallel more or less formal groups of Knesset members, such as that led by Amnon Rubinstein, were organized as well. They all sought to use Netanyahu's ineffectual government as a lever to amend the Direct Election Law.

Timing is critical in bringing an issue to public attention. Timing worked to the benefit of the PDA and similar groups because they identified the social crisis—Netanyahu's dependence on the small partisan parties, unworkable in number, sitting in the Knesset—immediately after the 1996 elections. Timing worked again in March 1997, when Carmon identified a political crisis regarding the Minister of Foreign Affairs, David Levy, who was being undermined by Netanyahu's office as well as Netanyahu's damaged relationship with Ariel.[62] Another instance took place in 1998, when discussion of the proposition to cancel the Direct Election Law, now passed to the Committee on the Constitution, Justice and Law, was constantly delayed. It was then that Carmon convinced the media to call the continual postponements a "dirty trick," a phrase that had become a symbol of parliamentary corruption.[63] Use of the phrase quickly and effective stigmatized all those who voted against cancellation of the law, and so employed again in 2000, when Barak's government came to an end. At that point, Professor Zeev Segal, a specialist in administrative law, defined Israel's system of government as "the worst possible."[64] Rubinstein spoke about the need for a different elections system but without mentioning cancellation of the prime minister's direct election[65] and Carmon repeated that the prime minister would not be able to rule unless the system determining his election was changed.[66] All these statements were, in essence, part of a vast media campaign.

## *Crisis Utilization*

By its nature, the collective action problem leads to public silence until nongovernability reaches crisis proportions. We will now show that abatement of the initial crisis (which led to passage of the Direct Election Law) led to a reduced sense of urgency, during which the political entrepreneurs involved awaited a new crisis to recreate a context in which they could stimulate another episode of collective action.[67]

To briefly reiterate, with the decline of a crisis, social initiatives decline as well. The subsequent period constitutes an interim period during which entrepreneurs wait for new crises to revive their power.[68] In the case under study, the pivotal event dampening the crisis took place in November 1996 when the Beilin, Shahal and Landau attempt to pass their proposition nullifying the Direct Election Law failed. A vast array of other events pushed and kept the proposition off the public agenda. By December 1998, however, their waiting period ending with the upcoming elections pitting Barak against Netanyahu, and the entrepreneurs were able to pass their proposition in its first Knesset vote. The animated public debate initiated by Carmon[69] included those who opposed the law's cancellation, calling it "exchanging one bad idea for another."[70]

It follows that entrepreneurs prefer ongoing crises, which enable them to retain their electoral capital by staying in the public eye. In 2000, the Knesset went for its summer recess. After the failure in Camp David, Barak was presented in the press as a person incapable of negotiating, a trait that only increased criticism of his policy. His pronouncements of a sudden civil (nonreligious) revolution, right after the religious party Shas quit his coalition, were greeted in the press as proof of unreliability, thus undermining the Israel One-Labor Party's as well as his own image as party chair.[71] One of Israel's leading political journalists, Zvi Lavie, called Ehud Barak's first year in the Fifteenth Knesset as the year when "democracy declined and corruption flourished."[72]

Revocation of the Direct Election Law remained high on the public agenda throughout the summer recess due to the activities of entrepreneurs and other political players who saw the issue as a minefield for the electoral capital that might help them promote their own status in Labor. Thus, Beilin renewed his sharp criticism of the existing electoral system.[73] Avraham (Avrum) Burg (*Labor*), the sitting Knesset's Chair, organized a meeting of 1,000 backers on September 19, 2000, in a bid for the leadership of his party. With Barak in the audience (the gathering had been defined as a celebration of "the coming new year"), Burg criticized the direct election of the prime minister and spoke in favor of the return to party democracy.[74] The crisis had been enflamed once more.

### *Incentives for Cooperation*

In order to gain public cooperation, the entrepreneur needs to use different incentives. On the other hand, the smaller the group, fewer incentives are needed because the group has internalized the need for a solution, allowing them to overcome the collective action problem. This feeling characterized the Parliamentary Democracy Association members.[75] Unlike Reichmann, Carmon enjoyed a common belief among large parts of the public in favor of his solution—the cancellation of the Direct Election Law. Furthermore, the repeated political crisis due to Netanyahu's inability to govern, also true of Barak in short periods, was cleverly used by Carmon and strengthened his alleged proposal. In that situation the use of incentives such as singers and demonstration is not much in need.

This section dealt with the different strategies the entrepreneur uses in order to recruit public support. The next section examines the implementation of these practices with regard to politicians.

## 4.6 Level 2: Entrepreneurs—Interest Groups—Politicians

In the following analysis, we highlight how cooperation between outside and inside parliamentary entrepreneurs was conducted with respect to revocation of the Direct Election Law.

### *Politicians' Time Perception: Short-Term Considerations*

Revocation of the law determining direct election of Israel's prime minister, as should be clear by this point, did not follow theoretical expectations regarding either long-term considerations or the effect of a formal institutional change on their chances of re-election. The structural and cultural conditions that had sidetracked orderly and rational decision-making continued to have their effect. A few examples illustrate this point.

At the end of December 1998, the proposal to revoke direct election of the prime minister was submitted for the first time by Beilin, Shahal and Landau. At that particular moment, Labor's chair Ehud Barak, as well as the prime minister and chair of the Likud, Binyamin Netanyahu, opposed the law's cancellation because, in light of previous election results, they both believed the law, as it stood, would serve their own but separate interests. Their opposition to its cancellation led to postponement of the debate on the proposition.

Later on, consider the demise of Barak's government. This was the basis for renewed activity by Parliamentary Democracy Association members.[76] Their interests were identical with those of other Knesset players, such as Avraham Burg, the Knesset's Chair. His interest seems to have been in holding early elections, which he saw as an opportunity for his replacement of Barak as Labor's chair. Burg had been elected the Knesset's Chair despite Barak's opposition, who preferred a member of his own faction within the party, Shalom Simhon, for the position. As a member of the Peres faction, Burg had originally supported postponement of the Direct Election Law (1995), but he had simultaneously nurtured other options as well. Beginning in January 1995 he had allied himself with Reichmann and the Constitution for Israel movement in furthering the proposal combining personal with regional elections of Knesset members simultaneously with direct election of the prime minister. Now, as another round of elections approached, he abandoned the idea of amendment of the Direct Election Law and, against Barak's will, began campaigning for the law's nullification. He therefore joined the PDA campaign. On June 13, 2000, he assembled Knesset members from the left and the right wing in his office to promote the struggle while he announced that he would demand that Barak allow free voting.[77] By doing so, he reopened the debate regarding the law.

Eventually, though, several short-term considerations led Knesset members not to vote for nullification at that time. Barak's resignation in late 2000 led to speculation in the press and the political system about whether the Direct Election Law could be revoked. While some claimed that the chances for this happening were greater than ever, others thought that a miracle was needed.[78] The alternative was not very appealing: voting for a proposition dissolving the Knesset as initiated by Barak and supported by Arik Sharon (which meant holding elections solely for the prime minister). Small parties opposed nullification because such a change would reduce their chances of re-election. Experience had shown that split voting increased the number of Knesset mandates won by smaller parties at the same time that it reduced those of larger parties. Corroboration for this view came from Eliyahu Yishai, the new leader of Shas, who stated that the law's revocation would be a "hard blow for Shas."[79] As far as Likud Knesset members are concerned, the main factor explaining Knesset members' opposition to the law's nullification was their lack of desire to dissolve the Knesset for fear of losing their seats if elections were held. This and jockeying for appointments should their allies win resulted in the passage of a proposal to hold early elections.

In 2001, after being elected prime minister, Ariel Sharon supported revocation of the Direct Election Law as part of his battle with Netanyahu over party control. Labor was also split between Barak, who opposed revocation, and Peres, who had replaced Barak as chair and preferred revocation. Whatever their substantive reasons for taking their respective positions—in addition to their attitudes toward establishing a coalition government with the Likud—represented another arena in which competition over the party's control could be waged.[80]

## *Lobbying Knesset Members*

Political entrepreneurship is often akin to lobbying.[81] Thus, in 1998, Beilin and Landau were recruiting supporters for a parliamentary lobby to assist the PDA in presenting its case during an upcoming Knesset debate. They recruited the special majority needed to revoke the law on the first reading: 62 Knesset members voted for the proposition. Few in the Labor Party opposed the proposition, but those who did were Barak supporters. Those who opposed the law from the right-wing camp were led by Binyamin Netanyahu, now the prime minister. The entrepreneurs were successful because they utilized structural conditions—such as internal party struggles over Labor Party leadership between Peres and Barak, the weakening of Netanyahu's status relative to that of Sharon in the Likud, coalition crises with Shas and the attempts of individual Knesset members, such as David Levy (Likud) to ensure their power within the political system—that might benefit them early in the campaign. Subsequently, however, when Netanyahu and Barak understood that Netanyahu's government would not hold, they altered their positions and proposed holding early elections earlier, which was approved. Ultimately, then, lobbying failed when the leaders of both major parties, Labor and Likud, discovered their short-term interests to be mutual and contrary to the political entrepreneur's goals.

Lobbying is not unidimensional; it is an activity that adopts numerous guises, all designed to put maximum pressure directly on policy-makers, including structural conditions, especially coalition government crises. For instance, in June 2000, a coalitional crisis was sparked when the Tal Commission, headed by a former justice of the Supreme Court, the Honorable Justice Zvi Tal, proposed the "Tal Law" that re-created new conditions allowing the draft of students continuing their religious studies in ultra-Orthodox learning institutions. The religious party taking greatest offense was Shas. Avraham Burg used this crisis to support his demand, made with political entrepreneurs, that Barak allow free voting on the bill calling for the Direct Election Law to be repealed. In an article published in *Globes*, a major financial newspaper, Arik Carmon explained how Shas's behavior proved that the law should be voided:

> Despite the opinion that Shas's statements deserve criticism, one cannot hide the central issue: Israeli democracy is on the verge of a deep government crisis... because broad sectors of Israeli society—with Shas representing one sector... and other groups occupying another—have not accepted nor internalized one of democracy's basic principles: the principle of inclusiveness... This crisis has increased and is reflected in the inability of the government to

> govern... the reason being... a bad system—the Direct Election of the Prime Minister Law. It is difficult to complain about Shas' use of the political power it received as a result of the new system—a power that is disproportionately large when compared to its share of the population. The direct elections system that has already caused the collapse of parties, the weakening of the Knesset with the change of common for sectoral interests... Cancellation of the Direct Election Law may pave the way to moderation in the cultural arena as well.[82]

Another crisis, this time utilized by Yossi Beilin, appeared with notification of the new summit talks to be held at Camp David (July 2000) between President Bill Clinton, Yaasir Arafat and Ehud Barak. The event prodded Beilin to change his strategy. He now proposed postponing the debate on his proposition. At a meeting of his faction of the *Labor* Party held in Tel Aviv, he called upon Barak to allow the debate to be shifted to the Committee on Constitution, Law and Justice prior to its second reading. Beilin also suggested that discussion of the proposal be brought before the party's Executive Committee only after the Knesset committee had concluded its debate.[83]

However, with the failure of the Camp David summit, it was announced that elections would be moved earlier. This rescheduling forced Beilin to change his mind once more and announced that, despite Barak's opposition, he would submit his proposition for the law's repeal in time for its second and third reading.

Still another structural condition that forced political entrepreneurs to make haste was the Continuity Law requiring all readings of the budget law to be completed during one Knesset term. A year earlier, Beilin had managed to obtain a special majority on his proposal's first reading. Due to the change of government, the Continuity Law's stipulations forced Beilin to bring the issue before the Knesset assembly less than a month away. Beilin's position as Minister of Justice was an advantage because it allowed him to call for a meeting of all the Labor Party Knesset members who supported him. At the meeting, he asked them to apply pressure on Barak to allow them to vote freely, a necessary condition if the proposal was to pass.

Barak's absence from Israel during the summit provided a good opportunity for the practice of "procedural alacrity."[84] With Rubinstein as chair of the Committee on the Constitution, Law and Justice, the entrepreneurs switched submission tactics and chose the alternative of filing a new legislative proposal in place of the previous one, thereby avoiding submission of the text to that committee. And so, the proposal for voiding the Direct Election Law was sent to the Knesset for its first reading on July 12, 2000. It passed without difficulty because, at least in part, the vote for the proposal was treated as a protest vote against Barak's behavior on the international and political level. Had the proposal been submitted in Barak's presence, it was doubted that it would pass.[85]

## 4.7 Level 3: Political Entrepreneurs and Legislative Bodies

According to the model proposed in chapter two, after politicians establish their positions regarding a policy and manage to reduce the opposition posed by administrators, they have to pass their programs in the form of parliamentary legislation. Here we describe the actions taken by inside political entrepreneurs with respect to Knesset members as well as their interactions with political entrepreneurs. The parameters stressed are: Key players (e.g., prime ministers, party institutions, committee chairs); Ideology, Strategy profession and experience; Compromises between the objective and the positive aspects of legislative propositions.

### *Key Players: Prime Ministers, Party Institutions, Committee Chairs*

Within the context of Israel's parliamentary democracy, prime ministers represent the central political players.[86] Under the circumstances of the case in question, the prime minister thus became a structural obstacle to revocation of the Direct Election Law. For instance, in 1999, Ehud Barak, as Labor's chair and Binyamin Netanyahu, as prime minister and the Likud's chair, preferred early elections, which would naturally lead to postponement of the debate on the law's repeal.

The prime minister, a structural position as well as a personality, clearly constitutes an important factor in any political entrepreneur's strategy. For instancc, in 2000, one saw cooperation between entrepreneurs and Avraham Burg—the Knesset's Chair—over convening the meeting during which the demand was raised that Barak allow free voting by Knesset members.[87] The same occurred when Yossi Beilin, as Minister of Justice, gathered together those of Labor's Knesset members who supported the law's nullification. During that meeting, we should recall, he asked the participants to pressure Barak on the free voting issue, necessary to block passage of the law.[88]

The prime minister has a number of structural instruments at his disposal that can be applied to affect the design of institutional change. The main instrument, which has become a recognized delaying strategy, is establishment of committees. For instance, at the beginning of his term in 1999, Barak asked/forced Beilin to wait nine months before raising the issue of the law's revocation. He promised Beilin that a committee would be established in the interim. Professor David Libai would sit at its head as it examined the Direct Election Law and found a solution on which both sides could agree. Libai, in turn, used his power as committee chair to abstain from convening the committee. Only when the PDA applied intense public pressure did the prime minister instruct Libai to convene the committee, which was late in filing its recommendations.

The prime minister's centrality comes from the place of the office in the parliamentary structure and, it follows, his or her capacity to influence how the political rules of the game are applied. However, as a political figure, prime ministers are obviously interested in being elected, an objective that reinforces the priority of short-term considerations. When the effective structural conditions contribute to the stability of a prime minister's term, the cost of agreeing to a change in the political rules that allowed him or her to be elected (or appointed, as in the old system) exceeds the benefits of change. Nevertheless, a change in structural design can affect the prime minister's actions. As Haim Assa has noted, a prime minister will generally support passage of any law preferred by a major segment of the electorate.[89]

On February 6, 2001, Ariel Sharon (*Likud*) defeated Ehud Barak in elections for the prime minister's office. Sharon was elected even though the Likud was not the largest party in the Knesset. The *Likud* had seven fewer seats (19) than did *Labor* (26, including the *Gesher* and *Meimad* lists). It was clear that the electoral reform was not fulfilling its objective of stable government. The two previous prime ministers elected under the direct election system, Binyamin Netanyahu and Ehud Barak, had not completed their four-year terms. In the duration of one more or less legal tenure, elections had been conducted three times and new governments chosen twice. The law had not neutralized the exaggerated power of smaller parties; the opposite had occurred, with that power growing as larger but not absolutely dominant parties were forced into constructing ever more complex—and therefore fragile—coalition governments. This situation allowed the small parties to extract ever larger concessions.[90]

In the background lingered another threat, that of Netanyahu. Netanyahu was believed to have an edge in direct elections because of his communication skills. The search for political stability and the desire to weaken Netanyahu motivated Ariel Sharon—who had supported revocation of the Direct Election Law prior to the elections—to agree to its repeal as a part of a deal enabling him to seat a coalition government with *Labor*. The defeated Barak was replaced by Shimon Peres as *Labor* chair acting as Minister of Foreign Affairs and Deputy Prime Minister in Sharon's Government and Binyamin (Fouad) Ben-Eliezer as Minister of Defense, who also favored the law's nullification, who were most intent on retaining control of their own parties as well as the coalition government.[91] We therefore see that in this episode as well, decisions related to political rule change were heavily weighted by immediate, short-term considerations.

Building on the literature as well as Assa's comment regarding passage of laws, it becomes clear that success in passing a formal institutional change in parliament increases the probability that the change will be regarded as electoral capital in the eyes of members of parliament. Knesset members could not disregard the institutional change or its implications if they wished to benefit from it. Hence, as Sharon, Ben-Eliezer and Peres were putting their coalition government together in 2001, Knesset members began evaluating the chances that direct election for the prime minister would be voided. On March 7, 2001, the Knesset voted to cancel the Direct Election Law (the vote was 72 for, 37 against and three abstentions) and to return to the older one-ballot system. The law revoking the reform took effect with elections for the Sixteenth Knesset.

### *The Parties and Their Institutions*

Israel's political parties constitute crucial structural factors regarding political rule change. Despite the decrease in the power of parties since the 1970s, their ability to serve as societal communication channels, mechanisms for recruiting leaders or arenas for public debate continue. Under the existing rules of the game, political parties are key factors in Knesset elections. And, because internal party institutions formulate party policy and strategies together with their leaders, they remain subject to critical analysis.[92]

The central role played by the parties was quite evident in the struggle over revocation of the Direct Election Law. In many cases, these bodies made decisions that contradicted their platforms.[93] Their power forced political entrepreneurs to take internal institutions into consideration within their strategies. For instance, in 2000, Beilin tried to recruit Labor's Central Committee, which he believed was powerful enough to influence the prime minister. He sent letters to all its members, asking them to demand the right to vote freely. Barak was active in other directions. He helped David Libai disseminate the Libai Committee's recommendations regarding continuation of the electoral reform, which were to be read at the Central Committee's meeting.[94]

Barak tried to convince Central Committee members to reject free voting.[95] He also met with leaders supporting the Constitution for Israel movement, e.g. Uriel Reichmann, Haim Ramon and Fuad Ben-Eliezer (the latter two Knesset members). Together they formulated an alternate proposition for electoral system change, specifically, separate dates for election of the prime minister and the Knesset, with Knesset members elected in regional elections; the no-confidence vote threshold would be raised, with a majority of 65 members (four more than the number required in the Direct Election Law) needed for a vote to pass. The Constitution for Israel members thereupon initiated a campaign to promote the new proposal through the press and among party members. The group published an invited Gallop poll whose results showed that 52 percent of the public supported direct elections for the prime minister; 37 percent opposed it and the remainder had not yet decided. *Iki Elner*, president of Constitution for Israel, pointed out that polls conducted over the past three years consistently showed majority support for the Direct Election Law. As to Yossi Beilin, *Elner* added: "Yossi Beilin is trying to punish Barak because the latter undermined his position."[96]

Beilin and his faction, "Truth 21" were well aware that *Labor*'s Central Committee would not vote against the prime minister. They therefore focused their efforts on attempts to convince the committee's members. Eitan Cabel, a major figure sitting on the committee, warned Beilin's group as follows: "You may be as enthusiastic as you like, but never in history did a prime minister bring an issue for a voting in the committee and have it rejected".

Beilin and his group were supported by the PDA as well as some Knesset members from the *Labor*. The Knesset's chair, Avraham Burg, assembled about 200 activists and called on them to support repeal of the Direct Elections Law. The coalition chair, Ofir Pines, also urged his supports to back Beilin's proposal.[97]

## *Committee Chairs*

Shepsle and Weingast (1981) have described the role of parliamentary committee chairs as that of a "structural catalyst," being in the position to confirm a committee's agenda. The chair plays an important role in the promotion—and the neglect or even rejection—of legislative proposals. A chair's approval of a proposal increases the probability that a political entrepreneurs' campaign will be successful, and vice versa: a lack of interest increases the probability of the campaign's demise. With respect to nullification of direct election of the prime minister, the chair of the Knesset Constitution, Law and Justice Committee played that role to the fullest.

Consider the following incident. In 1998, the Committee's chair was Hanan Porat (*Mafdal*), whose party was a member of the Netanyahu coalition. Porat announced his support of the Direct Election Law but promised not to bury the Beilin-Landau proposal for its revocation. He nonetheless estimated that the debate would continue into the winter.[98] By not outright rejecting the proposal, he allowed the institutional rule change to take place.

Because parliamentary chairs are also sitting Knesset members, the chair's primary interest is, as a rule, the use of this position as re-election capital.[99] And so, on March 6, 2001, the constitution Committee, with Amnon Rubinstein as its head, approved revocation of the Direct Election Law, sending it on the road to confirmation. Why did Rubinstein do so? It was well-known that he opposed repeal of the law and that, as the Committee's chair, he could delay the proposal's progress. The answer lies in a combination of normative and strategic interests. Rubinstein believed that using his authority to further personal preferences was wrong. The veracity of this belief is supported by his actions as a politician: He entered politics to promote his party, Shinui, on the basis of his personal prestige as an expert in constitutional law. As his career continued, his political power came to be based on media attention centered on his personality and credibility. If he had halted the law's revocation, this act would have undermined the foundations of his electoral appeal. Alternatively, there was the need for Rubinstein to survive the test of political results. The Labor-Likud coalition would have meted out considerable penalties had Rubinstein decided to use his power to stall the proposal. Alternatively, by not stopping the proposal, Rubinstein was left with another option, that of proposing amendments in the spirit of his original proposals to Basic Law: The Government, an objective he wished to fulfill before he retired from political life.[100]

From the point of view of political entrepreneurs, the centrality of committee chairs places these positions as the targets of pressure tactics or circumvention strategies. For instance, in July 2000, just before

Barak went to Camp David, Carmon and Beilin assumed that he would attempt to postpone the Knesset debate on the Direct Election Law's repeal to the following session beginning in September.[101] Yet, it was Rubinstein, the Constitution, Law and Justice Committee chair. who filed the postponement request. Those entrepreneurs intent on repealing the law had to overcome this structural barrier in order to schedule the debate for the second and third readings. There was also the threat of consecutiveness, another structural obstacle to be confronted, especially because the government's longevity was in question. With the summer recess approaching (August 1, 2000) and the need to file the legislative proposal before the current session ended, Rubinstein's agreement to the move became crucial. In order to evade these hurdles, Beilin and his partners filed the proposal anew, making it eligible for a preliminary reading, a status that bypassed the Constitution Committee chair as well as the consecutiveness clause. The proposal was indeed heard during a preliminary reading on July 12, 2000. It passed easily due to the support of the two largest parties despite Barak's disfavor.[102] The resubmission also saved Rubinstein from using his position as chair to thwart the proposal's progress, a step that benefited everyone.

## *Ideology, Strategy, Profession and Experience*

The tension between ideology and strategy as factors in political decision-making reflects the built-in friction between objective policies that maximize efficiency and social benefit, and subjective policies that reflect the decision-makers' personal political interests.[103] We do not claim here that any one parameter is of primary or secondary importance. What we do argue is that the parameters interact and are directly related to other parameters to create a network.

This does not, of course, subtract from the interesting way they affected the way in which the Direct Election Law was revoked in 2001. Throughout the process, both opposing groups—Beilin-Carmon-Peres versus Rubinstein-Reichmann-Barak-Netanyahu—shared a similar liberal ideology. This situation differed significantly from the struggle to legislate direct elections in 1992, when Shamir led the conservative camp while Reichmann, Rubinstein and Libai led the liberal camp. The common denominator shared by both episodes was the ideological discontinuity between the original and the subsequent struggle. Passage of the direct election law reflected attempts to accumulate electoral capital in a struggle between players motivated by short-term considerations with respect to their (re-)election. Their political values resulted from their perceptions of the peace process with the Palestinians and the ideological worth of the "land for peace" equation. This conflict (or competition) increased when extremist parties such as Meretz and Israel's Arab parties on the one hand and the Mafdal and extreme nationalist parties on the other joined the fray. Alternatively, the struggle to revoke the Direct Election Law, which included the struggle to pass the respective legislation into law in 1992–2000, represented a mixture of professional and ideological parameters together with attempts to maximize chances of re-election and achieving control of the government.

In its final phase, the personal political interests of the politicians involved explain those compromises.

A politician's ability to apply long-term considerations when formulating a fundamental, formal institutional change is a function of the depth of a society's internalization of essential democratic norms. These structural and cultural factors bridge the gap between ideology and strategic approaches. For instance, on March 6, 2001, Rubinstein, who was the constitution committee chairman, chose not to delay the law proposition. The explanation for his actions combines both ideological and strategic considerations. On the one hand, Rubinstein perceived the use of his authority as committee chairman in order to further his personal preferences as inappropriate. On the other hand, his approach was the source of his prestige that enabled him to maximize his chances of being elected.[104]

On March 6, 2001, the proposal to revoke the Direct Election Law was accepted by the Knesset Constitution Committee after a violent debate that included Knesset members shouting at each other and several attempts to restore order. The proposal's final version reflected several compromises orchestrated by Rubinstein, for example, a paragraph in the new law referred to "a constructive no-confidence motion," according to which a vote of 61 Knesset members was sufficient to remove the prime minister but only if an alternative candidate could be suggested. Another compromise provision stipulated that the prime minister could dissolve the Knesset only after receiving the president's approval.

## 4.8 Summary

When the legislation repealing the direct election of the prime minister was finally passed on March 7, 2001, Arik Carmon summarized the process that had materialized over the last two decades: "We raised the bar high but there is still a long way to go. Other changes are needed; however, they should be introduced gradually." It seems that that the alleged institutional change was only temporary and based on short-term considerations. Such an institutional change is bound to be unstable. The history of Basic Law: The Government (Direct Election of the Prime Minister) proves that point: In 1992, just a year after implementation of the Direct Election Law, the Israeli public began to feel that this political rule change had not solved the problems of either government centralization or nongovernability. This feeling was, in part, a result of Rabin's assassination, Netanyahu's difficulty in establishing a coalition, his inability to govern, and the activity of political entrepreneurs with respect to the Direct Elections Law.

Contrary to the direct election process observed in the 1980s, elections during the 1990s evidenced confusion between inside parliamentary entrepreneurs and outside entrepreneurs. While institution of direct elections exhibited a clear distinction between outside entrepreneurs (Reichmann and the Constitution for Israel movement) and inside parliamentary entrepreneurs (Rubinstein and other Knesset members), the proposal to revoke the law reflected a mixture of inside and outside entrepreneurs on each side (e.g., the Parliamentary Democracy Association had members from inside the Knesset as well as outside, private persons). This behavior reflects the transformations undergone by Israeli society beginning in the 1980s. At present, politicians are increasingly engaged in alternative political behavior meant to overcome what appears to be entrenched nongovernability, caused by the structural conditions that enforce the prominence of short-term considerations during political decision-making.

In parallel, political entrepreneurs—Yossi Beilin, Arik Carmon, Uzi Landau, and Moshe Shahal, Uriel Reichmann and Amnon Rubinstein—continued to play salient roles in the political rule change. These entrepreneurs sensed the public's distress, defined its source as a social problem, and identified a solution—revocation of the Direct Election Law, the subject of this chapter.

We have also shown that unlike the situation in 1992 when the Direct Election Law was legislated, the political arena of the 1990s was characterized by high levels of procedural democratic norms along with political instability. These structural and cultural conditions re-enforced the trend among the change agents toward short-term considerations, which increased the collective action problem. Privileged groups were consequently able to promote an institutional process that did not depend on the organization of collective action or the raising of public consciousness. The Parliamentary Democracy Association was a specific example of a privileged group that, due to these and environmental structural conditions, had no need to broaden the scope of public support in order to pressure politicians. As a small cohesive group, its members had internalized its message, which allowed Carmon to act with few resources while stressing the marketing aspects of institutional change. This situation contrasted with that of Reichmann, in whose case adoption of a marketing strategy undermined the message he was attempting to convey.

Lastly, we have shown that interactions between politicians had crucial influence on the outcome of the legislative process. Our focus was therefore on inside entrepreneurs, the politicians sitting inside the Knesset. While analyzing parameters, such as time perceptions, maximization of their chances of re-election, the prime minister's position, value perceptions, profession and experience, we were able to conclude that the institutional change in question reflected numerous last-minute compromises between the objective and substantive aspects of the proposed law and its resulting positivistic features.

# CHAPTER FIVE

# *Comparative Aspects of Institutional Changes: the Cases of Argentina, Italy and New Zealand*

## 5.1 Introduction

In this chapter we examine three institutional changes in three different countries—electoral reform in New Zealand and Italy, both from 1993, as well as judicial reforms in Argentina in 1994 and 1997. These institutional changes constitute political rules that redefine the political framework as well as the power relations among various players.[1]

The present study is not a complete comparative study of the three countries analyzed. The analysis of comparative changes is more circumscribed than the one used to analyze the Israeli cases. The aim of this work is to present a theoretical framework for institutional change and analyze examples in Israel. Therefore, the comparative chapter is meant to strengthen the theoretical claim exemplified via the Israeli case.

Information about these cases was collected from secondary studies. Regarding the institutional change that took place in New Zealand, the analysis was based upon the works of scholars.[2] The institutional change in Italy was analyzed as well on the basis of the works of scholars.[3] The institutional change in Argentina was similarly analyzed on the basis of the works of scholars.[4]

We compared the change in political rules pertaining to elections and the judicial system. We chose the electoral reform adopted in New Zealand on November 6, 1993. The reform was adopted as a result of a referendum, according to which a majority elections system called FPP (First Past the Post) was replaced by a relative system called MMP (Mixed Member Proportional), also known as the "German system."[5] This type of institutional change is an aggregation type of rule that redefines the decision function, which, in turn, translates preferences into political results from a majority to a relative elections system.

Another electoral reform was adopted in Italy in August 1993 whereby the relative system (PR) was replaced by a mixed-mode one (SMD-PR). The latter includes a component of single-representative districts—when the candidate elected receives most votes and seats. The total number of seats is divided among the party lists according to a relativity formula that depends upon the results of the division in single-representative districts.[6] This institutional change is an aggregation rule type that redefines the decision function, which translates preferences into political results, from a relative into a mixed-mode system.

An additional case is Argentina in 1994. It adopted a judicial reform as an amendment to the Argentine constitution, leading to the establishment of an independent national judicial council. Its duty was: to consider low-ranking federal judges and with, the approval of the senate, elect one of them as president of the council; to be responsible for funding the courts and supervising judges; to increase the percentage of senators required for approval of the appointment of high court judges by the president to two-thirds; and to increase the protection of human rights by establishing the post of a public servant (Ombudsman) whose job was to safeguard human rights. The operative parts of the change were supposed to be implemented via legislation in the congress. Nevertheless, it took three years for the reform to pass in the Argentine congress.[7] This institutional change is an authority rule type that redefines the system of actions that those who hold different social and political positions are allowed to take. As noted earlier, such institutional changes redefine the framework of the political discussion as well as the power relations between players.[8]

The choice of comparative cases was made in full cognizance of the fact that it is difficult to locate a common denominator for a group of countries according to any quantitative measurement—population size, geographical location, native cultures, seniority of the country as a democracy, the level of economic development, the structure of the society and type of government—that would indicate a common structural problem that could have led to the adoption of certain changes in those specific countries.[9] For instance, Israel is a unitary democracy with an agreement government, while New Zealand is a unitary democracy with a majority government. In contrast, Italy is closer to the center of the federal-unitary-majority-agreement spectrum.

The theoretical question to be examined in the context of the given cases is: why and under which conditions do formal basic institutional changes in the political system take place? How is the character and design of such a basic formal institutional change determined? What are the factors that explain the stability of such a change?

This chapter is divided into a number of parts in which we examine the comparative cases according to constant factors that will allow us to draw a number of conclusions regarding the design and stability of institutional change in general. The conclusions will be presented in a concluding section. Moreover, conclusions concerning the Israeli case analyzed in chapters three and four shall be presented in comparison with the cases analyzed in this chapter: the electoral reforms that took place in New Zealand and Italy, as well as the judicial reform in Argentina.

There are a number of ways to present the results of this comparative study. One possibility is to divide the chapter into three parts, each part analyzing a change in each state separately, according to constant parameters. Another possibility is to divide the chapter according to factors, each part discussing one factor and comparing the three cases. We chose the second approach. In other words, we analyze the comparative cases according to the factors decided on in the model presented in the first chapter and discussed in more detail in the second chapter. The reason for this choice is that the first possibility might mislead the reader into focusing more on the descriptive section rather than on the section about the factors. Moreover, we maintain that after the analysis based on factors presented in chapters three and four concerning the Israeli cases, this chapter should reflect the comparative aspect, also based on factors. We would like to stress that the comparative chapter has been added in order to strengthen the theoretical claim examined in the Israeli case.

In the first part of this chapter (5.2.1), we present a brief summary of the process of designing and determining political rules and their stability. We will apply this description to the empirical cases of New Zealand, Italy and Argentina and describe the feeling among the public that precedes the change in political rules. We shall include a description of the political and economic stability in these countries, as well as the degree of cultural centralization. In the second part (5.2.2), we describe the appearance of political entrepreneurs. In the third part (5.2.3), we explain the process of an institutional change design and conclude with a short summary (5.3).

## 5.2 The Feeling among the Public of a Need for a Political Rule Change

As mentioned, the claim concerning the analysis of political rule determination and the design process and ultimate stability is based upon two variables: the level of political economic stability on the one hand, and the political culture, characterized by the society's attitude to democratic norms, on the other. These variables enable us to develop a bivariate scale for measurement and analysis of the structural conditions affecting the short-term considerations of the change's design. This measurement will help us explain the stability of an institutional change. Such structural variables constitute the framework for the activity of the various players—politicians, interest groups, bureaucrats and the broad public—and affect their time perception when they attempt to bring about an institutional change.

The process of institutional change involves three main variables: the development of a feeling among the public of the need for a change; the appearance of political entrepreneurs, who, by their actions, define the institutional change as electoral capital; and the actions of players who make use of the electoral capital in order to maximize their benefit. Thus, the change is a balanced result of the actions of various players.

As we will demonstrate in the following section, in all three cases, institutional changes were preceded by a feeling among the public that a change was needed.

### *5.2.1 Argentina: The Judicial Reforms from 1994 and 1997*

In 1994, Argentina adopted a judicial reform as an amendment to its constitution. As a result of the reform, an independent national judicial council was formed. Its job was to choose a slate of low-ranking federal judges from which the president would be chosen, whose candidature had to be confirmed by the senate. The council would be responsible for funding the court system and supervising judges. In addition, the voting percentage in the senate needed to approve the appointment of a high court judge by the president was increased to two-thirds and additional safeguards against government repression of human rights were enacted in the form of a public servant (Ombudsman) whose job was to serve as a watchdog over these rights. The operative parts of the change were supposed to be implemented by legislation in the congress. However, it was not until three years later, in 1997, that the Argentine congress finally passed the legislation.[10] This institutional change is an authority rule type that redefines the system of actions that those who hold various social and political positions are allowed to take.

This change might have undermined the interests of politicians, who, prior to the judicial reform, appointed federal judges on low levels and decided the budget of the court system. In addition to judicial appointments, the reform strengthened the judicial system, because some of the functions of the executive authority were passed to the judicial branch of government. This change prompts us to ask, why would the politicians vote for an institutional change that limited their authority? What determined the character and design of this basic formal institutional change? And what are the factors explaining the stability of the change?

The literature explains the adoption of the judicial reform as an outcome of the motivations of politicians.[11] Thus, the amendment in Argentina, in 1994, was the result of an agreement between the two larger parties, the Radical party (the opposition) and the Peronists, led by President Carlos Menem. The "Radicals" were given the judicial reform, and the Peronists received a constitutional amendment that allowed Menem to run in the 1995 elections. The second phase, in 1997, took place when the Peronists, led by the re-elected President Menem, who had avoided implementing the judicial reform in congressional legislation, understood that the reform would increase the dominance of their party. The explanation offered in the literature that the judicial reform benefited the opposition because it limited the power of the ruling party is sufficient. The question is why would the Radicals demand an institutional change that would harm their interests if they became the ruling party? Why would they seek to establish a judicial reform in 1994, when the rationale was the same as before? What were the circumstances that forced Menem to legislate the judicial reform in congress, after four year's postponement?

Analysis of the reform in Argentina shows political and economic instability on the one hand, and a political culture characterized by procedural democratic norms, on the other. The political economic instability might have resulted from the shift from a military regime to a democracy in the 1980s, a shift characterized by the adoption of procedural democratic norms. Several other factors were at play here as well including the nongovernability of Alfonsin's (1984–1989) and Menem's (1989–1995) governments, the economic crisis that increased nongovernability, and fast-moving events in the high court, beginning with judicial activism that supported Alfonsin's government, and ending with judicial restraint that resulted from legislative restraint by Menem when he intervened in the high court. These actions reflect the political and economic instability, as well as procedural democratic centralization. These structural conditions constitute the framework for the development of a feeling that an institutional change was needed, a feeling that fed the rise of political entrepreneurs and the activities of the players in a dynamic process that resulted in judicial reform in Argentina.

### *The Development of a Desire for an Institutional Change*

The political history of Argentina in the twentieth century was shaped by an interchanging civil and military rule. These changes were not reflected in the adoption of essential democratic norms. In October 1983, after seven years of military oppression, Argentina returned to democratic rule with Raul Alfonsin from the Radical party as its president.

When Alfonsin was elected, five of the high court members resigned to enable the advent of the new Argentine democracy. Alfonsin appointed five professional candidates in their stead. Three of them were identified with the Radical party, one with the socialist faction and another with the traditional Peronists. As the president of the court, Alfonsin proposed the candidature of his Peronist opponent, Italo Luder, for court presidency. Luder turned the offer down.

The period between 1983 and 1989 marked the relative independence of the high court, which implemented a liberal interpretation of human rights.[12] This relative independence was possibly due to the support of the executive authority, which preferred to solve the issue of nongovernability through the court, despite the fact that on most occasions the court confirmed the legality of its actions.

However, due to the economic crisis that plagued the country in the 1980s, Carlos Menem, a candidate from the Peronist party, was elected president in 1989. For decades, the Argentine economy was characterized by alternating periods of economic crisis and prosperity. Since the 1970s, every six or seven years, reforms were made leading to a short-lived improvement in the economy and rising prices. Ultimately, there was a crisis and a lowering of prices, leading to the devaluation of assets and lands. As a result, Argentines and foreign investors lost their faith in the financial system. Citizens had learned that in order to preserve their funds, they should transfer them abroad. Approximately 130 billion dollars were deposited in accounts outside Argentina, a sum close to the overall Argentinean debt.[13] Menem's period was one of immense centralization on the part of the executive authority. He promoted his political and economic goals instead of those of other government institutions. Despite his promises during the election campaign, Menem instituted radical economic reforms, including price stabilization, a constant rate of one peso to one dollar (offering no possibility of changing the rate), privatization that resulted in the sale of almost all of the government firms, and the lifting of restrictions on imports. These reforms reflect the adoption of procedural democratic norms, despite the public's discontent, expressed in demonstrations and appeals to the high court against Menem's economic program.[14] The high court criticized Menem's actions. In response, contrary to his pre-election promises, Menem tried to intervene in the high court. His moves were made possible because the majority of the senate supported him. In April 1990, the senate approved his proposal to add four more judges to the high court. When the high court president and an additional judge resigned, Menem's judges became the majority. As a result, the high court changed its tactics from intervention to restraint.[15]

When the 1995 elections were approaching, Menem wanted to be re-elected. To be eligible to run again, he had to amend Argentine law. Doing so involved receiving the approval of a majority of two-thirds in both houses of parliament, the congress and the senate. He had the support of the majority in the senate, but not in the congress. Thus, he needed the support of the opposition parties. He preferred to negotiate with the Radical party because an alliance with them would legitimize his running in the 1995 elections.[16] However, the Radical party, led by Alfonsin, opposed the constitution amendment. Despite this obstacle, Menem stuck to his plan. In October 1993, the senate provided a legal draft of a declaratory law to be approved by the congress. This law was needed in order to assemble the parliament to amend the constitution. Menem threatened that he would conduct a referendum regarding the constitutional amendment at the end of November. Polls of the period showed that 70 percent of the public supported the constitutional gathering that would promote constitutional changes. Thus, Menem applied pressure on Alfonsin, who signed the agreement concerning the constitutional changes that called for the constitutional gathering, a week before the referendum.

The incompetence of the Radical party, revealed as a result of Menem's strategy, and the feelings of the public indicated that the

Peronist party candidate would be elected president. Drastic structural reforms undertaken by Menem that had halted inflation and an increase in investments being made in Argentina also contributed to Menem's popularity. His success at the polls could keep the Radicals in the opposition for six more years, until 2001.[17]

Nevertheless, there was also dissatisfaction with Menem's centralization and his intervention with the high court. The strategy of restraint that the high court adopted led all public activity to a dead-end and contrasted sharply with the high court's open-minded approach during Alfonsin's administration, which served various interest groups. These groups saw the high court as being able to confront the government's arbitrary actions. Now, the restraint of the high court increased the public's dissatisfaction. The economic prosperity did not last long either. The rate of exchange with the dollar was artificially maintained, leading to a gradual collapse of the local manufacturing system. Most of the funds received from privatization disappeared as a result of corruption. Public services continued to be inefficient. In order to provide them, Argentina had to take out loans. In the meantime, the rate of unemployment increased, and Argentina became the state with the highest unemployment and poverty rates in South America.[18]

Alfonsin defined the social problem as the centralization of the ruling party, which allowed Menem to rule while the political demands of other groups in Argentina remain unheeded. This social problem had to be solved. As a leading political entrepreneur, Alfonsin identified a number of reforms including shortening the president's term to four years, which would enable him to be elected in 1999, as well as implementing a judicial reform that would constitutionally block the ruling party from radical socioeconomic centralization.

From this analysis we can see how economic and political instability interacted with procedural democratic norms. The combination of these two variables led to the adoption of an institutional change based on short-term considerations. Political instability was evident in the frequent changes from a military regime to democratic rule, from the nongovernability of Alfonsin (1984–1989) to that of Menem (1989–1995). In addition, there were the rapid changes in the high court's behavior from judicial activism during Alfonsin's government, to judicial restraint, due to legislation interfering with the high court during Menem's rule. Economic instability was evident in the frequent economic crises and reforms, the collapse of production in the 1990s and ever-increasing unemployment. The rapid shift from a military regime to civil-democratic rule demonstrated political centralization.

We pointed out the use of a referendum as a strategy meant to maximize Menem's own interests.

The combination of these structural and cultural factors contributed to the dominance of short-term considerations. Pablo Spiller and Mariano Tommasi (2007: 6) wrote:

> One of the most noticeable features of Argentine politics and policy making is that key political actors tend to have short political horizons. The unusual democratic instability that characterized Argentina for most of the twentieth century has contributed to the shortness of horizons, even after the return to democracy in 1983. Democratic instability has left an imprint through path-dependent behavior in Congress, the courts, the bureaucracy, the federal fiscal system, and the actions and expectations of nongovernmental actors.

An institutional change based on such considerations is bound to be unstable, meaning that it will not be fully implemented and there will be attempts made to change it. As opposed to Argentina, Italy and New Zealand adopted an institutional change based on long-term considerations.

### *5.2.2 Italy: The 1993 Electoral Reform*

In August 1993, Italy adopted a reform of the electoral system in which the older, relative system (PR) was replaced by a mixed-mode one (SMD-PR). The latter combines a component of single-representative districts in which whoever receives the highest number of votes is elected, and the seats are divided among factions according to a relative formula.[19] This institutional change is an aggregation rule type, which redefines the decision function that translates preferences into political results, from the relative to a mixed-mode system.

This change can undermine the interests of serving politicians chosen via the old system, who rejected earlier attempts to design a formula agreed upon in the parliament. Therefore, the question is why would the politicians who used to oppose the change vote in 1991 be in favor of submitting the decision regarding an institutional change to a referendum? And why would the politicians decide to submit the decision to another referendum in 1993? As a result of the referendum outcomes in 1991, a bi-house committee was established to design a mutually acceptable formula for change. That attempt failed, leading to the second referendum in 1993. The paradox increases when we consider that, during the second half of 1992 and at the beginning of 1993, the government parties lost the local elections, making it clear that they would suffer if a majority system were adopted. So, why would they decide to submit the decision about the institutional change to a referendum, despite the harm it might cause them?[20] In this regard, the question arises, what determines the character and design of such a basic formal institutional change?

*Development of a Feeling that an Institutional Change is Needed*

Dissatisfaction with the functioning of the political system has been a common phenomenon in Italy since the end of the 1940s. Issues of governability, corruption and clientalism[21] were common characteristics of the Italian government for years. Moreover, the Italian government was characterized by the centralized rule of a single dominant party. The party system was perceived as functioning according to anachronistic guidelines.[22] However, the expression of this dissatisfaction began only in the beginning of the 1990s. Until that point, Italians had only two political choices—the Communism of the left or the Fascism of the right—so the current situation was presented (by politicians) as the lesser evil.[23] The crumbling of the Communist faction at the end of the 1980s and the development of secularization processes in Italian society led to the weakening of these dimensions, while issues that had long been marginalized—nongovernability, corruption, and clientalism—became key issues on the public agenda. The structural centralization led to an overload of demands on the government and its inability to satisfy them.[24]

During the 1980s the Italian public came to understand that the government was unable to provide or implement policies that would provide for their demands. The continuous dissatisfaction, the parties' rigidity, as well as the dominance of the ruling party, were key factors that kept Italy from meeting the demands of the European Union's criteria concerning the national debt and the government's inability to supply economic demands. The failure to meet these criteria prevented Italy from joining the European Union. In an attempt to reduce public criticism about governability issues in the political and economic spheres, in the early 1990s, the politicians promoted a reform of the local authority electoral system. The nongovernability continued, and even increased, as a result of the corruption exposed by the investigating judges. The elections reflected the tremendous dissatisfaction of the public and led to the collapse of the old party system as well as the creation of a new one. In this new party system, the coalition parties weakened, largely due to the increasing protests from groups led by the "Northern League."[25] Thus, the public expressed its desire for a change in the electoral system by voting in referendums in favor of all the institutional reforms, including changes in portions of the electoral system.[26]

This dissatisfaction was identified by political entrepreneurs, who defined the social problem as centralization and single-party rule that prevented the creation and implementation of policies that could supply public demands. This social problem demanded a solution, and the entrepreneurs proposed the examination of rule type, which meant a change of political rules—the assumption being that changing the system would weaken the ruling party.[27]

Italy was suffering from extremely high economic and political instability. Unlike Argentina, it enacted a series of democratic norms. The combination of these variables led to the adoption of long-term institutional change. Some may claim that the fact that the changes came about under pressure from the European Union shows that there has been no internalization of these democratic norms, but rather a solution based on immediate benefits. That could have been true if the behavior reflected in submitting the changes to a referendum was a strategic one (as was the case in Argentina) or a single occurrence after which the implementation of the reform was postponed. However, Italy continued to use referendums to enact changes, so pressure from the European Union did not constitute the main factor in the decision by the Italian public, politicians and judges to make significant changes in their political system.

Like Italy and unlike Argentina, the electoral reform in New Zealand reflects the adoption of a long-term institutional change. However, as opposed to Italy, the democratic culture in New Zealand was more inherent in the country's culture.[28] Therefore, it had greater effect upon the process of reform design

### *5.2.3 New Zealand: The 1993 Electoral Reform*

On November 6, 1993, as a result of a referendum, New Zealand adopted a reform of its electoral system. The single-representative majority elections system, the FPP (First Past the Post), was replaced by the MMP (Mixed Member Proportional) or the "German" system. This latter system uses a component of single-representative districts so that whoever gains the highest number of votes is elected, and seats are divided among factions according to a relative formula that depends upon the division results in single-representative districts.[29] This institutional change is an aggregation rule type that redefines the decision function, which, in turn, translates preferences into political outcomes, from majority to relative elections.

This change might potentially undermine the interests of the serving politicians, most of whom opposed the change. Therefore, we must ask, why would politicians who voted against the change in 1992 submit it to a referendum? And why did they do the same in 1993? Another question is why did the Labor party form the Royal Commission, the aim of which was to examine rule structure, despite the fact that the change might do the Labor party harm?[30] And why would the two parties with the majority of members against the change choose to promote an institutional change? In this regard, another question arises. How would the character and design of such an institutional change be determined, and what factors explain the stability of the change?

### *The Development of a Desire for an Institutional Change*

The two decades prior to the reform marked a distancing of the public from the two large parties: the National and Labor parties. The public felt that the government was unresponsive to its needs and requests. The rate of support for the two large parties continuously declined over the decades prior to the reform. Their radical socioeconomic policy elicited strong criticism from the public.[31] Most of the criticism was directed at the fact that a socioeconomic policy was not included in the platform of the parties that were used to a government culture of responding to and keeping promises made during the elections. During the 1980s, the government adopted a bill of rights and a reform of the referendum, in an attempt to appease the public, which allowed referendums to be held whenever the public wanted.[32] However, the phenomenon of government centralization continued, with a small group at the top dictating to the rest. The referendums of 1992 and 1993 were used as a means to protest against and punish the politicians from the two large parties, most of whom were against the reform. In his analysis, David Denemark (1998) presents evidence pointing to the decline of membership in and identification with the parties, the lack of faith in the parties and the parliament, the reduction in the rate of participation and the perceived ability to influence, the increase in the mobility of votes between elections, the rise in the rate of votes for smaller parties, and strategic, "insincere" voting for the large parties in order not to waste votes. The indicators point to the increase in political instability and the public's dissatisfaction with the political system and the ruling parties in New Zealand. This dissatisfaction smoldered for two decades. It also led to a process of learning among different groups in the public regarding the government's inability to determine and implement a policy that would meet the demands of the groups.

This dissatisfaction was identified by the political entrepreneurs, who defined the social problem as centralization of the ruling party. According to them, it prevented the government from implementing a policy that would meet public demands. As a solution, the entrepreneurs suggested an examination of the rule structure, in other words, a solution via political rule change. The assumption was that increasing representation through the adoption of a relative system would prevent the government from continuing with its radical socioeconomic centralization.[33]

New Zealand is a case where the structural conditions were characterized by a lower level of economic instability and a higher level of political instability. As opposed to Argentina and Italy, the cultural conditions were characterized by greater adoption of essential democratic norms. The combination of these variables led to the adoption of institutional change with long-term characteristics. In all three countries there were certain levels of democratic culture, as well as economic and political instability. In Argentina, the internalization of democratic norms was the lowest. Such conditions reflect the tendency for frequent institutional changes (in 1994 and 1997) coupled with low levels of actual implementation. As opposed to Argentina, New Zealand had the highest level of essential democratic norms as well as a lower level of political economic stability. Italy is an intermediate case.

Against the backdrop of these structural and cultural conditions, political entrepreneurs appeared who defined the social problem and pointed out the solution (section 5.2.2). The resulting change design comes from the combined actions of a number of players: politicians, interest groups, bureaucrats, and the public, all acting under structural and cultural conditions that promote an institutional change.

## 5.3 Political Entrepreneurs

The importance of political entrepreneurs lies in their ability to link public dissatisfaction resulting from nongovernability to the institutional change. The political entrepreneur defines the social problem and proposes the institutional change as a solution. However, there is no guarantee that the proposed change will be adopted by politicians. Its adoption depends upon its capability to become what we call "electoral capital." Whether it turns into such or not depends on the entrepreneurs' ability to make the politicians realize that its adoption would maximize their prestige and increase their chances of being elected. We pointed out that identification and design of the institutional change as electoral capital by the entrepreneurs depends upon a complex interaction that includes a number of players against a backdrop of various structural and cultural conditions. Within this context, the entrepreneur translates the social problem into a problem to be solved by a policy that expresses the feelings of the public, but does not create them. In the following section, we discuss in detail the appearance of entrepreneurs in these three comparative cases.

### *5.3.1 Argentina—Political Entrepreneurship*

The dissatisfaction with Menem's government led Alfonsin, the leader of the Radical party, to intervene. He identified the signs coming from the public and his own party, as dissatisfaction. He then defined the social problem as centralization of the ruling party, preventing the creation of a policy that could meet the demands of the public, for example, the prevention of a radical economic plan and the interference with the high court. This situation demanded a solution, and Alfonsin presented a number of demands for constitutional reforms as part of the negotiations held in November and December 1993.

Alfonsin demanded a reduction in the president's term from six to four years; an increase in the high court's independence; the establishment of a cabinet level position of chief of staff, responsible to the president and the congress; direct elections for the mayor of Buenos Aires; an increase in the number of seats in the senate in favor of the opposition; and the establishment of an auditor general's office to be led by the largest opposition party. Alfonsin's demands reflected his desire to maximize his benefits as a politician as well as those of his party, in part due to the projected decline in the power of the Radicals in the upcoming elections, as well as the expected triumph of the Radicals' candidate in Buenos Aires over his Peronist opponent.

This situation reflects the short-term considerations in the design of the reform in 1993. However, why would Alfonsin propose a judicial reform that passed control to the high court? The explanation stresses once more the short-term considerations in the design of the reform. In addition to the aforementioned demands, Alfonsin requested that control of the high court be given to judges appointed by the Radical party. He believed that the introduction of judges appointed by his party into the high court would maximize his control. In George Tsebelis's (1990) terms, Alfonsin's actions supply an explanation–all considerations taken into account–according to which the preferred alternative was to maximize the benefit of the Radicals.

After six weeks of negotiations, the sides reached a basic agreement that included 13 paragraphs of institutional changes, called the Nucleus of Basic Agreements. In addition, the two parties reached a basic agreement that gave control of the judicial majority to the Radical party in exchange for its support of a constitutional amendment enabling Menem to run for president again. Not all the Radical party members agreed with Alfonsin's initiative. However, most of party members voted for the proposal (December 1993). Three judges resigned and in their stead two of Alfonsin's judges and one Peronist judge were appointed. This created a majority of five to four in favor of the Radical party judges, and the constitutional amendment was passed as well. The decision to vote in favor of the bill in the congress led to a period where there was a split in the Radical party. In addition, the law determined that all of the 13 paragraphs are to be voted on in one go. This decision prevented both parties from backing away from keeping the agreement.

Thus, the judicial reform as a part of a number of institutional reforms was the result of a political settlement between two parties hoping to maximize their control and increase their chances of being elected. For Menem, agreeing to promote the reform was a response to signs coming from the voters as well as a way to enhance his personal and party interests.

The high court assembly issue was solved according to Alfonsin's request. The process for appointing judges to the high court was amended to reduce the influence of the executive authority. The establishment of a judicial council (but not its assembly) was decided upon. Another safeguard for human rights was legislated in the form of a ban on political repression and the creation of the office of ombudsman, whose duty it was to ensure that human rights were observed. However, a constitutional amendment had to be passed by the congress. That was a structural restriction, which made it easier for Menem, because the cost of this institutional compromise was postponed. Moreover, as far as Menem was concerned, the judicial reforms met the demands of the

International Monetary Fund (IMF), so Argentina could transfer funds, invest money abroad, and develop economically.

Another factor that affected the final reform design was the World Bank. The issue of a judicial council was not brought up during the initial negotiations between the two parties. The idea of such a council had been adopted by Adrian Ventura, one of the constitutional committee members who were supposed to implement the agreement between the two parties. Ventura proposed the idea of a judicial council after examining the World Bank report from September 1993. The report suggested the option of judicial reform in Argentina including the establishment of a judicial council.

Thus, the judicial reform appeared to be a solution to a social problem that affected most of the Argentine public. Nevertheless, that was only an initial phase of the judicial reform. To actually implement the reform, legislation had to be passed in the congress. The importance of political entrepreneurs lies in their ability to link the dissatisfaction level of the public and the proposed solution. In terms of the social choice theory, this link means making the various players understand the costs and benefits of such a solution. After that, the structural, cultural, systemic, and social conditions become the factors that propel the change,[34] if the various players see a correlation between public dissatisfaction and the proposed solution.[35]

To conclude, the signs emanating from the public, especially the left faction, were translated by Alfonsin into a social problem that demanded a solution. The solution suggested reflected a maximization of personal and partisan interests, because the high court was to be under their control. The constitutional compromise fit Menem's interests. The combination of these interests and preferences created a balance that led to the acceptance of the electoral reform in December 1997.

### *5.3.2 Italy—Political Entrepreneurship*

The dissatisfaction with the Italian government's functioning also led a number of political entrepreneurs to intervene. They came from the establishment—a small group of politicians led by Mariotto (Mario) Segni, a parliament member from the Christian-Democratic party.[36] Segni defined the social problem as the centralization of the ruling party that prevented the creation of a policy that could have satisfied public demands. The solution Segni proposed was a change in the electoral system. He believed, at least at the beginning, that the majority system would make his party the dominant one among the right and the center. Segni's group collected petitions requesting the holding of the two referendums. During these referendums, the public voted in favor of an electoral system change.[37]

By his actions, Segni had, among other things, maximized his benefit as a politician. However, as opposed to the previous initiatives of rule change that were directed inward, his initiative was aimed at distributing control. Even during the 1980s there were initiatives aimed at rule structure change. However, these were meant to strengthen the control of the serving policy makers. For instance, the prime minister, Benedetto (Bettino) Craxi, a Socialist party leader raised the idea of adopting presidential rule. This initiative met with opposition because people suspected it originated from personal motives. However, his initiative presented an alternative to the existing representative democracy and the rule of anachronistic parties.[38] Later on, Francesco Cossiga, the president of Italy, proposed the alternative of presidential rule. His radical conduct as well as his use of the veto led to a confrontation with the congress and great antagonism for the presidential system, eventually leading to his resignation. This event indirectly turned the electoral reform[39] into electoral capital for various players.

### 5.3.3 New Zealand—Political Entrepreneurship

The dissatisfaction with the New Zealand government's functioning led a small group of political entrepreneurs, who came from the establishment, to intervene. The most prominent was Geoffrey Palmer. He had been a professor of constitutional law, served as a parliament member, government minister, and for a short period even as prime minister (on behalf of the Labor party). He identified the dissatisfaction and defined the social problem as centralization of the ruling party, which prevented the creation of a policy that could meet public demands. As a solution to this social problem, Palmer initiated the establishment of a Royal Commission. At first it was only a paragraph mentioned in the platform of the Labor party when it was part of the opposition, but in 1984 it was actually carried out. While serving as Minister of Justice, Palmer made sure a Royal Commission was established for the purpose of examining rule structure. He influenced its composition, which was mostly nonpolitical, and even allowed it to take a broad range of actions.[40]

By his actions Palmer maximized, among other things, his benefit as a politician, while his being a professor of constitutional law lent credibility to his actions. The establishment of a Royal Commission was carried out as a part of the decentralization process of rule structure change when it was approved in the referendums of 1992 and 1993.

The possibility of change promotion depends upon structural, systemic and social conditions. These function as catalysts that the entrepreneur uses to promote the change and turn the electoral reform into electoral capital that becomes internalized among various players. For instance, before the 1984 elections, Palmer recognized the dissatisfaction among Labor party members from the number of seats they won after the 1978 and 1981 elections. Both public dissatisfaction with the radical economic policy and the Labor party members' dissatisfaction enabled Palmer to include the establishment of a Royal Commission for the purpose of rule examination in the election platform of the Labor party.

After the 1984 elections, while serving as Minister of Justice, he established the committee and conducted its meetings. In 1986, the recommendations of the Royal Commission were published, leading to a dispute within the party regarding the best way to proceed. In order to delay the decision, a parliamentary committee was established to examine the recommendations of the royal one. This took considerable time and the publishing of its results was postponed until after the 1987 elections. For this reason the issue of rule structure change was taken off the agenda. In order to bring the issue back to the agenda, Palmer took advantage of the words of the prime minister, who was the leader of the Labor party. During a debate that took place before the 1987 elections, the latter promised to hold a referendum concerning the recommendations of the Royal Commission, a pledge that did not appear in the party platform. Using that pledge, Palmer wanted to bring the issue of a rule structure change to the agenda. The National party representatives also used the prime minister's words regarding the electoral reform for their own purposes in the upcoming elections. So did various interest groups in their attempt to keep the reform on the agenda.

Political entrepreneurs have all played a role in Argentina, Italy and New Zealand. In Argentina and New Zealand, the entrepreneurs were politicians from the parliament, while in Italy they came both from the parliament and from the outside. These entrepreneurs sensed the feelings among the public, defined the social problem as government centralization, and proposed the reform as a solution. In fact, they took advantage of the structural and social conditions in order to put the issue of reform on the agenda. Their aim was to turn the reform into electoral capital for the use of various players in the process of institutional change determination. In the next section, we examine the actions of these various players, given the structural and cultural conditions that come into play in the interactions around the determination and design of an institutional change.

## 5.4 Determination of the Character and Design of a Basic Formal Institutional Change: Players' Activity as Determined via Structural and Cultural Constraints

This part examines the determination of the character and design of a basic formal institutional change in the three countries under consideration. In this regard, the analysis shall stress the activity of the players, including politicians, bureaucrats, the public and interest groups. All of these use their influence as far as structural and cultural constraints allow them. We shall examine their behavior—whether it is characterized by the adoption of short-term or long-term considerations. Note that according to the model, the activity of players depends upon structural and cultural factors that influence and determine the players' choice. The more unstable the structural and cultural conditions economically and politically and in terms of centralization of procedural norms, the more the players tend to adopt short-term considerations when determining and designing institutional changes. An institutional change that results from short-term considerations will tend to be less stable.

### *5.4.1 Argentina—Institutional Change Design*

In November 1995, Menem was re-elected and the Peronist party continued to control the senate. His actions concerning Judge Levenne reflected his intentions as well as his tendency to behave in certain ways. Levenne, the third Peronist judge, was supposed to resign according to the agreement between the Peronists and the Radical parties. However, he would not resign, upsetting Alfonsin and his associates. Nevertheless, they decided to uphold the agreement with Menem for the upcoming assembly of a constitutional conference in May 1994. The public's pleasure with the judicial reform and the Radicals' desire not to be perceived as interested solely in high court control, made them go along with the initial agreement.

Levenne resigned in November 1995, after Menem was re-elected. As agreed, Menem suggested the candidate from the Radicals, Hector Masnatta, for the job, for whom he also proposed a prestigious appointment at the United Nations office in Vienna. He also proposed his friend, Adolfo Vazques, to take the judicial position in the court. The latter asserted his undying support for Menem and his plans. Despite Masnatta's refusal to take the position at the UN, Menem quickly sought approval for Vazques for a judicial position in the high court. In a rushed vote held on December 7, 1995, the intermediate senate approved Vazques's appointment by a three to two majority, to the disappointment of the Radicals. This meant that the balance in the high court was now five to four, in Menem's favor.

For as long as Menem continued serving as Prime Minister, Alfonsin and his associates kept demanding that he change the assembly of the high court, but in vain. Menem now controlled both the high court and the senate, a control he would not give up. His behavior reflects, more than anything, adoption of the short-term strategy.

The judicial council appointment reflects, as well, Menem's adoption of short-term considerations. According to the new constitution, the judicial council was supposed to be established within one year. The deadline was August 24, 1995. The proposal was sent to the senate council, but the discussion was delayed. Not until March 1996 was the proposal concerning the establishment of a judicial council accepted by the senate. The council included 23 members, 13 of whom were Menem's people. Still, the proposal required the approval of the chamber of deputies, where Menem did not have a majority. In an unprecedented move, Menem threatened to make use of his authority to appoint federal judges. At that time, 21 federal judges were supposed to be appointed. The intention was for the new judicial council to appoint federal judges, as was within its authority. However, the council was not yet established, and judges had to be appointed. If Menem's threat had worked, it would have reflected the depth of procedural democratic norms in Argentina. However, the threat did not work. Interest groups, especially those from the left, protested and demonstrated against Menem. Their protest made Menem abandon his idea, but it did not make him speed up the establishment of a judicial council, as promised. Instead, he chose to freeze the establishment of the judicial council with the excuse that there was real disagreement about the council's assembly and operation.

Another factor that put pressure on Menem, however unsuccessfully, was the International Monetary Fund. In July 1997, Menem approached the fund, asking for a loan. He was reproached by the fund's representatives for delaying the establishment of the judicial council. However, the IMF did not sanction him, so he continued to delay the establishment of the judicial council. Where the IMF failed, the protests of various interest groups succeeded. Their activity left the issue of the establishment of the judicial council on the public agenda. Thus, the judicial council remained electoral capital—an object of cost/benefit for the Radical party members, who wanted to maximize their prestige.

In October 1997, intermediate elections for the congress were held. Their outcome reflected more than ever the feelings of the public toward Menem's government and behavior concerning the implementation of the judicial reform, his restriction of the high court and his radical economic policy. The Radical party knew the feelings of the public, and used the judicial reform as electoral capital, warning against Menem's centralization. It demanded a change in the high court as well as the immediate implementation of the judicial reform. Together with the left party, Frepaso, the Radicals ran for congressional elections and, in a center-left coalition, triumphed over the Peronists (45.7 percent to 36.2 percent), becoming the majority in the chamber of deputies. In the city of Buenos Aires, the Peronists were defeated (17.98 percent to 56.7 percent). Similar scenes took place in the states of Buenos Aires (41.3 percent to 48 percent), Santa Fe and Entre Rios, which had always been pro-Peronist. The results of the intermediate elections in 1997 sent a clear message to Menem. The Peronists' chances of winning the 1999 elections were fading. Such a message forced Menem to support the establishment of a judicial council.

As the judges were sworn in, the coalition approved the establishment of a judicial council in the chamber of deputies and turned it over to the senate for approval. On December 18, 1997, the senate approved the establishment of a judicial council. The council included 20 members, who were the representatives of three government authorities: the majority and minority parties and the legal system. This was done to make sure that no political group had exclusive control. Menem still had control of the senate, but due to the upcoming elections in 1999 and the polls that predicted the Peronists' loss in the 1999 elections (40.3 percent Coalition, and 27.6 percent Peronists), he allowed passage of the law. However, he delayed the selection of members. Only a year later, on November 18, 1998, were the representatives sworn in as members of the judicial council. At the beginning of February 1999, the council began its activity, and, at the end of 1999, it made the first appointments for federal judges.

Thus, the process of the determination and design of a judicial reform in Argentina was characterized by the adoption of behavior based on short-term considerations. As we will see in the next section, the process of determining and designing a reform in Italy also made use of short-term considerations, but to a lesser extent.

### *5.4.2 Italy—Institutional Change Design*

The dissatisfaction of the citizens in Italy led to the formation of a small group of politicians led by Mario Segni, which managed to bring the idea of a reform back to the agenda. From this moment on, a process of overall institutional change began, leading to the referendum in 1993, the establishment of a bi-parliament council intended to design an agreed-upon change formula, the referendum in 1993, and legislation for the electoral system change. The design and acceptance of the electoral reform was the result of the actions of a number of players, including politicians, public, interest groups, and bureaucrats, all of whom functioned under the given structural and cultural constraints. All of the actions, interests and preferences of the above players achieved a balance in August 1993, when electoral reform was approved.[41]

As opposed to the initiatives of rule structure change from the 1980s, the one in 1993 was characterized by a higher level of long-term considerations. Those earlier initiatives of rule change were directed at strengthening the control of the policy makers; e.g., Francesco Cossiga, president of Italy proposed the adoption of presidential rule. The initiatives were met with great opposition and aroused suspicions of personal motives.[42]

After the failure of parliamentary actions to promote a reform of rule structure, Segni chose the path of referendum and began to collect the necessary signatures. The group's aim was to use the public in order to affect the political system. Until that time, the referendum as a way of solving conflicts had been limited to social issues. In 1991, when the first referendum was due to be held, the court refused to allow a referendum concerning the electoral system for the senate to take place. It allowed only the cancellation of vote preference. Referendums in Italy are of a canceling type, meaning that a majority of 50 percent and above leads to the cancellation of rules or parts of rules, leaving the decision concerning the details in the hands of the politicians. In the 1991 referendum, the personal preference vote linked to political corruption was cancelled by a vast majority (95.6 percent) of voters. The supporters of the change, most of whom came from the left, the president and his allies, publicly supported and seemed enthusiastic about the change. They managed to overcome their opponents, most of whom came from the Democratic-Christian and the Socialist parties.

The results of the 1991 referendum led to the establishment of a bi-parliament council that was supposed to design an agreed-upon change formula, but it failed to do so. The initiators of the reform continued the successful strategy of referendum use as a way to force the politicians to accept the change. This path was possible after the court permitted the holding of a referendum about the electoral system for the senate. A possible explanation for the change in the court's decision came from public pressure reflected in the unequivocal results of the 1991 referendum.

Various structural, systemic and social conditions helped keep the idea of reform on the agenda. The 1991 elections introduced the traditional coalition into the government. However, for the first time it did not receive the majority of votes, so it was threatened with the loss of public support, especially from the "Northern League." The Northern League started a campaign, mostly through newspaper advertisements. Its activity helped the issue to remain on the agenda and turned the electoral reform into electoral capital illustrating the importance of the activity of interest groups. These groups overcome the problem of collective action that characterizes the general public, and, according to the informational approach, constitute an important component in the supply of information by the decision makers.

In the second half of 1992 and the beginning of 1993, elections for local authorities were held. The government parties suffered considerable losses in these elections. The results of the elections created additional pressure upon the government. These results reflected the dissatisfaction of the public with government policy. These results also reflected the demands of the public for a change, making clear that government parties could lose by adopting the majority system. This rationale encouraged the government parties to seek out a formula that would reduce the extent of the damage.

Another factor was the investigations into alleged political corruption. They started in 1992 in Milan as the result of an inquiry into a vacation taken by an official and the usurpation of the positions of authority by the Northern League. The bureaucrats who gained the support of the public and the local politicians initiated an enthusiastic and stubborn fight to eliminate political corruption. While the investigation went on, one of the investigating judges, Giovanni Falcone, was assassinated. This event reflected the deep involvement of the Italian Mafia in politics, affecting the further promotion of change.

As the 1993 referendum neared, both the government and the social-democratic parties, supported the change. The activity of entrepreneurs made it possible for the issue to remain on the agenda by means of a referendum. Those who opposed the change were the radical parties—on the left, the Communist Resurrection party established by a rigid faction of the Communist party, and on the right, the Neo-Fascist party.

In 1993, another referendum was conducted. The voters supported the institutional reform by voting overwhelmingly for all of the questions presented in the referendum. Electoral system change was supported by 87 percent of the voters, with 77 percent of the electorate participating, a very high number. The results of the referendum turned the electoral system into a three-fourths-of-senate-seats majority, single-representative system. As a result, the senate had to arrive at an agreed-upon formula for change within the parliament. This had to be done because the government depended on the trust of both the senate and the parliament. Thus, the parliament decided upon the adoption of an electoral system similar to that of the senate.

In August 1993, the electoral system change was enacted into law. The formulation adopted attempted to combine small parties into an essentially majority electoral system. The final system adopted was the result of a compromise between different formulae, some of which tended toward a relative system, while others wanted to adopt a majority system. The compromise was reached mostly between the old government parties. Thus, despite the desire to adopt the majority system reflected in the referendum, there was an opening left for the survival of smaller parties. During the final call on the bill (in the senate and the parliament), the representatives of the government parties and the Northern League voted in favor; the representatives of the social-democratic parties withheld their vote; the Green, the Net, the Neo-Fascist factions and the Communist Resurrection voted against it.[43]

In conclusion, The Italian case is characterized by long-term considerations among the different players concerning determination for reform (referendum). On the other hand, it is characterized by short-term considerations concerning the design of the specific institutional change. This dichotomy existed because of the structural conditions reflected in the canceling format of the referendum, which left the final decisions in the hands of the politicians. Long-term considerations are evident in the choice of the referendum alternative. Such a choice emerged from the instilling of deep-rooted essential democratic norms during the eighties. These norms led the political entrepreneurs to choose a referendum as a way of determining change. The constitutional court in Italy chose to cooperate partially with these initiatives, taking a step toward the 1993 referendum. The choice of a referendum as a way to solve social and economic issues reflected the existing democratic culture. In New Zealand, too, electoral reform was characterized by the adoption of long-term considerations reflecting social flexibility as well as the ability to adapt the decisions to the demands of the public.

### *5.4.3 New Zealand—Institutional Change Design*

Citizens' dissatisfaction led to the formation of a small group of politicians led by Geoffrey Palmer. This group managed to bring the issue of reform to the agenda. It made use of the protests from the public against the government. From this moment on, there began a process of general institutional change: establishment of a Royal Commission for the purpose of rule examination by the Labor party, inter-party argument regarding an indicative referendum in 1992, and the referendums in 1992 and 1993. The design and acceptance of the electoral reform was the result of the actions of a number of players, including politicians, the public, interest groups, and bureaucrats. All of these function under cultural and structural constraints. The overall actions, interests, and preferences of the above players achieved a balance that led to the acceptance of the electoral reform on November 6, 1993.

The Labor government adopted the idea of establishing a Royal Commission to examine the possibility of rule structure. Geoffrey Palmer, as central player, with a small group of politicians, initiated the establishment of the committee and was the personality behind it. The committee was composed of nonpolitical experts, who lent it professional legitimacy. The establishment of the Royal Commission was the continuation of the tradition of referendums customary in New Zealand as a way of solving conflicts. In the 1980s, the referendum mechanism was broadened: the government parties adopted a bill of rights and a reform of the referendum mechanism that allowed them to be held at the public's request.[44] This change was made in order to appease the public. Salzberger and Voigt (2002) call this type of decision "a decision not to decide" that reflects the best possible preference the politicians can choose from the possible strategies they have.

In 1986, the recommendations of the Royal Commission were published. They started an inter-party argument about how to proceed. In order to postpone the decision, a parliamentary committee was established. Its work and recommendations were delayed and published only after the 1987 elections. The rejection of the committee's recommendations led to the establishment of a group of citizens called the "Electoral Reform Campaign." This group started a propaganda campaign to promote the reform of government structure. Its actions enabled the reform to remain on the agenda, turning it into "electoral capital," which was used by various players to maximize their prestige and increase their chances of being elected. The activity of the group was supported by Palmer and his associates, who made use of the idea of the reform as electoral capital to maximize their prestige. For instance, before the 1987 elections, the prime minister (the Labor party leader) promised to conduct a referendum on reform. His promise was perceived as a slip of the tongue, since it was not mentioned in the party's platform. Palmer made use of the slip, in order to return reform to the agenda.

A group of citizens focused on transferring the decision about reform to an indicative referendum in 1992. Their activity was carried out using propaganda and publicity. In terms of social choice theory, these citizens overcame the collective action problem that characterizes the public in general and constitutes an important ingredient in the supply of information by the policy makers. The latter saw the shift in the decision to use a referendum as a decision that reflected the greatest possible benefit for them at that period of time.[45]

The politicians agreed to the referendum in 1992, all the while expecting it to fail. They did not suspect the real extent of public dissatisfaction.[46] The feeling among the politicians was that the use of reform as electoral capital by the Labor party (1987) and the National party (1990) was intended only as mutual taunting by the two parties. The results of the 1992 referendum made clear the extent of the public's dissatisfaction with the government's conduct.

Various systemic and social conditions helped keep the idea of reform on the agenda. The establishment of an independent panel, which organized propaganda prior to the referendums, served as a neutral channel of information. The elections brought the idea of the reform onto the agenda through the parties. The parties wanted to maximize their image with the voters by taunting each other and proclaiming that the promises to implement the reform had not been acted upon. Such proclamations on the part of the politicians from both parties struck a chord in the public, who saw the electoral reform as the solution to the problem of nongovernability.

As the 1993 referendum neared, another pressure group was formed, calling for the preservation of the majority single-representative system. It was called the "Campaign for Better Government." It enjoyed the privilege of being business elite, and promoted a widespread advertising campaign against the idea of reform. However, the results of the 1992 referendum, the late formation of the group, and the elitist image it had, turned the confrontation between those in favor of and those against reform, into a struggle between capital that represents the existing government that opposed the reform against the employees who represent the best of the reform's ideas.[47] Such behavior reflects the adoption of essential democratic norms as a part of a learning process during which the public is actively involved in the provision of political products.

## 5.5 Summary

In this chapter we examined the process of basic formal institutional change from a comparative perspective. The examination was made in a number of phases. In the first, we examined the political and economic instability and the centralization of essential democracy in the given states. The design of institutional change takes place within the context of structural and cultural conditions. They constitute a reward and constraint system that impacts the behavior of various players in the political sphere. In the second phase, we examined the dynamics of the design of an institutional change.

Concerning the first phase, we claimed that the greater the political and economic instability and the less the centralization of essential norms, the greater the chance for an unstable institutional change. Its stability is measured by its frequency of change and the extent of its implementation. In the three states discussed, Argentina, Italy and New Zealand, we identified the extent of each democratic culture and political and economic instability. Argentina had the lowest extent of political and economic stability and the least internalization of essential democratic norms. These conditions led to frequent institutional changes—for instance, those of 1994 and 1997—combined with limited implementation of changes. In contrast to Argentina, New Zealand had the highest level of essential democratic norms as well as lower political and economic stability. Italy was an intermediate case.

Given these structural and cultural conditions, we described the development of a desire for an institutional change among the public. This desire led to the appearance of political entrepreneurs. These individuals defined the social problem and proposed a reform of government structure as a possible solution. In addition, acting within various structural and social conditions, the entrepreneurs made sure that the reform idea stayed on the agenda. Thus, they turned the reform into electoral capital used by various political players in order to maximize their prestige and increase their chances of being elected. The design of the change was the result of the actions of these players, including politicians, interest groups, bureaucrats, and the public, all of whom functioned under the given structural and cultural conditions while designing and determining the institutional change.

# CHAPTER SIX

# *Summary and Conclusions*

## 6.1 Preface

The focus of this book has been on several questions. Why and under what conditions do basic formal institutional changes in the political system take place? What determines the character and design of such basic formal institutional changes? What are the factors that contribute to the stability of such changes?

In this last chapter we discuss conclusions about the Israeli case (6.2). In the second section (6.3), we present conclusions of the comparative analysis between New Zealand, Argentina, Italy and Israel.

## 6.2 Institutional Changes in Israel

Our main claim is that there are two major factors that explain the formation and the stability of an institutional change. These factors are:

1. The level of economic and political stability.
2. Centralization of essential democratic norms—the character of political culture as reflected in the attitude of citizens in a given society toward democratic norms.

According to the claim, the lower the levels of economic and political stability as well as the centralization of essential democratic norms, the greater the tendency toward institutional changes. Low levels of economic and political stability and of essential democratic norms lead to the enforcement of short-term considerations among change agents.

The model assumes that the time considerations of the players affect the stability of change, as reflected in the extent of its implementation and the attempts to undo it. Therefore, in situations of initial instability and procedural rather than internalized democratic norms, the institutional change will be more unstable.

We have shown that Israel is characterized by systemic centralization that led to political and economic instability.[1] Such structural conditions enforced short-term considerations among people. In addition, the political culture is characterized by a more instrumental approach to democratic norms. This procedural democracy also explains the existence of short-term considerations concerning institutional changes to a democratic rule system. The combination of structural and cultural conditions leads to the dominance of short-term considerations. Therefore, changes are expected to be both unstable and frequent. Short-term considerations help preserve the existing system. Furthermore, there is less willingness on the part of the society to accept the basic institutional changes needed to cope with nongovernability. Refusal to deal with this issue may lead to an overload of demands and a tendency to look for alternative approaches to governing, including even the adoption of a military regime. The tendency to adopt a military regime depends on the extent of procedural democratic norms as well as the level of economic and political stability, both of which increase the tendency to accept institutional changes. In addition, there must be a correspondence between the solution of a dictatorship and public preferences in a given society. The claim that each politician aspires, by definition, to maximize his prestige and increase his chances of being elected (which he can then transform into electoral capital and use to be elected over and over again) depends upon structural and cultural conditions. Greater internalization of democratic norms in a given society leads to institutional changes based on long-term considerations, despite the tendency of politicians to focus on the short-term ones. In such societies, we expect a politician interested in promoting an institutional change to design the change according to long-term considerations. These fit the democratic norms in the society, and therefore also match the logic of maximizing his chances of being re-elected.

These structural and cultural conditions are essential in order to design a process of institutional change. They constitute the system of constraints and rewards, which impacts the behavior of various players in the political sphere. Given these specific initial conditions, we pointed out two phases in the analysis of the process of institutional change design.

In the first phase, we identified the existence of a feeling that a change is needed among the change agents. Such a feeling is essential for the design of an institutional change to begin. In the second phase, we noted the involvement of political entrepreneurs. They identify both the need for and the benefits the change might bring them. The importance of political entrepreneurs lies in their ability to link public dissatisfaction and the institutional change they propose as a solution to the social problem. We defined this as the creation of electoral capital. Electoral capital means the accumulation of assets (image, real resources, support of different groups) one can use when running for office. Thus, the support of a constitutional change in the electoral system, such as the direct elections law, may under certain conditions be translated into electoral capital. From the entrepreneur's point of view, his promotion of change reflects, among other things, his desire to gain the political support of those who favor the change. However, it is not obvious that the institutional change proposed by a political entrepreneur as a solution to the social problem will be adopted as electoral capital by other players as well. The ability of the entrepreneur to turn the change into electoral capital depends on his ability to spread the understanding that the adoption of the institutional change will bring about the maximization of other players' chances of being elected as well.

We identified a number of action strategies the political entrepreneur adopts in the process of institutional change determination and design. These strategies share the characteristic of short-term considerations:

1. Focusing the institutional change. This strategy is meant to enable the acceptance of a more limited institutional change, which entails reduced costs.
2. Blurring or creating chaos in the process of decision-making. A strategy that obscures the principal issue might lead to an inadequate decision-making process, especially when coupled with structural elements of player fatigue.
3. Recruitment of public support, such as the use of the media to affect public opinion and keep the public focused on the issue, choosing a general objective that fits a broader range of public groups and the use of rewards and by-products.
4. Manipulations of the agenda, such as utilization of the full Knesset assembly in order to apply pressure on Knesset members, or the use of a Knesset majority while voting for another law proposal for the purpose of promoting an institutional change.
5. "Procedural alacrity," the entrepreneur makes use of the complexity of parliamentary processes in order to promote his idea swiftly. In such a manner, the parliamentary entrepreneur chooses to mask his true moves, either by the promotion of another legal proposal

(that of his opponents), or by utilizing an existing situation that concerns his opponents as well. Underhanded opportunism also makes use of timing by taking advantage of changes in structural conditions that have heretofore blocked the entrepreneurs.

6. Recruiting the parties as a resource while making use of the structural conditions.
7. Focusing lobbying efforts on specific Knesset members in order to apply pressure and signal the possibility of harming their chances of being elected.

In the Israeli context, there was no significant influence of bureaucrats (administrators) during the acceptance and cancellation process of direct elections. One of the explanations for this absence is that the change in political rules did not directly touch upon the authority of bureaucrats. Therefore, the level of resistance by the bureaucrats is expected to be small. However, when the institutional change does affect an area where the bureaucrats have authority, their resistance is expected to be greater. Nevertheless, we found some involvement of bureaucrats in the process of the Israeli institutional change, namely, the high court, which in social choice theory is known as a special choice bureaucracy. The high court played a meaningful part in the process of the law's acceptance and cancellation. Its activity was not in specific appeals concerning the struggle between interest groups to promote or cancel the Direct Elections Law, but in the creation of a social background. We pointed out that since the 1908s and especially the 1990s, as a result of structural and cultural conditions, the high court has occupied the central place as a provider of alternative policy. Its centrality, coupled with the government's inability to govern, contributed to the public's dissatisfaction with public policy. This dissatisfaction led to the appearance of political entrepreneurs. How does the situation in Israel compare with that in New Zealand, Italy and Argentina?

## 6.3 Institutional Changes—A Comparative Perspective

The process of designing and determining political rule changes and the level of their stability is based upon the combination of two factors: the level of political and economic instability and the type of political culture, characterized by the attitude of people in a given society to democratic norms. These factors allow us to develop a bivariate scale to measure and analyze the structural conditions that affect the design

**Table 6.1** Institutional Changes—A Comparative Perspective

| | *Level of Economic Stability* | *Level of Political Stability* | *Depth of Democratic Norms* | *Short-Term Time Frame* | *Rule Stability* | *Entrepreneurs* |
|---|---|---|---|---|---|---|
| Argentina 1994 1997 | Very Low | Very Low | Procedural | Very High | Very Low | Parliamentary |
| Israel 1992 | Low | Low | Procedural | High | Low | Outside and Parliamentary |
| Israel 2001 | Low | Low | Procedural | High | Low | Outside and Parliamentary |
| Italy 1993 | Medium | Medium | Medium Essential | Medium | Medium | Parliamentary |
| New Zealand 1993 | High | High | High Essential | Low | High | Outside and Parliamentary |

*Notes*:

By_*Level of Economic Stability* we mean people's perceptions of the government's ability to provide economic public goods such as jobs, and an improved standard of living (poverty). We use measures such as the unemployment rate, poverty forecasts, size of mortgages and frequency of changes in government policy. These variables will be analyzed according to how well they comply with predetermined estimates. Other measures to be examined include secondary variables such as the Arian and Nachmias (2003) Democracy Index and the Gastil (1990) Freedom Index, which includes the level of political-economic stability. This issue is further elaborated in Section/Chapter 3, 4.

By *the Level of Political Stability* we refer to people's perceptions of the government's ability to provide public services based on current rules of the political game. The measures used are: number of electoral change in a given election both within political units and between them, the number and size of new parties, the length of governmental or parliamentary office terms and the frequency of changes in political appointment procedures, such as the process for appointing members of Parliament to particular posts. This factor is also analyzed according to the measures cited for the assessment of economic stability.

By *Depth of Democratic Norms* we refer to people's perceptions of the democratic system. Do democratic values constitute the core beliefs regarding the nature of society (essential democracy) or are they considered only as tools for the maximization of other values or interests (procedural democracy) (De Haan & Siermann, 1995; Gastil, 1990; Scully & Slottje, 1991; Wittmann, 1989)? According to De Haan and Clemens (1995), a country is democratic if there is considerable competition between individuals and organized groups for election and/or appointment to government office. For a nation to be democratic, competition must be free of violence, all sizeable groups can compete, and those political and civil liberties that ensure political participation and competition are embraced. By civil rights we mean that individual rights, such as freedom of the press and the right to organize and demonstrate, are freely exhibited. In democratic societies, these perceptions, developed over time, represent the consensus (Mantzavinos, North, and Shariq, 2004). Gatsil (1990) rates political rights, defined as the extent to which an individual is allowed to participate in or control the decisions made by government policy makers, from 1 (high) to 7 (low). In order to examine this factor, we again rely on the Democracy Measure (Arian and Nachmias, 2003) and the Freedom Measure (Gastil, 1990).

By *Players' Time Frame* we refer to the players' time frames varies from short term at one end of the scale to long term at the opposite end of the scale. Short-term scales are associated with the immediate maximization of prestige as well as the probability of being elected. The long-term scales are associated with intensive discussions, public hearings, collaboration of interest groups.

*Political Rule Stability*: reflected in the extent of rule implementation and the attempts to change it.

*Political Entrepreneurs*: the "political entrepreneur" as a person or a group intent on changing political reality by changing the political rules of the game or policy regulation within the existing rules of the game (Doron and Sened, 2001; Christopoulos, 2006; Meydani, 2008).

**Table 6.2** The Extent of Democratic Norms Internalization—A Comparative Aspect

**Democratic Norms**

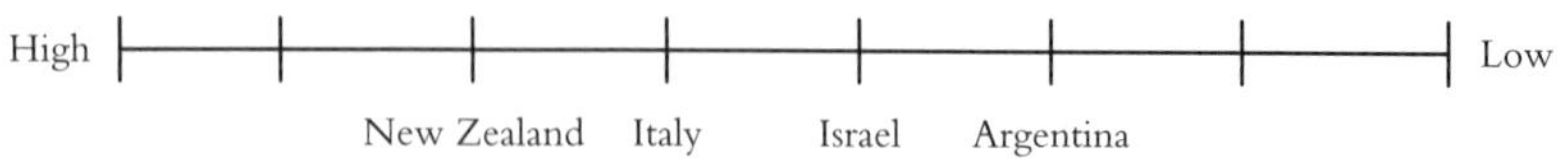


*Notes*:
Low: a low level of essential democratic norms (procedural democratic norms).
High: a high level of essential democratic norms.
* The ranking was made on the basis of a political cultural analysis that was presented in chapters 3 and 4 (Israel p.88 and p.160), and chapter 5 (Argentina p.208, Italy p.213, New Zealand p.215).
* On the basis of the democracy measure of Arian and Nachmias 2003 (except Argentina).
* On the basis of the measure of freedom of Gastil (1990).
* On the basis of the measure of freedom presented in Scully and Slottje (1989).

**Table 6.3** The Extent of the Political Economic Stability—Comparative Aspects

**Economic and Political Stability**

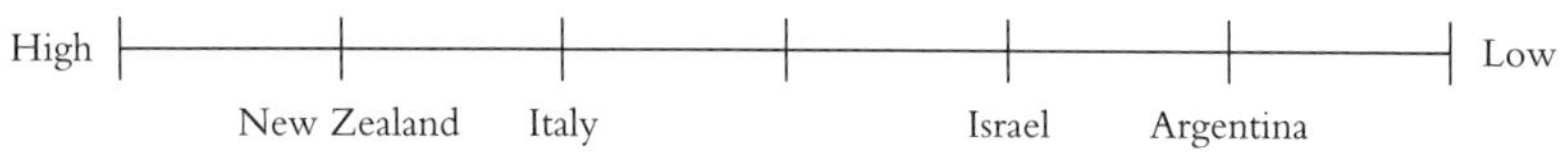


*Notes*:
Low: a low level of essential democratic norms (procedural democratic norms).
High: a high level of essential democratic norms.
The rating was made on the basis of a number of secondary measures concerning the level of economic stability. We made use of the following measures: increase/decrease in unemployment, poverty, disability payments, mortgages taken, frequency of changes in the government's economic policy. Concerning the level of political stability, we made use of the following measures: the extent of electoral change from one election to the next inside political coalitions and between them; the number and size of new parties; the length of government and parliamentary terms; the frequency of change in political policy, for instance, a change in the process of appointing members of parliament. Israel, see p. 88 and 160, Argentina see p. 208, Italy, see p. 213 and New Zealand, see p. 215.
* On the basis of the democracy measure of Arian and Nachmias 2003 (except Argentina).
* On the basis of the measure of freedom of Gastil (1990).
* On the basis of the measure of freedom presented in Scully and Slottje (1989).

of time considerations as reflected in the behavior of people, and thus explain the stability of an institutional change.

In order to make the comparative discussion clearer, we present a table that rates the reforms in the given states according to the following parameters: economic and political stability, the extent of democratic norm centralization, short-term time perception, political rule stability and the type of political entrepreneurs (outside or parliamentary). In addition, we present two scales that rate the countries according to the extent of democratic norm centralization and the level of political and economic stability.

A comparison of the four countries strengthens the claim about the design and stability of institutional change in a political system. We found that Israel is characterized by a high level of economic and political instability as well as low essential democratic norm internalization. These factors affect the strong tendency toward institutional changes, as reflected in the electoral reform in 1992, the postponement of its implementation to 1996, and its cancellation in 2001 (and the return to the previous elections system, with minor changes).

Similar yet deeper structural and cultural conditions were found in Argentina—high levels of economic and political instability and a low level of essential democratic norms. These factors led to the acceptance of a constitutional reform based on short-term considerations: the adoption of reform in the Argentine constitution in 1993, the result of Alfonsin's desire to maximize his benefit and benefit his party. Alfonsin's desire to include new positions such as a head of the general staff and a state controller's office in the constitution, and increase the number of seats in the senate, were in part due to the expected decline in the power of the Radicals in the upcoming elections for the congress. Similarly, the independence of the high court resulted from Alfonsin's desire to have the court under his party's control. In 1997, the promotion of judicial reform in the congress was the result of the decline of Menem's and the Peronist party power.

Like Israel and Argentina, Italy has suffered from economic and political instability as a result of political and economic centralization. However, unlike Argentina and Israel, the political culture of the Italian public was characterized by a greater adoption of essential democratic norms.[2] The referendum, in fact, was the means by which the public could express its desire for an institutional change. Politicians and the constitutional court turned to referendums as a means of affecting the government. Social choice theory calls this kind of decision "a decision not to decide," reflecting the best possible choice a politician can make from a number of options. A possible explanation for this preference lies, among other things, in the depth of the internalization of democratic norms among citizens and their representatives in the constitutional court.

Unlike Israel, the Italian case reflected the involvement of an outside structural condition that affected the public's attitude toward the design of the change. The pressure to join the European Union necessitated the adoption of reforms that would fit the demands of the European market. This structural constraint constitutes a cardinal stage in the development of the public's feelings, reflected in calls from the interest groups and the activity of politicians. Argentina also had some international pressure in the form of the World Bank. However, this pressure did not create a change in the feelings of the public or of the politicians. We claim that the explanation for the difference between Argentina and Italy lies in the depth of the procedural norms centralization: the lower the norms are, the less the readiness to respond to outside influence.

New Zealand constitutes a case in which the structural conditions were characterized by a low level of economic instability on the one hand, and a high level of political instability on the other. However, unlike the other three countries, democratic norms were strongly ingrained in New Zealand. These norms promoted the design of a reform based on long-term considerations. We pointed out the choice of the referendum format, the establishment of a Royal Commission as a part of the reform, and the establishment of a parliamentary committee later on. In the absence of the ability to make decisions, the medium chosen was that of a referendum, accompanied by the public involvement of interest groups in the process of institutional change design. The process in New Zealand reflects the stability of the political rule system, because as a part of the democratic system there is an agreed-upon mechanism of basic institutional change. There is no guarantee that the reform will solve the issue of nongovernability. However, as the process shows, the institutional change is the result of a deep social agreement that took place after a learning process on the part of the public. Such social readiness results from the depth of essential democratic norms internalization, making sure institutional changes take place as a result of long-term considerations, in a flexible fashion and without unnecessary revolutions and crises.

Short-term considerations tend to preserve the existing systems, and there is a tendency on the part of the public to accept fewer basic institutional changes than needed-to-deal-with issues of intense nongovernability. When there is no capability to cope on the social level, there may be a situation of demand overload and the tendency to locate alternative "governability supplicants" and possibly even to adopt military regimes to meet the demands. The probability of embracing such regimes depends on the depth of procedural democratic centralization and the levels of political and economic stability that feed the desire for institutional change, as well as the match between the format of a dictatorship and public preferences in a given society.

Nevertheless, the passage into such a nondemocratic regime does not depend upon local dynamics alone, because in the age of globalization, outside conditions may interfere with and constrain changes made with long-term considerations in mind. The character of the normative system that exists in a society plays a major role as well. For instance, Italy responded to the pressure applied by the European Common Market and adopted a more stable rule model than Argentina. In the latter case, the pressure of the World Bank and its threat not to transfer funds did not affect the decision-making during the centralized regime of Carlos Menem. Of course, the pressure of the European Common Market differs from that of the World Bank. The former reflects the desire to be accepted into a framework that seemingly assures security and economic stability. This feeling affected the design and acceptance of the institutional change.

In all of the cases, political entrepreneurs played a role. The analysis shows that the importance of the political entrepreneur lies in the translation of the solution into electoral capital. When the structural conditions promote long-term considerations, the design and stability of the change is unaffected by whether the initiative was begun by a parliamentary or outside entrepreneur. On the other hand, when the structural conditions promote short-term considerations, the ability of focused outside entrepreneurs to promote an institutional change is greater. A possible explanation for this difference may be that the ability of the public to engage in a collective action is smaller. Note that there could be a gap between the institutional change adopted on the basis of short-term considerations and the political democratic norms in a given society. The lack of a match between the formal rule adopted and the nonformal rules in a society reflects the instability of the institutional change. The more internalized the system for changing rules is, the more likely the change process will be based upon long-term considerations. A process based on long-term considerations accepted by most of the population is bound to be more stable. While the basic institutional change created under such circumstances may not necessarily solve the nongovernability issues that led to its design, the change process will be promoted in a flexible and stable framework, without unnecessary crises, and with the certainty that it will be accepted by the majority of the public.

# NOTES

## 1 Introduction

1. Doron, 2006; Reichmann & Nachmias, 2006
2. Buchanan, 1990
3. Mackerras, 1994; Sakamoto, 1999
4. Dunleavy & Margetts, 1995; Sakamoto, 1999
5. Finkel, 2003; Larkins, 1998
6. Lijphart, 1984, 1999; Peters, 1999
7. Mantzavinos, North & Shariq, 2004
8. Doron & Sened, 2001; Schneider & Teske, 1992; López, 2002; Sheingate, 2003; Christopoulos, 2006; Meydani, 2008

## 2 Institutional Change as an Interaction between Political and Social Players—The Role of Political Entrepreneurs

1. Powell & DiMaggio, 1991
2. Knight, 1995
3. Selznick, 1949, 1957; Perrow, 1986
4. Selznick, 1957
5. Scott & Meyer, 1991
6. Powell & DiMaggio, 1991
7. Powell & DiMaggio, 1991
8. Colomer, 1995a, 1995b; Pridham & Vanhanen, 1994
9. North, 1986; Ostrom, 1986; Riker, 1980; Shepsle, 1986; Williamson, 1985
10. Buchanan, 1990; Doron & Sened, 2001; Gardner & Ostrom, 1991; Gavious & Mizrahi, 2003
11. Riker, 1980; Shepsle, 1986; Shepsle & Weingast, 1981; Weingast & Marshall, 1988
12. Moe, 1987: 291
13. De Haan & Siermann, 1995; Gastil, 1990; Scully & Slottje, 1991; Wittmann, 1989
14. Mantzavinos, North & Shariq, 2004
15. Gastil, 1990

16. Milgrom & Roberts, 1990
17. North, 1995; Nachmias & Sened, 1999
18. Mantzavinos, North & Shariq, 2004
19. Riker, 1980
20. Doron, 1988
21. Mantzavinos, North & Shariq, 2004
22. Dahl, 1961; Kingdon, 1995; Schneider & Teske, 1992; López, 2002; Doron & Sened, 2001
23. On social entrepreneurs see Offe, 1985; on economic entrepreneurs see Schumpeter, 1934; Salisbury, 1969
24. On the difference between fundamental ideology and operative ideology, see Naor, 1999; Seliger, 1977
25. See for example Weber, 1964; Kelsen, 1945; Edelman, 1994a, 1994b
26. Yishai, 1987
27. Doron & Sened, 2001
28. Doron, 1988; Baumgartner & Jones, 1993; Kingdon, 1995; Doron & Lebel, 2005
29. Spector & Kitsuse, 1987
30. Doron, 1986
31. Braybrooke & Lindblom, 1963
32. Cantril, 1963, 63; Doron & Lebel, 2005; Eliade, 1965, 174–177; Hirschman, 1970; Wallace, 1969
33. Spiller & Tommasi, 2007
34. Stewart, Watson, Carland & Carland, 1998
35. Hardin, 1982
36. Doron & Lebel, 2005; Nisbet, 1966; Offe, 1985
37. Breton &Breton, 1969; Calvert, 1992; Colomer, 1995a,b; Fiorina & Shepsle, 1989; Frohlich, Oppenheimer & Young, 1971; Salisbury, 1969; Wagner, 1966
38. Note that policy products are arrived at usually through rules, regulations, and court rulings, and in this respect we might claim that the legitimacy of the rules, prestige of the law system and the notion of stability as a function of the positive law, constitute the public product as defined in the works of Olson (1965)
39. Dahl, 1963
40. Jones, 1978
41. Sandler, 1992
42. Eliade, 1965; Doron & Lebel, 2005
43. Axelrod, 1984
44. Goode, 1957
45. Doron & Lebel, 2005
46. Downs, 1957
47. Doron, 1986; Fearn-Banks, 1996; Yishai, 1987; Millbrath, 1965
48. Blumer, 1971; Doron & Lebel, 2005; Spector & Kitsuse, 1987; Wolfsfeld, 1997
49. Arian, 1997
50. Olson, 1965
51. Hardin, 1982
52. Downs, 1957
53. Doron & Lebel, 2005; Yishai, 1987
54. Yishai, 1987
55. Berry, 1977; Eckstein, 1960; Hayes, 1981; McFarland, 1984; Ziegler, 1964
56. Hayes, 1981; Ziegler, 1964
57. Doron & Lebel, 2005
58. See also Riker, 1980; Sened, 1995; Shepsle & Weingast, 1981
59. Doron & Maor, 1989

60. Shepsle & Weingast, 1981
61. Doron, 1988; Laver & Shepsle, 1994; Tsebelis, 1990, 2002
62. Laver & Schofield, 1990
63. Policy evaluation studies highlight the built-in tension between objective policy that maximizes effectiveness and social profit and subjective policy evaluation that reflects the private political interests of the decision-makers (Browne & Wildavsky, 1983; Rist, 1995; Nagel, 1994; Lipsky, 1980; Golden, 1990; Sabatier, 1986).
64. See also Deri, 1993; Deri & Sharon, 1994; Vigoda, 2002
65. Bendor, 1990; Breton, 1995
66. Bendor, Taylor & van Gaalen, 1987a,b; Miller & Moe, 1983
67. Kramer, 1977; Monsen & Cannon, 1965
68. Barzilai, 1998; Dotan & Hofnung, 2001
69. Kremnitzer, 1999
70. Arian, Nachmias & Amir, 2002; Kimmerling, 2004
71. Knight, 1995
72. North, 1995; Powell & DiMaggio, 1991
73. Mantzavinos, North & Shariq, 2004
74. Buchanan, 1990
75. Braybrooke & Lindblom, 1963; Lindblom, 1959; Powell & DiMaggio, 1991
76. Doron & Lebel, 2005; Nisbet, 1966; Offe, 1985; Spector & Kitsuse, 1987
77. Begly & Boyd, 1987; Johnson, 1990; McClelland, 1987
78. Doron & Sened, 2001; Kingdon, 1995; Schneider & Teske, 1992; López, 2002; also as Adam Sheingate (2003: 191) mentioned, "one must understand how institutional complexity creates the conditions that make entrepreneurship possible. More important, a focus on complexity points to the characteristics of institutions themselves that provide the opportunities for speculation, the resources for creative recombination, and the assets entrepreneurs use to consolidate innovation into institutional change."
79. Rahat, 2006
80. Herman, 1996
81. Migdal, 2001
82. Shafir & Peled, 2002
83. Doron & Adiri, 1994; Hazan, 1996
84. Sheffer, 1999
85. Doron, 1996b; Korn, 1998; Levi-Faur, Sheffer & Vogel, 1999; Rahat, 2000; Dowty, 1998

## 3 Political Entrepreneurs and Institutional Change: The Case of Basic Law: The Government (1992)

1. Buchanan, 1990; Gardner & Ostrom, 1991; Gavious & Mizrahi, 2003
2. CA 6821/93 *United Mizrahi Bank v. Migdal Cooperative Village*, in Decisions, vol. 49, section 4, p. 221 (Hebrew)
3. Barak, 1993
4. Powell & DiMaggio, 1991
5. This task was usually assigned to the head of the party obtaining the most votes and thus Knesset seats in the current election. If the head of the majority party fails to form a government, the task is given to the head of the next-largest party or some other Knesset member.

6. Note that a bill must pass three readings and votes in the Knesset before it is passed into law.
7. Arian, 1997; Arieli, 1992; Barzilai, 1992; Beilin, 1984; Gutman, 1994; Horowitz & Lissak, 1989; Eisenstadt, 1989; Rubinstein, 1982
8. Barzilai, 1992
9. The Commission released its interim report on the circumstances leading to the outbreak of the Yom Kippur War in 1974.
10. This Commission investigated the 1982 massacre of Lebanese refugees at the Sabra and Shatila refugee camps by Phalangist militias during the Lebanese civil war. Arian, 1997; Eisenstadt, 1989; Shaham, 1998
11. Eisenstadt, 1989
12. A protest against the Israeli government started four months after the war ended. It was led by Motti Ashkenazi, commander of Budapest, the northernmost of the Bar-Lev forts and the only one during the war not to be captured by the Egyptians. Anger against the Israeli government (and Dayan in particular) was high. Shimon Agranat, President of the Israeli Supreme Court, was asked to lead an inquiry—the Agranat Commission—into the events leading up to the war and the setbacks of the first few days.
13. The Histadrut ("Federation" [of labor]) was founded in December 1920 in Haifa as a Jewish trade union that would also provide services for members, such as an employment exchange, sick pay, and consumer benefits. The Histradrut became one of the most powerful institutions in the state of Israel, a mainstay of the Labour-Zionist movement. With the increasing liberalization of the Israeli economy since the 1980s, the role and size of Histradrut has declined though it still remains a powerful force in Israeli society and the nation's economy.
14. The Dollar Account affair was a political scandal that broke in Israel in 1977, following the exposure of an illegal US Dollar bank account held by Israeli Prime Minister Yitzhak Rabin and his wife Leah. According to Israeli currency regulations at the time, it was illegal for citizens to maintain foreign bank accounts without prior authorization. In the wake of this disclosure, Rabin handed in his resignation from the party leadership and candidacy for prime minister, an act that earned him praise as a responsible person and a man of integrity.
15. Aharoni, 1991
16. Judicial review of the constitutionality of primary legislation was not explicitly defined in the basic laws, and has developed in Israel on the basis of the Supreme Court's interpretation of the constitutional documents. It is through this process that rights such as freedom of expression, freedom of election and freedom of protest have been established. Kretzmer, D.; The Path to Judicial Review in Human Rights Cases: From Bergman and Kol Ha'am to Mizrahi Bank. *Mishpatim*, 1997, 28, 359–385 (Hebrew).
17. Adam, 1995; Benvenisti, 2001; Dotan & Hofnung, 2001; Mizrahi & Meydani, 2003
18. Dror, 1989; Eisenstadt, 1989; Mautner, 1993
19. Lehman-Wilzig, 1991, 1992; Mizrahi & Meydani, 2003
20. Yishai, 1987
21. Shprinzak, 1986
22. Korn, 1998
23. In 1975, the municipal electoral system underwent major reform. According to the new system, local elections are held every five years, separately from national elections. In 1978, the new system in which voters cast a double ballot and were able to vote for both a candidate for mayor and for a party list on the city council was implemented for the first time. This led to the proliferation of independent lists and candidates on behalf of the national parties; see also Brichta, 1977.
24. Arian, Nachmias & Amir, 2002; see also Goldberg, 1994

25. Arian, Nachmias & Amir 2002: 103
26. Arian, Nachmias & Amir, 2002: 104
27. One Israeli party was formed by Labor Party leader Ehud Barak in the run-up to the 1999 elections with the aim of making the Labor Party appear more centrist and to reduce its secularist and elitist reputation among Mizrahi voters. (Gesher was led by prominent Mizrahi politician and former Likud MK David Levy, and Meimad is a religious party.)
28. Arian, Nachmias & Amir, 2002: 108
29. Rae, 1967: 47–58
30. Laakso & Taagepera, 1979
31. Knesset Archive, 2001
32. *Swirski* & Fraenkel, 2001; see also Moalem & Frisch, 1991
33. The majority of Israelis own rather than rent their homes and apartments.
34. *Swirski* & Konor-Attias, 2000
35. Swirski & Konor-Attias, 2000
36. The 1984 election was inconclusive and led to a power sharing agreement between Shimon Peres of the Alignment (*HaMa'arakh*) and Shamir of Likud. Peres was prime minister from 1984–1986 and Shamir from 1986–1988.
37. Eldar, March 21, 1985; Margalit, March 20, 1985, March 21, 1985, March 26, 1985
38. Markus, April 2, 1985
39. Naor, April 2, 1985
40. Bechor, 1996; Gerti, May 25, 1987; Reichmann, Interview, February 3, 2004; Rubinstein, Interview, December 31, 2003
41. Conger, 1991; Greenberg & Sexton, 1988; Moore, 1986; Naffziger et al., 1994
42. Bechor, 1996
43. Bechor, 1996; Doron, 1996b; Rubinstein, interview, December 31, 2003; Rubinstein, June 14, 1982, June 7, 1987, January 5, 1988, May 22, 1988, December 12, 1988, July 30, 1989, April 15, 1990, April 20, 1990, December 14, 1990
44. Rubinstein, 1982
45. Shinui is a Zionist, secular and anti-clerical free-market liberal party in Israel established in 1974; Dash—Democratic Movement for Change—a centrist party established in 1976 with great hopes for reforming Israeli politics in the wake of the disillusionment of the Yom Kippur War.
46. Reichmann, *Davar*, December 21, 1990; Reichmann, *Hadashot*, January 4, 1989; Reichmann, *Maariv*, July 10, 1988; Reichmann, Maariv, December 15, 1991; Reichmann, interview, February 3, 2004; Rubinstein, 1982; Reichmann, *Yediot Aharonot*, December 24, 1990
47. Bechor, 1996: 158; Lynn, *Maariv*, April 4, 1990, Lynn, *Maariv*, November 26, 1991, Lynn, *Maariv*, February 25, 1992; Lynn, *Yediot Aharonot*, January 16, 1992
48. Bechor, 1996: 156; Carmel, 2001: 944; Tsiddon, February 20, 1989, April 3, 1990, April 26, 1990, July 26, 1991, December 25, 1991
49. See for example Doron & Sened, 2001
50. Carmon, interview, 2004; Reichmann, interview, 2004; Rubinstein, interview, 2003
51. Bechor, 1996
52. See also Rahat, 2008
53. Doron, 1988
54. Bechor, 1996; Yishai, 1987
55. See for example Doron & Sened, 2001
56. Horowitz & Lissak, 1989; Eisenstadt, 1989; Rubinstein, 1982: 30–31
57. Rubinstein, 1982: 34
58. Bechor, 1996; Rubinstein, 1982: 34–35
59. Braybrooke & Lindblom, 1963; Lindblom, 1959; Doron, 1986

60. Rubinstein, 1982: 46
61. Bechor, 1996
62. Rubinstein, 1982: 59
63. Bechor, 1986: 16; Reichmann, interview, February 3, 2004
64. Berger, 1969: 23–24
65. Shragai, June 7, 1985; Shchori, June 7, 1985
66. The Public Committee for Economic Recovery, ad placed in *Haaretz*, August 16, 1985
67. Petition, *Haaretz*, August 3, 1985, p.7
68. Bracha, August 3, 1985
69. Reichmann, *Haaretz,* May 30, 1986
70. Olson, 1965; Taylor, 1987; Axelrod, 1984
71. Ainsworth & Sened, 1993; Austen-Smith, 1998; Lohmann, 1993
72. Nisbet, 1966
73. Doron, 1988; Kingdon, 1995
74. Reichmann, Interview, February 3, 2004
75. Rubinstein, Interview, 2003; Reichmann, Interview, 2004
76. See Doron, 1988; Kingdon, 1995
77. See Frohlich, Oppenheimer & Young, 1971
78. Bechor, 1996
79. Doron, 1988
80. Sandler, 1992
81. Bechor, 1995; Reichmann, interview, February 3, 2004
82. Eliade, 1965
83. Bechor, 1996
84. Olson, 1965
85. *HaIr*, May 5, 1989
86. *Galilee Yediot*, May 5, 1989
87. Reichmann, Interview, February 3, 2004
88. Bechor, 1996; Alon, 1995
89. Bechor, 1996: 34
90. Reichmann, February 3, 2004
91. Reichmann, Interview, February 3, 2004
92. Beilin, 1996: 201
93. Reichmann, interview, February 3, 2004; Reaction to the publicity campaign was mostly critical. Negative comments were received from publicists (for example: Samet Gideon, July, 2 1987; Schwitzer Abraham, September 3, 1987, January, 2 1989; Segev Tom, January 15, 1988), academics (for example: Barnea Josef, May 1, 1989; Brichta Abraham, February 17, 1988; Carmon Arik, August 8, 1989; Gutman, Emanuel, August 8, 1989; Doron Gideon, August 8, 1989; Dror Yehezkel, July 30, 1989; Gavison Ruth, December 1, 1987; Prokacha Uriel, October 16, 1987), judges (Shamgar Meir, 1988; Landoi, Moshe 1988 see in Bechor, 1996), politicians from the religious sector (a team of lawyers associated with the *Mafdal*, the National Religious Party, determined that *A* constitution undermined the Jewish character of the state; daily religious and orthodox papers attacked the very idea of a constitution) and representatives of various interest groups (Shalvi Alice, the Women's Lobby, October 9, 1987). These reactions evoked an alternative debate meant to support the idea (Zamir Yitzhak, October 7, 1987; August 28, 1987; Barak, 1987; see Bechor, 1996)
94. Bechor, 1996: 136; Rahat, 2000; Reichmann, February 3, 2004
95. Bechor, 1996
96. Melamed & Kalfon, 1992
97. Pori poll, April 30, 1987

98. Eldar, *Haaretz*, April 23, 1987
99. Gerti, *Haaretz*, May 25, 1987
100. Rubinstein, *Haaretz*, June 7, 1987
101. Samet, *Haaretz*, July 2, 1987
102. Shoval, *Haaretz*, June 18, 1987
103. Reichmann, interview, February 3, 2004
104. Bechor, 1996: 34
105. Yishai, 1987
106. Shchori, *Haaretz* April 11, 1985
107. *Haaretz*, May 27, 1990
108. Bechor, 1996: 150
109. *Haaretz*, May 27, 1990
110. This rational consideration was made by steering committee members who believed that it would be easier to influence the public if the struggle focused on three specific items rather than the vague concept of a constitution. Reichmann has himself stated (interview, February 3, 2004) that this new focus helped him achieve two goals: It highlighted his future destination while lending legitimacy to those same goals.
111. Cantril, 1963: 63; Eliade, 1965; Hirschman, 1970; Wallace, 1969: 174–177
112. Eliade (1965) states that exposure to facts contrary to accepted ideologies and beliefs can lead to collective action. Hence, an entrepreneur interested in defining a social problem should first reveal it—this is a necessary action if he is to succeed. Crises may also be uncovered as a result of external factors. An adept entrepreneur will utilize them to promote his objectives and views. For instance, to the Israeli public, suicide bombers highlighted the failings of the system by revealing the violent outcomes of an inconsistent security policy that was colored by indecision and coalition pressures.
113. Cantril, 1963: 63; Eliade, 1965
114. In June, 1982 the Begin government authorized the "Shalom HaGalil Operation"in which the IDF was assigned the mission of eliminating all the terrorists who were firing upon Israel's settlements in Galilee from their stations in Lebanon. By July 14, 1982, when the number of the Israeli casualties had reached 214, the public debate about the war's objectives had lessened, to be replaced by intensive protest demonstrations organized by Peace Now (Shalom Ach'shav), the Ratz party and others. Left-leaning Knesset members turned to the government in an attempt to stop the action and begin the search for a political solution. As a part of these attempts, Shinui asked the Knesset to authorize humanitarian aid to the residents of the Lebanese cities damaged during the war (Rubinstein, *Haaretz* June 14, 1982).
115. Bechor, 1996; Reichmann, interview February 3, 2004
116. Ad: Israeli-Palestinian Peace Now: "Stop the Occupation," *Haaretz*, January 7, 1988; Rubinstein, January 5, 1988; Ad: "There is No Replacement for a Political Solution," Centralist Movement, *Haaretz*, January 8, 1988; Ad: "Petition the Israeli Government to Avoid Using Live Ammunition While Dispersing Demonstrations, *Haaretz*, January 8, 1988; Labor began building its platform on the basis of a prosperity-promoting economic program. Shinui paired up with the Independent Liberals. The public was against the government policy in the occupied territories. Therefore, the leftist factions filed a vote of no confidence, while Shalom Ach'shav and other civil groups demonstrated against government policy.
117. The incident's name was taken from a comment made by Yitzhak Rabin, who accused Peres of playing a "dirty trick" for his own rather than national purposes.
118. Beilin, 1996: 200
119. Bechor, 1996
120. On April 4, 1990, when Peres thought he had managed to form a coalition, he discovered that Knesset members Abraham Vardinger and Eliezer Mizrachi, of Agudat Israel, did not

appear at the Knesset's plenary session by order of the Lubovitch Rabbi, the party's spiritual leader, in opposition to the Rabbinical Council. The Knesset, in which the new government was to be presented, was forced to disperse in disgrace.

121. "The new system should determine that the candidate for the prime minister's position does not get elected in the centers of the parties, but in preliminary elections between all of the party's members, so that there is no need to bribe the members of the party's executive committee. The new election system should allow one party to gain the solid majority, otherwise, we will continue to straddle between the Likud and Labor for many years to come" (Strasler, *Haaretz* March 16, 1990).
122. Blumer, 1971; Wolfsfeld, 1997
123. In an article published in *Haaretz*, Rubinstein wrote: "Everyone looking at our political system sees its crack... The crack is twofold: First, the dependence of the prime ministers or whoever attempts to establish a government on small factions that can change their political loyalty and thus have the power to sustain the given government. Second, the readiness of a few Knesset members to sell themselves to whoever offers the higher price." Rubinstein continued to explain why direct election of the prime minister was the way "that would save democracy from those ready to humiliate it": "The reform in local government—the Direct Election of Community Leaders Law—changed the situation almost overnight: from rule of *law* based on arguments... we had a period of stability and relative political cleanliness... If we adopt an elections system that designates a number of electoral regions in which contestants would run for a few vacancies, the Knesset would be different. This Knesset would have a different relative representation, and it would be possible to establish a government without needing a small number of voices" (Rubinstein, *Haaretz*, March 18, 1990).
124. Editorial, *Haaretz*, March 20, 1990
125. *Galnoor*, Yediot Aharonot, March 26, 1990; Carmon, *Haaretz*, April 2, 1990
126. Peres put significant effort into negotiations with the members of the *New Liberal Party* led by Yitzhak Moda'i then Minister of Economics and Planning who had left the *Likud* together with three more other MKs (all of them former members of the *Liberal Party*) to form the *Party for the Advancement of the Zionist Idea*, later renamed the *New Liberal Party*. He managed to convince only one Knesset member belonging to the faction to switch sides—Abraham Sharir. The agreement with Sharir included a promise that he would be appointed a minister in the Peres government after the 1992 elections, which greatly angered the public (Korn & Shapira, 1997).
127. Doron, 1988
128. *Hadashot Daily* November 30, 1990
129. The key events included for examples: (1) Israel's Minister of Internal Affairs, Aryeh Der (Shas) was investigated by the police in early 1990 due to alleged irregularities in financial transfers made to local authorities and religious institutions. Der'i refused to cooperate and labeled the entire incident as a case of discrimination against Oriental Jewry (Korn & Shapira, 1997; Shaham, 1998). (2) Another case was the "bunny speech" delivered by the ultra-Orthodox Rabbi Shach (founder of the *Degel HaTorah* party) in which he criticized the Kibbutz Movement (September 26, 1990). (3) In a November 1990 speech made by the Minister of Absorption Yitzhak Peretz (Shas), Peretz stated in that 30 percent of the immigrants from the former USSR were not Jewish (this problematic issue is rooted in Israel's Law of Return, the country's immigration policies as well as ethnic gaps and rivalries, a discussion of which goes beyond the limits of this book). (4) The ultra-Orthodox Agudat Israel party joined Shamir's coalition in November 1990, not after they were promised to approve three acts: Prohibition of the printing and display of "sensationalist" advertisements, prohibition of public transit, even if privately owned, on the Sabbath and prohibition of the sale of pork.
130. For example: In February 1991, the far-right Rechavam Ze'evi (Moledet) joined the government as Minister Without Portfolio, which caused considerable outrage due to his call

to transfer of Palestinian Arabs from Israel (including the West Bank & Gaza Strip) to the neighboring Arab countries; In 1991, the Shamir (Likud) government fell and early elections were called. Shamir, together with a narrow right-wing coalition, wanted to discontinue the negotiations with the Palestinians due to the outbreak of the *Intifada* and his refusal to succumb to US pressure to negotiate. This led to disputes among the coalition members (Tzomet, Techia & Moledet). A political breakthrough in the Madrid Conference (October 30, 1991) completely destabilized the coalition and brought on its demise (Korn & Shapira, 1997).

131. Hardin, 1982
132. Olson, 1965
133. This motivated the proposals for the direct election of the prime minister submitted by the other four parliamentary entrepreneurs—Rubinstein, Lynn, Libai & Tzidon—in 1990.
134. Doron, 1996b
135. Margalit, *Haaretz,* June 8, 1988
136. The issue of whether to apply Orthodox Jewish definitions to the Law of Return, which grants immediate citizenship and several other legal and economic benefits to those who meet the traditional definition of *Jewish* affiliation A person who complies is then listed as a Jew on his or her identity card, which all Israeli citizens are required to carry at all times.
137. Shchori, *Haaretz,* June 14, 1988
138. Shchori, Ben Vered & Alon, *Haaretz,* June 15, 1988
139. Rubinstein, *Haaretz,* May 22, 1988. The 1988 general elections saw Shinui joining the "Independent Liberals" (Lamed Ayin) and the "Liberal Center" (Hamerkaz Haliberali), getting two seats—MK Amnon Rubinstein and MK Avraham Poraz. Rubinstein became popular; he made a point of expressing his views only on matters of infringements of the rule of law in the occupied territories because it suited his attempt to garner the electoral center. In an article he published in *Haaretz* (May 25, 1988), Rubinstein wrote: "*How much longer will disruption of the rule of law continue in the occupied territories?... It is difficult to understand the silence of [legal institutions] in light of the occurrences. Whoever remains silent in these times is expressing an opinion... in the jargon of lawyers; this silence 'speaks for itself.'*"
140. See Rubinstein's remarks regarding a political solution to the security problem: Rubinstein, *Haaretz,* June 14, 1982; Rubinstein Interview, December 31, 2003
141. *Zrahya, Haaretz,* May 28, 1990
142. See Doron, 1988).
143. See Beilin, 1996: 202
144. Beilin, 1996: 201
145. Doron & Lebel, 2005
146. Yishai, 1987: 192
147. Zeev Segal, *Haaretz,* September 12, 1990
148. Advertisement (Ad.) *Hadashot,* May 20, 1988; Ad.*Yediot Aharonot,* March 3, 1988
149. Ad. *Maariv,* November 8, 1989; Ad. Corfo, December 2, 1991; Ad. Lynn, January 12, 1990; Ad. Shamir, July 26, 1989; Ad. Shilanski, November 21, 1991; Ad. *Yediot Aharonot,* December 29, 1989
150. Ad. Lynn December 15, 1989; Ad. Lynn & Horovitz, December 30, 1991; Ad. *Maariv,* November 14, 1988
151. Brichta, *Haaretz,* February 17, 1988; Schwitzer, *Haaretz,* February 29, 1988
152. Margalit, *Haaretz,* March 1, 1988; Shchori, *Haaretz,* March 1, 1988
153. Unification of resources reduces the cost of passing the proposition on second and third readings. In their activity, the entrepreneurs made use of the structural conditions that signified a stability crisis in Shamir's government: It was based upon an insufficient majority and distrust propositions were frequently filed by the Labor party. The struggle in the Likud took place between Shamir and Moshe Arens's close associates and those of Ariel Sharon and David Levy; Shamir's were for early elections and Sharon and Levy's were

against. The latter wanted to admit Agudat Israel in the coalition and thus to ensure the government's power (Shapira, *Haaretz*, 26/10/90).

154. The constitution steering Committee members sent personal letters to Knesset members in order to obtain information as to how they would vote. The results were published in the press. By late 1991, 65 Knesset members were in favor of the law. Kadish's movement displayed Knesset members and demonstrated in front of the homes of those who were not in favor of the law. Information stands were erected, with advertisements placed on billboards and in newspapers.
155. These structures are reflected in the mechanism of legislation, such as who determines the daily agenda, the order determining which suggestions will be raised, the way in which veto rights are distributed, variations in committee agendas, rules legal procedure and committee decision-making (Riker, 1980; Ostrom, 1986; Shepsle, 1986; Shepsle & Weingast, 1981; Weingast & Marshall, 1988).
156. Ben Vered, *Haaretz*, June 8, 1988
157. Bechor, 1996
158. Margalit, *Haaretz*, June 15, 1988
159. Bechor, 1996; Margalit, *Haaretz*, June 15, 1988
160. Ben Vered, March 20, 1990
161. "Four Knesset members forgo partisan considerations." *Haaretz*, May 28, 1990
162. Editorial: "Likud negotiations for Shamir's replacement," *Haaretz*, March 16, 1990
163. Shchori, *Haaretz*, May 27, 1990; Tal, *Haaretz*, May 28, 1990a,b
164. Bechor, 1996
165. Reichmann, Interview, February 3, 2004
166. Editorial Article, *Haaretz*, March 20, 1990
167. Banzhaf, 1965; Coleman, 1971; Laver & Schofield, 1990; Schofield, 1995; Sened, 1996; Shapley, 1953; Shapley & Shubik, 1954
168. Doron, 1988
169. Shchori, *Haaretz*, November 15, 1990
170. Alon, *Haaretz*, November 20, 1990
171. See also Advertisement, "Stop religious extortion," *Haaretz*, November 20, 1990; Galili, *Haaretz*, November 18, 1990; Galili & Alon, *Haaretz*, November 18, 1990
172. Shchori, *Haaretz*, November 13, 1990, November 14, 1990
173. Shchori, *Haaretz*, November 14, 1990
174. Reichmann, interview, February 3, 2004
175. The Teleseker Institute, June 23, 1991, July 16, 1991
176. Veteran Likud member Uzi Landau, belonging to the party's right wing, had also formulated a proposal for reform, but Reichmann's group explained that it served the interests of the left wing.
177. Bechor, 1996
178. Thus, three Mapam members voted in support of paragraph 13 even though they claimed that they had intended to vote against it.
179. Bechor, 1996
180. These structures are reflected in the different parliamentary committee agendas, the rules of the game that define application of legal regulations and the committees' decisions (Riker, 1980; Shepsle & Weingast, 1981; Weingast & Marshall, 1988).
181. Arian, Nachmias & Amir, 2002; Such rules exist in all democracies; hence, this analysis may further our understanding of the roles played by prime ministers and party leaders in other political environments. In Israel, prime ministers usually share power with members of their parties as well as their coalitional partners. However, despite the fact that the latter may complicate the process concluding in the government's agenda, most often, prime ministers have sufficient power to do so independently. Because the prime minister is often simultaneously the head of the executive branch, the leader of the largest party and the leader of a governing coalition—the majority of political questions and state decisions

reach him or his close associates in search of decisions. But, just like any other politician, prime ministers tend to act according to short-term considerations.

182. Doron, 1996a,b
183. Advertisement, *Haaretz*, March 4, 1988, p. 8
184. Liberty to civilians or submission to the orthodox, *Hadashot*, November 15, 1989; They will continue the plunder, *Yediot Aharonot*, March 29, 1991; We are made fun of, *Yediot Aharonot* May 6, 1990
185. The Yaacobi Committee, which served as an outlet for public anger, included 5 Knesset Members from each bloc: Yaacobi, Shachal, Edri, Marom and Libai of the Alignment/Labor, and Meridor, Moday, Olmert, Lynn and Landau of the Likud. The Committee's head, Gad Yaacobi, had the power to control the committee's agenda and thus was the structural factor that could set the pace of the process (Ben Vered, *Haaretz*, August 1, 1989). The Yaacobi Committee was indeed deadlocked, but not only because of the political stalemate of its members but also due to the doubt regarding the party leaders' acquiescence to change. Other committee heads encouraged him to be very active but he did not heed their advice. He seldom held meetings, thereby turning the committee into a kind of academic forum for lectures and exchange of opinion (Bechor, 1996). The committee discussed two alternatives only: that formulated by Mordechai Virshubski (Ratz) and Reichmann's. The committee consulted three groups of experts: those sponsored by Reichmann, those by Arye Carmon (representing the Israel Institute for Democracy) and those by Dan Elazar (Bar-Ilan University) as well as independent analysts. In May 17, 1989 the committee published its recommendations, which constituted a compromise of the proposed system changes. These were, specifically, election of 60 Knesset members in 60 electoral districts, and 60 more according to nationwide lists (Ben Vered, *Haaretz*, August 1, 1989). The committee's recommendations did not deal with the direct election of the prime minister, leading the constitutional steering committee members to publish an appeal, in the form of a newspaper advertisement, calling for the law's completion with respect to this issue.
186. Assa, 1996: 167
187. Doron, 1996a,b
188. Doron, 1996a,b
189. Reichmann, Interview, February 3, 2004
190. Toward the end of the Twelfth Knesset, the Mapam, Ratz, and Shinui parliamentary groups merged into single parliamentary group. The common denominator among the three was their advocacy for an agreement with the Palestinians on the basis of a territorial compromise, and the establishment of a Palestinian state, civil and human rights, and the separation of religion and state.
191. Bechor, 1996
192. Shchori, *Haaretz*, November 12, 1990
193. The Labor Party, whose status, according to the polls, had declined after the "dirty trick" (Shchori, November 12, 1990), had given its support to the Constitution for Israel movement in two stages. At first, movement members applied pressure to the members of Labor's Central Committee via a telephone and newspaper ad campaign to persuade them to vote for the reform. In the first stage, the Labor Central Committee voted for the reform (November 29, 1990); in the second, 65 percent of the Labor Committee voted for the Direct Elections Law (December 23, 1990). Shimon Peres and Yitzhak Rabin supported it, whereas Moshe Shachal, Abraham Catz-Oz, Shimon Shetreet, Emanuel Zisman and Yossi Beilin opposed it. The latter chose to vote for an alternative proposal formulated by Dr. Arye Carmon, former minister of justice Chaim Tzadok and the editor of *Davar* (a left-wing paper historically associated with the party), Yoram Peri (Peri, Davar, April 2, 1990; Shahal, Davar, December 18, 1990; Reichmann, Davar, December 21, 1990; Reichmann, Yediot Aharonot, December 24, 1990). Peres, whose reputation had waned due to the "dirty trick," preferred to act according to public preferences as a result of his competition with Yitzhak Rabin (Doron, 1988).

194. Alon, 1996; Uriel Lynn, David Magen and Binyamin Netanyahu supported the law. They believed that such support would maximize their personal prestige prior to the impending leadership struggle. Moshe Arens, Uzi Landau, Benny Begin and Haim Corfo, chair of the Knesset Constitution, Law and Justice Committee, opposed the proposal. (Shamir was prime minister and Likud the governing party at the time.) Haim Corfo was supposed to help Shamir carry out his decision. Corfo turned the mission into a personal crusade: He introduced a number of delaying tactics such as postponing votes on discussions, submitting numerous propositions, turning to the press, denouncing committee members who supported the law and so forth. The lawyer Aharon Papo joined Corfo in the struggle (Papo, Yediot Aharonot, December 16, 1991). The Constitution steering committee reacted by publishing denouncements of Corfo in *Haaretz*, to which Corfo replied by filing a slander suit (civil file number 19769/91, denied in May 1994).
195. HCJ 637/89, ruling 46 (1) 191
196. Alon, 1995; Bechor, 1996
197. Reichmann, Interview, March 3, 2004
198. Doron & Maor, 1989
199. Shepsle & Weingast, 1981.
200. Together with this proposal, the Committee decided to file the Virshubski proposal. This proposal had evolved in Alignment-Labor circles for twenty years. It entailed electing 40 Knesset members through the existent proportional system and 80 more in a proportional-regional system. Kulas approved of this proposal because he believed it would attract religious parties' support. In addition, Reichmann's constitutional steering committee decided to file both propositions in the hope that their adherents would cooperate in order to pass the voting barrier: 61 Knesset votes (Bechor, 1996).
201. Bechor, 1996
202. Downs, 1957
203. Margalit, *Haaretz*, June 7, 1988
204. Shchori, *Haaretz*, June 9, 1988
205. Shchori, *Haaretz*, June 10, 1988
206. *Haaretz*, November 21, 1991
207. Bechor, 1996
208. Nagel, 1994; Rist, 1995
209. Dye, 2002: 19
210. Beilin, 1996: 199
211. Bechor, 1996: 194
212. Yaacobi, 1996: 221
213. Reichmann, Interview, February 3, 2004
214. Peleg, 1996: 119
215. Bechor, 1996
216. Lynn, *Yediot Aharonot*, January 16, 1992
217. Reichmann, interview February 3, 2004

## 4 Political Entrepreneurs and Institutional Change: Cancellation of the Direct Election of the Prime Minister

1. Buchanan, 1990; Gardner & Ostrom, 1991; Gavious & Mizrahi, 2003
2. On Basic Law: The Government (2001) see website of Israel Ministry of Foreign Affairs http://www.mfa.gov.il/MFA.

3. Arian, 1997; Mizrahi & Meydani, 2003
4. Carmon, Interview, 2004
5. Doron, 1996a,b
6. Korn & Shapira, 1997
7. For instance, contentious remarks made by Shulamit Aloni (Meretz), the Minister of Education, Avraham Poraz's (Meretz) attempt to legalize prostitution and the sale of non-kosher pork, as well as homo-lesbian discussion groups by Yael Dayan all demonstrate the schizophrenia of the coalition (Korn & Shapira, 1997: 344; Shaham, 1998: 535).
8. Shaham, 1998: 525
9. For further details, see Barzilai, 1998; Dotan & Hofnung, 2001; Mautner, 1993; Shamir, 1994
10. Israel's major labor union cover organization
11. Shaham, 1998
12. Brichta, 1998
13. Arian, Nachmias & Amir, 2002: 107
14. For detailed accounts of these developments see Doron, 1996a,b
15. Barzilai, 1998; Dotan & Hofnung, 2001; Mizrahi & Meydani, 2003
16. Arian, Nachmias & Amir, 2002
17. Its full name: Gesher—National Social Movement. An ethnic parliamentary group established by MKs David Levy and David Magen towards the end of the Thirteenth Knesset after they left the Likud.
18. Shaham, 1998: 564
19. Carmon, Interview, 2004
20. Beilin, 1996; Carmon, Interview, 2004
21. Conger, 1991; Greenberg & Sexton, 1988; Moore, 1986; Naffziger et al., 1994
22. In the course of the Sixteenth Knesset, the parliamentary group Meretz-Democratic Choice-Shahar changed its name to "Yahad and the Democratic Choice."
23. A platform identified with the political origins of the Labor Party (Mapai) and the late Mapam.
24. See http:// www.nfc.co.il.
25. Doron, 1996a
26. Bechor, 1996: 98; Carmon, Interview, February 25, 2004
27. Carmel, 2001: 1076
28. Knesset, 11; 12 Until March 15, 1990
29. Knesset 13
30. Until January 9, 1995
31. Carmel, 2001: 595; Landau, *Yediot Aharonot*, December 12, 1991
32. Beilin, 1996: 206
33. Begly & Boyd, 1987; Birley & Westhead, 1994; Doron & Sened, 2001; Johnson, 1990; McClelland, 1987; Scheinberg & MacMillan, 1988; Stewart et al., 1998
34. Carmel, 2001
35. Lynn, *Haaretz*, June 8, 1995
36. Yossi Beilin was charged with being "Peres's poodle" in the media on several occasions a term coined by Peres's political rival, Yitzhak Rabin in the early 1990s.
37. See Carmel, 2001
38. Carmel, 2001
39. Carmon, *Haaretz*, June 10, 1998
40. Beilin, 1996: 201
41. Rubinstein, Interview, December 31, 2003
42. Vardi, *Globes*, March 8, 2001
43. Reichmann, Interview, February 3, 2004
44. Mantzavinos, North & Shariq, 2004

45. Vardi, *Globes*, March, 8, 2001
46. Carmon, Interview, February 25, 2004
47. Doron & Sened, 2001
48. Alon, *Haaretz*, March 10, 1997
49. A nationalist list, made up of new immigrants and old-timers and headed by MK Avigdor Lieberman
50. Barak was in power during the appointment of the Tal committee which dealt with the controversial issue of *haredi,* Jews' exemption from military service. After the religious parties Mafdal and Shas quit his coalition he called for a civil nonreligious revolution.
51. Rubinstein, Interview, December 31, 2003
52. Carmon, February 25, 2004; Reichmann, Interview, February 3, 2004; Rubinstein, Interview, December 31, 2003
53. Breton & Breton, 1969; Calvert, 1992; Colomer, 1995b; Fiorina & Shepsle, 1989; Frohlich, Oppenheimer & Young, 1971; Salisbury, 1969; Wagner, 1966
54. Jones, 1978
55. Sandler, 1992
56. Axelrod, 1984
57. Carmon, interview, February 25, 2004
58. Arian & Shamir, 1999; Nachmias & Sened, 1999
59. *Parliament*, September 29, 2000, Jerusalem: The Israeli Democracy Institute (in Hebrew).
60. See for example, Doron, 1996a
61. Vardi, Globes, 8 February 2001
62. Alon, *Haaretz*, March 10, 1997
63. Carmon, Harts, June 10, 1998
64. Segal, *Haaretz*, November 6, 2000
65. Rubinstein, *Haaretz,* November 11, 2000
66. Carmon, interview, February 25, 2004
67. Eliade, 1965
68. Doron & Lebel, 2005
69. Carmon, *Haaretz*, June 10, 1998
70. Steinberg, *Haaretz*, June 25, 1998
71. Lavie, *Globes*, August 1, 2000
72. Lavie, *Globes*, August 1, 2000
73. Shadmi, *Haaretz*, August 28, 2000
74. Shadmi, *Haaretz*, September 20, 2000
75. Carmon, Interview 25 February, 2004
76. Carmon, interview, February 25, 2004
77. Shadmi, *Haaretz*, June 13, 2000
78. Alon, *Haaretz*, November 30, 2000
79. Bar Gefen, *Y-net*, March 8, 2001
80. Rubinstein, Interview, December 31, 2003
81. Doron & Lebel, 2005
82. Carmon, Globes, June 15, 2000
83. Bar Gefen, *Y-net*, July, 6, 2000
84. Arian, Nachmias & Amir, 2002
85. Rubishtein, Interview, December 31, 2003
86. Arian, Nachmias & Amir, 2002
87. Shadmi, *Haaretz*, June 13, 2000
88. Bar Gefen, *Y-net*, July, 6, 2000
89. Assa, 1996: 167
90. Arian & Shamir, 2002

91. Rubinstein, Interview December 31, 2003
92. Korn & Shapira, 1997
93. Banzhaf, 1965; Coleman, 1971; Laver & Schofield, 1990; Schofield, 1995; Sened, 1996; Shapley, 1953; Shapley & Shubik, 1954
94. Bar Gefen, *Y-net*, July 6, 2000
95. Verter, *Haaretz*, July 5, 2000
96. Bar Gefen, *Y-net*, July 6, 2000; Ottolenghi, 2001
97. Bar Gefen, *Y-net*, July 6, 2000
98. Alon, *Haaretz*, June 29, 1998
99. Downs, 1957
100. Rubinstein, Interview, December 31, 2003
101. Bar Gefen, *Y-net*, July 6, 2000
102. Bar Gefen, *Y-net*, July 6, 2000; Carmon, interview, February 25, 2004
103. Nagel, 1994; Rist, 1995
104. Rubinstein, Interview December 31, 2003

## 5 Comparative Aspects of Institutional Changes: the Cases of Argentina, Italy and New Zealand

1. Buchanan, 1990; Gardner & Ostrom, 1991; Gavious & Mizrahi, 2003
2. Catt, 1996; Denemark, 1998; Mackerras, 1994; Rahat, 2000; Sakamoto, 1999; Shugart & Wattenberg, 2000
3. Donoven, 1995, 1996; Dunleavy & Margetts, 1995; Ginsborg, 1996; Hine, 1996; Katz, 1996, 1998; Morlino & Tarchi, 1996; Parker, 1996; Rahat, 2000; Sakamoto, 1999; Sidoti, 1993
4. Finkel, 2003; Larkins, 1998; Spiller & Tommasi, 2007
5. Mackerras, 1994; Sakamoto, 1999
6. Dunleavy & Margetts, 1995; Sakamoto, 1999
7. Finkel, 2003; Larkins, 1998
8. Buchanan, 1990; Gardner & Ostrom, 1991; Gavious & Mizrahi, 2003
9. Lijphart, 1984; 1999
10. Finkel, 2003; Larkins, 1998
11. Finkel, 2003
12. Larkins, 1998
13. Spiller & Tommasi, 2007
14. Finkel, 2003
15. Larkins, 1998
16. Finkel, 2003: 13
17. Finkel, 2003: 14, 27
18. Spiller & Tommasi, 2007
19. Dunleavy & Margetts, 1995; Sakamoto, 1999
20. Sakamoto, 1999
21. Political system based, usually informally, on the ability of political leaders (patrons or "bosses") to provide jobs, local investment, or services for their supporters (clients).
22. Donoven, 1995, 1996; Katz, 1996, 1998
23. Katz, 1996, 1998; Morlino & Tarchi, 1996; Parker, 1996
24. Hine, 1996; Morlino & Tarchi, 1996; Sidoti, 1993
25. Katz, 1996, 1998; Parker, 1996

26. Donoven, 1995, 1996; Ginsborg, 1996; Hine, 1996; Katz, 1996, 1998; Morlino& Tarchi, 1996; Parker, 1996; Sidoti, 1993
27. Rahat, 2000: 333
28. Arian & Nachmias, 2003
29. Mackerras, 1994; Sakamoto, 1999
30. Mackerras, 1994; Sakamoto, 1999
31. Catt, 1996; Shugart & Wittenberg, 2000
32. Catt, 1996
33. Rahat, 2000: 326
34. Sakamoto, 1999
35. Rahat, 2000: 330
36. Morlino & Tarchi, 1996; Parker, 1996; Sidoti, 1993
37. Rahat, 2000: 333
38. Morlino & Tarchi, 1996; Sidoti, 1993
39. Della Sala, 1993
40. Castels, 1994; Goff, 1993; Ingle, 1995; Mackerras, 1994
41. Donoven, 1995, 1996; Ginsborg, 1996; Hine, 1996; Katz, 1996, 1998; Morlino & Tarchi, 1996; Parker, 1996; Sidoti, 1993
42. Della Sala, 1993; Morlino & Tarchi, 1996; Sidoti, 1993
43. Katz, 1998
44. Castels, 1994; Goff, 1993; Ingle, 1995; Mackerras, 1994
45. Sakamoto, 1999
46. Sakamoto, 1999
47. Rahat, 2000: 333

## 6 Summary and Conclusions

1. Arian, Nachmias & Amir, 2002
2. Hine, 1996; Morlino & Tarchi, 1996; Nachmias & Arian, 2003; Sidoti, 1993

# BIBLIOGRAPHY

## Articles and Books in English


Ainsworth, S. & I. Sened (1993) "The Role of Lobby-ists: Entrepreneurs with Two Audiences," *American Journal of Political Science,* 37: 834–866.

Alchian, A.A. & H. Demsetz (1972) "Production, Information Cost, and Economic Organization," *American Economic Review,* 62: 777–795

Alexander, J. (1987) *Twenty Lectures: Sociological Theory since World War II,* New York: Columbia University Press.

Arian, A. & M. Shamir (eds.) (1999) *The Elections in Israel—1996*, Albany: SUNY Press.

Arian, A. & M. Shamir (eds.) (2002) *The Elections in Israel—2001*, Jerusalem: Israel Democracy Institute (in Hebrew).

Austen-Smith, D. (1998) "Allocating Access for Information and Contributions," *Journal of Law Economics and Organization*, 14: 277–303.

Axelrod, R. (1984) *The Evolution of Cooperation*, New York: Basic Books.

Banzhaf, J.F. III (1965) "Weighted Voting Doesn't Work: A Mathematical Analysis," *Rutgers Law Review*, 19: 317–343.

Baumgartner, F. & B.D. Jones (1993) *Agendas and Instability in American Politics*, Chicago: Chicago University press.

Begly, T.M. & D.P. Boyd (1987) "Psychological Characteristics Associated with Performance in Entrepreneurial Firms and Smaller Business," *Journal of Business Venturing*, 2(2): 79–93.

Bendor, J. (1990) "Formal Models of Bureaucracy: A Review," in: N.B. Lynn & A. Wildavsky (eds.) *Public Administration: The State of the Discipline,* Chatham, NJ: Chatham House.

Bendor, J., S. Taylor & R. van Gaalen (1987a) "Politicians, Bureaucrats and Asymmetric Information," American *Journal of Political Science,* 31: 796–828.

Bendor, J., S. Taylor & R. van Gaalen (1987b) "Stacking the Deck: Bureaucratic Missions and the Search for Alternatives," *American Political Science Review,* 81: 873–896.

Berger, P. (1969) *The Social Reality of Religion*, London: Faber and Faber.

Berry, J.M. (1977) *Lobbying for the People*, Princeton, NJ: Princeton University Press.

Birley, S. & P. Westhead (1994) "A Taxonomy of Business Start-Up Reasons and Their Impact on Firm Growth and Size," *Journal of Business Venturing*, 9(1): 7–31.

Blumer, H. (1971) "Social Problems as Collective Behavior," *Social Problems,* 18: 298–306.

Braybrooke, D. & C.E. Lindblom (1963) *A Strategy of Decision,* Albany: SUNY Press.

*Breton, A. (1995) "Organizational Hierarchies and Bureaucracies: An* Integrative Essay," *European Journal of Political Economy,* 11(3): 411–440.

Breton, A. & R. Breton (1969) "An Economic Theory of Social Movements," *American Economic Review,* 59: 198–205.

*Brichta,* A. (*1998*) "The New Premier-Parliamentary System in Israel," *Annals, AAPSS,* 555: 180–192

Browne, A. & A. Wildavsky (1983) "Implementation as Exploration," in: J.L. Pressman & A. Wildavsky (eds.) *Implementation* (3rd ed.), Los Angeles: University of California Press, pp. 232–256

Buchanan, J.M. (1990) "The Domain of Constitutional Economics," *Constitutional Political Economy,* 1: 1–18.

Burns, T. & H. Flam (1987) *The Shaping of Social Organization,* Hewbury Park, CA: Sage.

Calvert, R.L. (1992) "Leadership and Its Basis in Problems of Social Coordination," *International Political Science Review,* 13(1): 7–24.

Cantril, H. (1963) *The Psychology of Social Movement,* New York: John Wiley and Sons.

Castels, F.G. (1994) "The Policy Consequences of Proportional Representation: A Sceptical Commentary," *Political Science,* 46(2): 161–171.

Catt, H. (1996) "The Other Democratic Experiment: New Zealand's Experience with Citizens Initiated Referendum," *Political Science,* 48(1): 29–47.

Christopoulos, D.C. (2006) "Relational Attributes of Political Entrepreneurs: A Network Perspective," *Journal of European Public Policy,* 13(5): 757–778 .

Coase, R.H. (1937) "The Nature of the Firm," *Economica,* 16: 386–405.

Coase, R.H. (1960) "The Problem of Sofial Cost," *Journal of Law and Economics,* 3: 1–44.

Coleman, J.S. (1971) "Control of Collectivities and the Power of a Collectivity to Act," in: B. Lieberman (ed.) *Social Choice,* New York: Gordon and Breach.

Colomer, J.M. (1995a) *Game Theory and the Transition to Democracy: The Spanish Model,* Aldershot, UK: Edward Elger.

Colomer, J.M. (1995b) "Leadership Games in Collective Action," *Rationality and Society,* 7(2): 225–246.

Conger, J.A. (1991) *The Charismatic Leader: Beyond the Mystique of Exceptional Leadership,* San Francisco: Jossey- Bass.

Dahl, R.A. (1961) *Who Governs? Democracy and Power in an American City,* New Haven, CN: Yale University Press.

Dahl, R.A. (1963) *Modern Political Analysis,* Englewood Cliffs, NJ: Prentice Hall.

De Haan, J. & C.L.J. Siermann (1995) "New Evidence on the Relationship between Democracy and Economic Growth," *Public Choice,* 86: 175–198.

Della Sala, V. (1993) "The Cossiga Legacy and Scalfaro's Elections: In the Shadow of Presidentialism?" *Italian Politics: A Review,* 8: 34–49.

Denemark, D. (1998) *Choosing MMP in New Zealand: Explaining Electoral System Change in 1993* (Prepared for Delivery at the conference on "Mixed" Electoral Systems, December 11–13, 1998, Newport Beach, California)

Donoven, M. (1995) "The Politics of Electoral Reform in Italy," *International Political Science Review,* 16(1): 47–64

Donoven, M. (1996) "Electoral Reform in Italy," *Representation,* 33(4): 141–147

Doron, G. & A. Adiri (1994) *Privatization of Service Delivery in Israeli Local Governments,* Jerusalem: Institute for Advanced Strategic and Political Studies.

Doron, G. & I. Sened (2001) *Political Bargaining: Theory, Practice, and Process,* London: Sage.

Dotan, Y. & M. Hofnung (2001) "Interest Groups in the Israeli High Court of Justice: Measuring Success in Litigation and In-Out-Of Court Settlements," *Law and Policy,* 23: 1–27.

Downs, A. (1957) *An Economic Theory of Democracy*, New York: Harper and Roe.

Dowty, A. (1998) *Thye Jewish State: A Century Later*, Los Angeles: University of California Press.

Dunleavy, P. & H. Margetts (1995) "Understanding the Dynamics of Electoral Reform," *International Political Science Review*, 16(1): 9–29.

Dye, T.R. (2002) *Understanding Public Policy* (10th ed.), Upper Saddle River, NJ: Prentice Hall.

Hardin, R. (1982) *Collective Action,* Baltimore: Johns Hopkins University Press.

Eckstein, H. (1960) *Pressure Groups Politics: The Case of the British Medical Association*, Stanford: Stanford University Press.

Edelman, M. (1994a) *Courts, Politics, and Culture in Israel*, Charlottesville: University Press of Virginia.

Edelman, M. (1994b) "The Judicialization of Politics in Israel," *International Political Science Review,* 15: 177–186.

Eliade, M. (1965) *The Myth of the Eternal Return*, New York: Pantheon Books.

Fearn-Banks, K. (1996) *Crisis Communication*, New York: Erlbaum, Mahwah.

Finkel, J. (2003) *Initiation versus Implementation: Judicial Reform in Argentina in the 1990's*, Paper presented at the American Political Science Association Conference, Philadelphia, August 25, 2003.

Fiorina, M. & K.A. Shepsle (1989) "Formal Theories of Leadership: Agents, Agenda Setter, and Entrepreneurs," in: B.D. Jones (ed.) *Leadership and Politics: New Perspectives in Political Science*, Kansas: University Press of Kansas.

Frohlich, N., J.A. Oppenheimer & O. Young (1971) *Political Leadership and Collective Goods*, Princeton, NJ: Princeton University Press.

Gardner, R. & E. Ostrom (1991) "Rules and Games," *Public Choice*, 70(2): 121–150.

Gastil, R.D. (1990) "The Comparative Survey of Freedom: Experiences and Suggestions," *Studies in Comparative International Development*, 25: 25–50.

Gavious, A. & S. Mizrahi (2003) "A Signaling Model of Peaceful Political Change," *Social Choice and Welfare*, 20: 119–136.

Ginsborg, P. (1996) "Explaining Italy's Crisis," in: S. Gundle & S. Parker (eds.) *The New Italian Republic*, London: Routledge, pp. 311–325.

Goff, P. (1993) "Voting for Change: New Zealand's Referendum on Voting Systems," *Parliamentarian*, 74(2): 84–87.

Golden, O. (1990) "Innovation in Public Sector Human Service Programs: The Implications of Innovation by 'Groping Along,'" *Journal of Policy Analysis and Management,* 9(2): 219–248.

Goode, W.J. (1957) "Community within a Community: The Professions," *ASR*, 22: 194–200.

Gramsci, A. (1971) *Selection from the Prison Notebook*. London: Lawrence and Wishart.

Greenberger, D.B. & D.L. Sexton (1988) "An Interactive Model of New Venture Initiation," *Journal of Small Business Management*, 26(3): 1–7.

Grossman, S.J. & O. Hart (1987) "The Costs and Benefits of Ownership: A Theory of Vertical and Lateral Integration," *Journal of Political Economy,* 94: 691–719.

Hayes, M.T. (1981) *Lobbyists and Legislatures: A Theory of Political Markets, New Brunswick*, New Jersey: Rutgers University Press.

Hazan, R. (1996) "Presidential Parliamentarism: Direct Popular Election of the Prime Minister, Israel's New Electoral and Political System," *Electoral Studies*, 15(1): 21–37.

Herman, T. (1996) "Do They Have a Chance? Protest and Political Structure of Opportunities in Israel," *Israel Studies*, 1(1): 144–170.

Hine, D. (1996) "Italian Political Reform in Comparative Perspective," in: G. Stephan & S. Parker (eds.) *The New Italian Republic*, London: Routledge, pp. 311–325.

Hirshman, A.O. (1945) *National Power and Structure of Foreign Trade*, Los Angeles: University of California Press.

Hirschman, A.O. (1970) *Exit, Voice & Loyalty*, Cambridge, MA: Harvard University Press
Horowitz, D. & M. Lissak (1989) *Trouble in Utopia*. Albany: SUNY Press.
Ingle, S. (1995) "Electoral Reform in New Zealand: The Implications for Westminster System," *Journal of Legislative Studies*, 1(4): 76–92.
Johnson, B. (1990) "Toward a Multidimensional of Entrepreneurship: The Case of Achievement Motivation and Entrepreneur," *Entrepreneurship: Theory and Practice*, 14(2): 139–161.
Jones, P. (1978) "The Appeal of the Political Entrepreneur," *British Journal of Political Science*, 8: 498–504.
Katz, R.S. (1996) "Electoral Reform and the Transformation of Party Politics in Italy," *Party Politics*, 2(1): 31–54.
Katz, R.S. (1998) *Reforming the Italian Electoral Law, 1993* (Prepared for Delivery at the conference on Mixed Electoral Systems, December 11–13, 1998, Newport Beach, California)
Kelsen, H. (1945) *General Theory of Law and State*. Cambridge, MA: Harvard University Press.
Kingdon, J.W. (1995) *Agendas, Alternatives and Public Policies* (2nd ed.), New York: Harper Collins.
Knight, J. (1995) "Models, Interpretations, and Theories: Constructing Explanations of Institutional Emergence and Change," in: J. Knight & I. Sened (eds.) *Explaining Social Institutions*. Ann Arbor: University of Michigan Press.
Kramer, F.A. (1977) *Dynamics of Public Bureaucracy*, Cambridge, MA: Winthrop.
Laakso, M. & R. Taagepera (1979) "Effective Number of Parties: A Measure with Application to West Europe," *Comparative Political Studies*, 12: 3–27.
Larkins, C. (1998) "The Judiciary and Delegative Democracy in Argentina," *Comparative Politics*, 30(4): 427.
Laver, M. & N. Schofield (1990) *Multiparty Government*, Oxford: Oxford University Press.
Laver, M. & K.A. Shepsle (1994) *Making and Breaking Governments: Cabinets and Legislatures in Parliamentary Democracies*, New York: Cambridge University Press.
Lehman-Wilzig, S.N. (1991) "Loyalty, Voice and Quasi-Exit." *Comparative Politics*, 24: 97–108.
Lehman-Wilzig, S.N. (1992) *Wildfire: Grassroots Revolts in Israel in the Post-Socialist Era*. Albany: SUNY Press.
Levi-Faur, D., G. Sheffer & D. Vogel (eds.) (1999) *Israel: The Dynamics of Change and Continuity*, London: Frank Cass.
Lindblom, C.E. (1959) "The Science of Muddling Through," *Public Administration Review*, 19: 79–99.
Lijphart, A. (1984) *Democracies: Patterns of Majoritarian and Consensus Government in Twenty-One Countries*, New Haven: Yale University Press.
Lijphart, A. (1999) *Patterns of Democracy: Government Forms and Performance in Thirty-Six Countries*, New Haven: Yale University Press
Lipsky, M. (1980) *Street Level Bureaucracy: Dilemmas of the Individual in Public Service* , New York: Russell Sage Foundation.
Lohmann, S. (1993) "A Signaling Model of Information and Manipulative Political Action," *American Political Science Review*, 87: 319–333.
López, Edward J. (2002) "The Legislator as Political Entrepreneur: Investment in Political Capital," *Review of Austrian Economics*, 15 (2–3): 211–228.
Mackerras, M. (1994) "Reform of New Zealand's Voting System 1985–1996," *Representation*, 32(118): 36–40.
Mantzavinos, C., D. North & S. Shariq (2004) "Learning, Institutions and Economic Performance," *Perspectives on Politics*, 2: 75–84.
McClelland, D.C. (1987) "Characteristics of Successful Entrepreneurs," *Journal of Creative Behavior*, 21(3): 219–233.

McFarland, A.S. (1984) *Common Cause: Lobbying in the Public Interest*, Chatham, NJ: Chatham House.

Meydani, A. (2008) "Political Entrepreneurs and Electoral Capital: The Case of the Israeli State Economy Arrangement Law," *Constitutional Political Economy,* 19(4): 301–312.

Migdal, J.S. (2001) *Through the Lens of Israel. Explorations in State and Society,* Albany: SUNY Press.

Milgrom, P & J. Roberts.(1990) "Bargaining Costs, Influence Costs, and the Organization of Economic Activity," in J.E. Alt & K.A. Shepsle (eds.) *Perspectives on Positive Political Economy,* Cambridge: Cambridge University Press.

Millbrath, L.W. (1965) *Political Participation,* Chicago: Rand McNally.

*Miller, G. & T. Moe (1983) "Bureaucrats, Legislators, and the Size of* Government," *American Political Science Review,* 77: 297–322.

Mizrahi, S. & A. Meydani (2003) "Political Participation via the Judicial System: Exit, Voice and Quasi-Exit in Israeli Society," *Israel Studies,* 8(2): 118–138.

Moe, T. (1987) "Interests, Institutions, and Positive Theory: The Politics of the NLRB," *Studies in American Political Development,* 2: 236–299.

Monsen, J.R. & M.W. Cannon (1965) *The Makers of Public Policy,* New York: McGraw Hill.

Moore, D. (1981) "Toward Anew Contingency Approach: The Search for Organizational Gestalts," *Journal of Management Studies,* 18(1): 1–26.

Morlino, L. & M. Tarchi (1996) "The Dissatisfied Society: The Roots of Political Change in Italy," *European Journal of Political Research,* 30(1): 41–63.

Nachmias, D. & I. Sened (1999) "The Bias of Pluralism: The Redistributional Effects of the New Electoral Law in Israel's 1996 Election," in: A. Arian & M. Shamir (eds.) *The Elections in Israel—1996,* Albany: SUNY Press.

Naffziger, D.W., J.S. Hornsby & D.F. Kuratko (1994) "A Proposed Research Model of Entrepreneurial Motivation," *Entrepreneurship Theory and Practice,* 18(3): 29–42.

Nagel, S.S. (1994) "Systematic Policy Evaluation," in: S.S. Nagel (ed.) *Encyclopedia of Policy Studies,* New York: Marcel Dekker, pp. 31–48.

Nelson, R. & S. Winter (1982) *An Evolutionary Theory of Economic Change,* Cambridge, MA: Harvard University Press.

Nisbet, R.A. (1966) *The Sociological Tradition,* New York: Basic Books.

Niskanen, W.A. (1971) *Bureaucracy and Repreventative Government,* New York: Aldine Atherton.

North, D.C. (1981) *Structure and Change in Economic History,* New York: W.W. Norton.

North, D.C. (1986) "The New Institutional Economics," *Journal of Institutional and Theoretical Economics,* 142: 230–237.

North, D.C. (1995) "Five propositions about Institutional Change," in: J. Knight & I. Sened (eds.) *Explaining Social Institutions,* Ann Arbor: University of Michigan Press.

Offe, C. (1985) "New Social Movements: Challenging the Boundaries of Institutional Politics," *Social Research,* 52(4): 871–868.

Olson, M. (1965) *The Logic of Collective Action,* Cambridge, MA: Harvard University Press.

Ostrom, E. (1986) "An Agenda for the Study of Institutions," *Public Choice,* 48: 3–25.

Ottolenghi, E. (2001) "Why Direct Election Failed in Israel," *Journal of Democracy,* 12(4): 109–122.

Parker, S. (1996) "Electoral Reform and Political Change in Italy 1991–1994," in: S. Gundle & S. Parker (eds.) *The New Italian Republic.* London: Routledge, 40–56.

Perrow, C. (1986) *Complex Organizations: A Critical Essay* (3rd ed.), New York: Longman.

Peters, G.B. (1999) *Institutional Theory in Political Science: The New Institutionalism,* London: Cssells.

Posner, R.A. (1981) *The Economics of Justice,* Cambridge, MA: Harvard University Press.

Powell, W.W. & P.J. DiMaggio (eds.) (1991) *The New Institutionalism in Organizational Analysis*, Chicago & London: University of Chicago Press.

Pridham, G. & T. Vanhanen (eds.) (1994) *Democratization in Eastern Europe*, London: Routledge.

Przeworsky, A. (1991) *Democracy and the Market*, Cambridge: Cambridge University Press.

Rae, D.W. (1967) *The Political Consequences of Electoral Laws*, New Haven: Yale University Press.

Rahat, G. (2006) "The Politics of Electoral Reform Abolition: The Informed Process of Israel's Return to Its Previous Electoral System," *Political Studies*, 54(1): 43

Rahat, G. (2008) *The Politics of Regime Structure Reform in Democracies: Israel in Comparative Perspective*, Albany: SUNY Press,.

Riker, W.H ( 1980 ) "Implications from the Disequilibrium of Majority Rule for the Study of Institutions," *American Political Science Review*, 74: 432–447.

Rist, R.C. (1995) "Introduction," in: R.C. Rist (ed.) *Policy Evaluation*, Aldershot, UK: Edward Elgar.

Sabatier, P. (1986) "Top-Down and Bottom-Up Approaches in Implementation Research: A Critical Analysis and Suggested Synthesis," *Journal of Public Policy*, 6(1): 21–48.

Sakamoto, T. (1999) "Explaining Electoral Reform: Japan versus Italy and New Zealand," *Party Polities*, 5(4): 419–438.

Salisbury, R.H. (1969) "An Exchange Theory of Interest Groups," *Midwest Journal of Political Science*, 13: 1–32.

Sandler, T. (1992) *Collective Action: Theory and Applications*, Ann Arbor: University of Michigan Press.

Scheinberg, S. & I.C. MacMillan (1988) "An 11-Country Study of Motivation to Start a Business," in: B.A. Kirchof, W.A. Long, W.A. McMullan, K.H. Vesper & W.E. Wetzel (eds.) *Frontiers of Entrepreneurship Research*, Wellesley, MA: Babson College, 669–687.

Schneider, M. and Teske, P. (1992) "Toward a Theory of the Political Entrepreneur: Evidence from Local Government," *American Political Science Review*, 86: 737–747.

Schofield, N. (1995) "Coalition Politics: A Formal Model and Empirical Analysis," *Journal of Theoretical Politics*, 7(3): 245–281.

Schotter, A. (1981) *The Economic Theory of Social Institution*. New York: Cambridge University Press.

Schumpeter, J.A. (1934) *The Theory of Economic Development—An Inquiry into Profits, Capital, Credit, Interest and the Business Cycle*, Oxford: Oxford University Press.

Scott, W.R. & J.W. Meyer (1991) "The Organization of Societal Sectors: Propositions and Early Evidence," in: W.W. Powell & P.J. DiMaggio (eds.) *The New Institutionalism in Organizational Analysis*, Chicago & London: University of Chicago Press.

Scully, G.W. & D.J. Slottje (1991) "Ranking Economic Liberty Across Countries," *Public Choice*, 69: 121–152.

Seliger, M. (1977) *Ideology and Politics*, London: George Allen & Unwin.

Selznick, P. (1949) *TVA and the Grass Roots*, Berkeley: University of California Press.

Selznick, P. (1957) *Leadership in Administration*, Evanston, IL: Row, Peterson.

Sened, I. (1995) "Equilibria in Weighted Voting Games with Side-Payments in Two Dimensional Spaces," *Journal of Theoretical Politics*, 7: 283–300.

Sened, I. (1996) "A Model of Coalition Formation: Theory and Evidence," *Journal of Politics*, 58(2): 350–372.

Shafir, G. & Y. Peled (2002) *Being Israeli: The Dinamics of Multiple Citizenship*, Cambridge: Cambridge University Press.

Shapley, L.S. (1953) "A Value for N-Person Games," in: H.W. Kuhn & A.W. Tucker (eds.) *Contributions to the Theory of Games*, Vol. 2: *Annals of Mathematics Studies* No. 28, Princeton, NJ: Princeton University Press.

Shapley, L.S. & M. Shubik (1954) "A Method of Evaluating the Distribution of Power in a Committee System," *American Political Science Review*, 48: 787–792.

Sheffer, G. (1999) "Political Change and Party System Transformation," *Israel Affairs*, 6(2): 148–171.

Sheingate, Adam D. (2003) "Political Entrepreneurship, Institutional Change, and American Political Development," *Studies in American Political Development*, 17: 185–203.

Shepsle, K.A. (1986) "Institutional Equilibrium Institutions," in: H. Weisburg (ed.) *Political Science: The Science of Politics*. New York: Agathon, pp. 51–82.

Shepsle, K.A. (1987) "The Institutional Foundations of Committee Power," *American Political Science Review*, 81: 85–104.

Shepsle, K.A. & B. Weingast (1981) "Structure—Induced Equilibria and Legislative Choice," *Public Choice*, 37: 502–519.

Shugart, M. & M.P. Wattenberg (2000) "Mixed Member Electoral Systems: A Definition and Typology, Are Mixed-Member Systems, the Best of Both Worlds?" in: M.S. Shugart & M.P. Wattenberg (eds.) *Mixed-Member Electoral Systems: The Best of Both Worlds?* Oxford: Oxford University Press.

Sidoti, F. (1993) "Italy: A Clean-Up after the Cold War," *Government and Opposition*, 28(1): 105–114.

Spector, M. & J.I. Kitsuse (1987) *Constructing Social Problems,* New York : Aldine de Gruyter

Spiller P.T. & M. Tommasi (2007) The *Institutional Foundations of Public Policy in Argentina.* Cambridge: Cambridge University Press.

Stewart, W.H., W.E. Watson, J.C. Carland & J.W. Carland (1998) "A Proclivity for Entrepreneurship: A Comparison of Entrepreneurs, Small Business Owners, and Corporate Managers," *Journal of Business Venturing*, 14(2): 189–214.

Taylor, M. (1987) *The Possibility of Cooperation.* Cambridge: Cambridge University Press, Chapter Five.

Tsebelis, G. (1990) *Nested Games, Rational Choice in Comparative Politics*, Los Angeles: University of California Press.

Tsebelis, G. (2002) *Veto Players: How Political Institutions Work*, Princeton, NJ: Princeton University Press.

Truman, D.B. (1971) *The Government Process* (2nd ed.), New York: Knopf.

Vigoda E. (ed.) (2002) *Public Administration: An Interdisciplinary Critical Analysis,* New York: Marcel Decker.

Voight, S. & E.M. Salzberger (2002) "Choosing Not to Choose: When Politicians Choose to Delegate Powers." *KYKLOS,* 55(2): 289–310.

Wagner, R. (1966) *Pressure Groups and Political Entrepreneurs.* Papers on Nonmarket Decision Making.

Wallace, A. (1969) "Revitalization Movement," in: B. Mclaughlin (ed.) *Studies in Social Movements*, New York: Free Press, 174–177.

Weber, M.(1964) *The Theory of Social and Economic Organization/Max Weber,* A.M. Henderson (trans.), T. Parsons (ed. with an intro.) Glencoe, IL: Free Press.

Weingast, B. & W. Marshall (1988) "The Industrial Organization of Congress; or, Why Legislatures, Like Firms, Are Not Organized as Markets," *Journal of Political Economy*, 96: 132–64.

Williamson, O.E. (1975) *Markets and Hierarchies,* New York: Free Press.

Williamson, O.E. (1985) *The Economic Institutions of Capitalism*, New York: Free Press.

Wittmann, D. (1989) "Why Democracies Produce Efficient Results," *Journal of Political Economy*, 97: 1395–1424.

Wolfsfeld, G. (1997) *Constructing News about Peace*, the Tami Steinmetz Center for Peace Research (Research Report no. 8), Tel-Aviv University.

Ziegler, H. (1964) *Interest Groups in American Society*, Englewood Cliffs, NJ: Prentice Hall.

## Articles and Books in Hebrew

Adam, R. (1995) *Petition to the High Court of Justice as Israeli Interest Groups Strategy*, Kesher (Magazine—The Andrea and Charles Bronfman Center for the Media of the Jewish People).

Aharoni, Y. (1991) *Political Economics in Israel*, Tel-Aviv: Am Oved (in Hebrew).

Alon, G. (1995) *Direct Election*, Tel-Aviv: Bitan (in Hebrew).

Arian, A. (1997) *The Second Republic*, Tel-Aviv: Zmora-Bitan.

Arian, A. & D. Nachmias (2003) *Democracy Index*, Jerusalem: Israeli Democracy Institute.

Arian, A., D. Nachmias & R. Amir (2002) *Executive Governance in Israel*, Jerusalem: Israel Democracy Institute (in Hebrew).

Arieli, Y. (1992) *History and Politics*, Tel-Aviv: Am Oved, Afikim Library (in Hebrew).

Assa, H. (1996) "Dmoctator Doll," in: G. Doron (ed.) *The Electoral Revolution*, Tel-Aviv: HaKibbutz Hameuchad, pp. 163–171 (in Hebrew).

Barak A. (1993) The Constitutional Revolution: Protected Human Rights, *Mishpat Umimshal*, 1(1): 9–10. (in Hebrew).

Barzilai, G. (1992) *A Democracy in Wartime: Conflict and Consensus in Israel*, Tel-Aviv: Sifriat Polaim (in Hebrew ).

Barzilai, G. (1998) "Courts as Hegemonic Institutions and Social Change," *Politics—Periodical for Political Science and International Relations*, 3: 31–51. (in Hebrew).

Bechor, G. (1996) *A Constitution for Israel*, Or Yehuda: Ma'ariv (in Hebrew).

Beilin, Y. (1984) *Sons in the Shadow of Their Fathers*, Tel-Aviv: Revivim (in Hebrew).

Beilin, Y. (1996) *Accident by Name Direct Election for Prime Minister*, in: G. Doron (ed.) *The Electoral Revolution*, Tel-Aviv: HaKibbutz Hameuchad, pp. 199–206 (in Hebrew).

Benvenisti, E. (2001) *Judicially Sponsored Checks and Balances*, 32 Mishpatim 797–819 (4) The Hebrew University, Law Rev. ( in Hebrew).

Brichta, A. (1977) *Democracy and Elections: On Changing the Electoral and Nomination Systems in Israel*. Tel-Aviv: Am Oved (in Hebrew).

Carmel, A. (2001) It's All Politics, Ganei-Aviv: Dvir (in Hebrew).

Deri, D. (1993) *Political Appointments in Israel*, Tel-Aviv: Israel Democracy Institute and Ha'Kibbutz Ha'Meuchad (in Hebrew).

Deri, D. & E. Sharon (1994) *Economics and Politics in State Budget*, Tel Aviv: Israel Democracy Institute and Ha'Kibbutz Ha'Meuchad (in Hebrew).

Diskin, A. & H. Diskin (1988) *How to Vote*, Jerusalem: Jerusalem Institute for Israel Studies (in Hebrew).

Doron, G. (1986) *To Decide and to Implement: Chapters in Public Policy*. Tel Aviv: Kivunim (in Hebrew).

Doron, G. (1988) *Rational Politics in Israel*, Tel-Aviv: Ramot (in Hebrew).

Doron, G. (ed.) (1996a) *The Electoral Revolution: Direct Election of the Prime Minster and Primaries*, Tel-Aviv: Ha'Kibbutz Ha'Meuchad (in Hebrew).

Doron, G. (1996b) Political Reason of Reforms in the Democratic Election Systems, in: G. Doron (ed.) *The Electoral Revolution*, Tel-Aviv: Ha'Kibbutz Ha'Meuchad, pp. 54–78 (in Hebrew).

Doron G. (2006) *A Presidential Regime for Israel*, Jerusalem: Carmel (in Hebrew).

Doron, G. & M. Maor (1989) *Barriers to Entry into a Political System*, Tel-Aviv: Papirus, Tel-Aviv University (in Hebrew).

Doron, G. & U. Lebel (2005) *The Politics of Bereavement* (2nd ed.), Tel-Aviv: HaKibbutz Hameuchad (in Hebrew).

Dror, Y. (1989) *Grand Strategy for Israel*, Academon: Hebrew University in Jerusalem, p. 3 (in Hebrew).

Dror, Y. (1996) "Governability as Criteria to Stabilize the Regime," in: G. Doron (ed.) *The Electoral Revolution*, Tel-Aviv, Israel: Ha'Kibbutz Ha'Meuchad, pp. 149–162 (in Hebrew).

Eisenstadt, S.N. (1989) *Social Change in Israeli Society*, Jerusalem: Hebrew University, Magness Press.

Goldberg, G. (1994) *The Israeli Voter*, Jerusalem: Magness Press, Hebrew University (in Hebrew).

Gutman, E. (1994) "Change of the Election System in Constitutional Reform," in: C. Hershkovitz (ed.) *Israel and Its Ramifications*, Jerusalem: Jerusalem Center for Public Affairs, pp. 56–59 (in Hebrew).

Kimmerling, B. (2004) *Immigrants, Settlers and Natives: Israel Between Plurality of Cultures and Cultural Wars*, Tel-Aviv: Am Oved/Alma. (in Hebrew).

Korn, D. (ed.) (1998) *The Decline of Parties*, Tel-Aviv: HaKibbutz Hameuchad (in Hebrew).

Korn, D. & B. Shapira (1997) *Coalitions*, Tel-Aviv: Zmora-Bitan (in Hebrew).

Kremnitzer, M. (1999) "The High Court of Justice and the Shaping of Public Policy: Equality between the Sexes," in: D. Nachmias & G. Menahem (eds.) *Public Policy in Israel, The Israel Institute for Democracy*, pp. 175–189 (in Hebrew).

Kretzmer, D (1997) "The Path to Judicial Review in Human Rights Cases: From Bergman and Kol Ha'am to Mizrahi Bank," *Mishpatim*, 28: 359–385 (in Hebrew).

*Mautner, M. (1993)* The Decline of Formalism and the Rise of Values in Israeli Law, *Tel-Aviv: Ma'agalay Da'at (in Hebrew).*

*Melamed, A. & D. Kalfon (1992) "The Role of Communication in Developing the Protest Movement for Governmental Change 12.6.90–13.3.90,"* Patuach, *1: 102–105 (in Hebrew).*

Moalem, Y. & R. Frisch (1991) *Increase in the Return on Schooling in Israel in 1976–1997*, Jerusalem: Bank of Israel Research Department (in Hebrew).

Naor, A. (1999) "The Security Argument in the Territorial Debate in Israel: Rhetoric and Policy," *Israel Studies*, 4 : 150–177 (in Hebrew).

Peleg, M. (1996) "Primaries and Government: Influence in Two Directions," in: G. Doron (ed.) *The Electoral Revolution*, Tel-Aviv: HaKibbutz Hameuchad, pp. 113–123 (in Hebrew).

Rahat, G. (2000) "The Politics of Regime Structure Reform," Ph.D. Dissertation, Jerusalem: Hebrew University (in Hebrew).

Reichmann, U. & D. Nachmias (eds.) (2006) *Reinventing Government in Israel*, Herzliya: Interdisciplinary Center (in Hebrew).

Rubinstein, A. (1982) *A Certain Political Experience*, Jerusalem: Edanim, Yediot Aharonot Books (in Hebrew).

Shaham, D. (1998) *Israel—50 Years*, Tel- Aviv: Am Oved (in Hebrew).

Shamir, *R. (1994)* "Without Limits: on the Supreme Court's Deportation Decision," *Plilim*, 26(6): 59–66 (in Hebrew).

Shprinzak, E. (1986) *Everyman Whatsoever Is Rright in His Own Eyes: Illegalism in Israeli Society*, Tel-Aviv: Sifriat Poalim (in Hebrew).

Swirski, S. & A. Fraenkel (2001) *Maintenance Wage,* Tel-Aviv: Adva Center

Swirski, S. & E. Konor-Attias (2000) *Israel: A Social Report*, Tel-Aviv: Adva Center (in Hebrew).

Yaacobi, G. (1996) "Political Reforms: Chances, Dangers and Price," in: G. Doron (ed.) *The Electoral Revolution*, Tel-Aviv: HaKibbutz Hameuchad, pp. 219– 223 (in Hebrew).

Yishai, Y. (1987) *Interest Groups in Israel: The Test of Democracy*, Tel-Aviv: Am Oved (in Hebrew).

## Interviews

Aloni, Shulamit (2001) Knesset Member in 1992–1996

Badash, Pini (2001) Knesset Member in 1992

Prof. Barzilai, Gad (January 10, 2002) An Expert in Politics, Law, and Society.

Dr. Carmon, Arye (February 25, 2004) External Entrepreneur

Dr. Hofnung, Menachem (January 15, 2002) Expert in Politics and Law

Prof. Nachmias, David (2002) An Expert on Public Administration, Policy and administrative reform, is a Senior Fellow Emeritus at the Israel Democracy Institute

Dr. Rahat, Gideon (2004) An Expert on Electoral Reforms

Prof. Reichmann, Uriel (February 3, 2004) External Entrepreneur

Prof. Rubinstein, Amnon (December 31, 2003) Internal Entrepreneur

Prof. Sened, Itay (2001) An Expert on Modern Political Economics

Prof. Shetreet, Shimon (January 15, 2002) Knesset Member in 1992

## Israeli Press in Hebrew

### *The Direct Election Law—1992*

Alon, G. (1990) The Knesset Plenum to Discuss Today the Likud Coalition Agreement with Agudath Israel, *Haaretz Daily*, November 20, 1990 (in Hebrew)

Barnea, Y. (1989) The Professors Are Not Drawing Up a Constitution, *Haaretz Daily*, May 1, 1989 (in Hebrew)

Ben Vered, A. (1988) The Joint Struggle of the Small and Orthodox Parties Postponed A Change to the Election System, *Haaretz Daily*, June 8, 1988 (in Hebrew)

Ben Vered, A. (1989) Celebrators Became Protestors, *Haaretz Daily*, August 1, 1989, p. 13 (in Hebrew)

Ben Vered, A. (1990) Four Bills Calling for Direct Prime Ministerial Elections Passed Primary Vote—The Orthodox Were Absent, *Haaretz Daily*, March 20, 1990 (in Hebrew)

Bracha, B. (1985) Sad Constitutional Considerations, *Haaretz Daily*, August 3, 1985 (in Hebrew)

Brichta, A. (1988) Why Should the Election System Be Changed, *Haaretz Daily*, February 17, 1988 (in Hebrew)

Carmon, A. (1989) Reform Is Not Revolution, *Haaretz Daily*, August 8, 1989 (in Hebrew)

Carmon, A. (1990) Direct Election as Populism, *Haaretz Daily*, April 2, 1990 (in Hebrew)

Dror, Y. (1989) Self-Destruction Mechanism, *Haaretz Daily*, July 30, 1989 (in Hebrew)

Editorial (1990a) Don't Despair from the System, *Haaretz Daily*, March 20, 1990 (in Hebrew)

Editorial (1990b) Likud Negotiations for Shamir's Replacement, *Haaretz*, March 16, 1990 (in Hebrew)

Eldar, A. (1985) Peres Ordered to Ease Tensions with the Likud, *Haaretz Daily*, March 21, 1985 (in Hebrew)

Eldar, A. (1987) Peres: Without a Majority for an International Convention There Is No Justification for This Government and No Alternative to Elections, *Haaretz Daily*, April 23, 1987 (in Hebrew)

Galili, L. (1990) Peace Now Movement (Shalom Ahshav) Held First Convention with Russian Immigrants, *Haaretz Daily*, November 18, 1990 p. 7a (in Hebrew)

Galili, L. & G. Alon (1990) Maarach, Ratz and Mapam Calling for Minister Peretz's Dismissal Due His Call for Change in the Law of Return, *Haaretz Daily*, November 18, 1990, p. 7a (in Hebrew)

*Galnoor Y.* (1990) Direct Election—No Thanks, *Yediot Aharonot Daily*, March 26, 1990 (in Hebrew)

Gavison, R. (1987) (Interview) Constitution Now?, *The Chamber*, December 1, 1987 (in Hebrew)

Gerti, M. (1987) Rubinstein Says Goodbye: I Cannot Be a Minister in This Government, *Haaretz Daily*, May 25, 1987 (in Hebrew)

Gideon, D. (1989) Change for the Sake of Change, *Haaretz Daily*, August 8, 1989 (in Hebrew)

Gilat, Z. (1990) They've Had Enough, *Hadashot Daily*, November 30, 1990 (in Hebrew)

Gutman, E. (1989) Excessive Personalization, *Haaretz Daily*, August 8, 1989 (in Hebrew)

Landau, U. (1991) Direct Election—Why It's Bad, *Yediot Aharonot Daily*, December 12, 1991 (in Hebrew)

Lynn, U. (1990) To Elect a New Prime Minister, *Maariv Daily*, April 4, 1990 (in Hebrew)

Lynn, U. (1991) Direct Election: Likud Contemplating—in Favor, *Maariv Daily,* November 26, 1991 (in Hebrew)

Lynn, U. (1992a) All I Wanted Was to Pass the Law in Peace, *Yediot Aharonot Daily*, January 16, 1992 (in Hebrew)

Lynn, U. (1992b) I'm Coming Home, *Maariv Daily*, February 25, 1992 (in Hebrew)

Marcus, Yoel (1985) The Weakest Link, *Haaretz Daily*, April 2, 1985 (in Hebrew)

Margalit, D. (1985a) Committee without a Goal, *Haaretz Daily,* March 20, 1985, p. 7 (in Hebrew)

Margalit, D. (1985b) Doron Raised Proposals to Ease the Frustrated Coalition Members, *Haaretz Daily*, March 26, 1985 (in Hebrew)

Margalit, D. (1985c) New Tension Due to Histadruth Elections, *Haaretz Daily,* March 21, 1985 (in Hebrew)

Margalit, D. (1988a) Likud and Maarach Directorates Aloud Magen and Ramon Propose Bill to Bring Forward the Elections, *Haaretz Daily*, March 1, 1988 (in Hebrew)

Margalit, D. (1988b) There was Nothing to Lose, *Haaretz Daily*, p. 1, June 15, 1988

Margalit, D. (1988c) Votes Cast Today on Changing Election System—A Slim Chance, *Haaretz Daily*, June 7, 1988

Naor, A. (1985) Coalition: Squabbling Children, *Haaretz Daily*, April 2, 1985 (in Hebrew)

Papo, A. (1991) Caution, Professor on the Loose, *Yediot Aharonot Daily,* December 16, 1991 (in Hebrew)

Peri, Y. (1990) Changing the System—121 Knesset Members, *Davar Daily*, April 2, 1990 (in Hebrew)

Procacha, U. (1987) Constitution Now? *Haaretz Daily*, October 16, 1987 (in Hebrew)

Reichmann, U. (1986) To Protect the Legal Advisor, *Haaretz Daily*, May 30, 1986 (in Hebrew)

Reichmann, U. (1987) Nevertheless, Constitution Now, *Haaretz Daily*, September 17, 1987 (in Hebrew)

Reichmann, U. (1988) All-Out War in the Wrong Battlefield, *Maariv Daily*, September 10, 1988 (in Hebrew)

Reichmann, U. (1989) Sometimes the Celebration Ends, *Hadashot Daily*, January 4, 1989 p. 14 (in Hebrew)

Reichmann, U. (1990a) How Will the Prime Minister Be Elected—There Are No Risks in This Chance, *Davar Daily*, December 21, 1990 (in Hebrew)

Reichmann, U. (1990b) What Are You Afraid of? *Yediot Aharonot*, December 24, 1990 (in Hebrew)

Reichmann, U. (1991) Where Does the Money Come From, *Maariv Daily*, December 15, 1991 (in Hebrew)

Rubinstein, A. (1982) Time for an Initiative, *Haaretz Daily*, June 14, 1982 (in Hebrew)

Rubinstein, A. (1987) Jurists in Space, *Haaretz Daily*, June 7, 1987 (in Hebrew)

Rubinstein, A. (1988a) Automatism in Gaza, *Haaretz Daily*, January 5, 1988 (in Hebrew)

Rubinstein, A. (1988b) It's Essential to Alter the System, *Haaretz Daily*, December 12, 1988 (in Hebrew)

Rubinstein, A. (1988c) Silence of the Jurists, *Haaretz Daily*, May 22, 1988 (in Hebrew)

Rubinstein, A. (1989) Despite It All the Knesset Is Strong, *Haaretz Daily*, July 30, 1989 (in Hebrew)

Rubinstein, A. (1990a) Changing the System—Some Questions and Answers, *Yediot Aharonot*, April 20, 1990, p. 14 (in Hebrew)

Rubinstein, A. (1990b) Political Crisis and Its Solution, *Haaretz Daily*, April 15, 1990 (in Hebrew)

Rubinstein, A. (1990c) Rescue the Democracy from Its Degraders, *Haaretz Daily*, March 18, 1990 (in Hebrew)

Rubinstein, A. (1990d) Thinking Against—Voting For, *Yediot Aharonot*, December 14, 1990 (in Hebrew)

Samet, G. (1987) Maybe It's Possible to Change the System, *Haaretz Daily*, July 2, 1987 (in Hebrew)

Schweitzer, A. (1987) The Blue Bird Hunters, *Haaretz Daily*, September 3, 1987 (in Hebrew)

Schweitzer, A. (1989) Androgynous at the Wheel, *Haaretz Daily*, January 2, 1989 (in Hebrew)

Segal, Z. (1990) Begin the Revolution, *Yediot Aharonot Daily*, September 12, 1990 (in Hebrew)

Segev, T. (1988) Constitution at the Square, *Haaretz Daily*, January 15, 1988 (in Hebrew)

Shahal, M. (1990) Bring Back Honor, *Davar Daily*, December 18, 1990 (in Hebrew)

Shalvi, A. (1987) Constitution—For Women as Well, *Haaretz Daily*, October 9, 1987 (in Hebrew)

Shapira, B. (1990) Gray Suits Him, *Haaretz Daily*, October 26, 1990, p. 2b (in Hebrew)

Shchori, I. (1985a) Shinui Party Considers Withdrawing from the Government in 6 Weeks, *Haaretz Daily*, June 7, 1985 (in Hebrew)

Shchori, I. (1985b) Shinui Party in Defensive Position, *Haaretz Daily*, April 11, 1985 (in Hebrew)

Shchori, I. (1988a) Forty Candidates in the Liberal Party, *Haaretz Daily*, June 9, 1988 p. 3 (in Hebrew)

Shchori, I. (1988b) Labor Party Relying on New Faces, *Haaretz Daily*, June 10, 1988, p. 2b (in Hebrew)

Shchori, I. (1988c) Likud Leaning towards Bringing Elections Forward If Shultz Applies Pressure to Accept His Plan, *Haaretz Daily*, March 1, 1988 (in Hebrew)

Shchori, I. (1988d) Today, Herut (Freedom) Party Applies Pressure on Liberals to Support "Who Is a Jew," *Haaretz Daily*, June 14, 1988, p. 1 (in Hebrew)

Shchori, I., A. Ben David & G. Alon (1988) Grand Treason, *Haaretz Daily*, June 15, 1988, p. 1 (in Hebrew)

Shchori, I. (1990a) Confusion Safeguards the Party, *Haaretz Daily*, November 12, 1990, p. 3b (in Hebrew)

Shchori, I. (1990b) Going Back to Counting on the Likud, *Haaretz Daily*, November 13, 1990, p. 1b (in Hebrew)

Shchori, I. (1990c) Labor Party Inquiry Commission, *Haaretz Daily*, May 27, 1990, p. 3 (in Hebrew)

Shchori, I. (1990d) Liberal Party Activists Call for Re-establishment of Party under Yitzhak Moday, *Haaretz Daily*, November 14, 1990, p. 3a (in Hebrew)

Shchori, I. (1990e) Likud Consents to Agudat Israel's Demand, *Haaretz Daily*, November 15, 1990 (in Hebrew)

Shragai, N. (1985) Hamaarach Offers Portfolios to Shas, Mafdal, Egoi, Mtzad, and Pai, *Haaretz Daily*, June 7, 1985 (in Hebrew)

Strasler, N. (1990) Only Changing the System Might Help, *Haaretz Daily*, March 16, 1990 (in Hebrew)

Tsiddon, Y. (1989) The Threat of the Third Republic, *Haaretz Daily,* February 20, 1989 (in Hebrew)

Tsiddon, Y. (1990a) Human Resources Government, *Haaretz Daily*, April 3, 1990(in Hebrew)

Tsiddon, Y. (1990b) Only the Price Rose, *Haaretz Daily*, April 26, 1990 (in Hebrew)

Tsiddon, Y. (1991a) Raful and I Are Fed Up with Tricks, *Maariv Daily*, December 25, 1991 (in Hebrew)

Tsiddon, Y. (1991b) Who Will Die First—The Villain or the Dog, *Maariv Daily*, July 26, 1991 (in Hebrew)

## Advertisements in Newspapers: Direct Election Law—1992

- To All Knesset Members: Your Stance Will Be Brought to Public Knowledge, *Yediot Aharonot Daily,* March 3, 1988 (in Hebrew)
- Who's in Favor and Who's Against Changing the Elections System? Those Supporters and Objectors Who Didn't Express Their Stance Yet, *Hadashot Daily*, May 20, 1988 (in Hebrew)
- According the Newly Proposed Election System, Tel-Aviv Residents Will Elect 6 Knesset Members Directly, *Ha'ir* (The City) *Weekly Local*, May 5, 1989 (in Hebrew)
- Galilee Residents Deserve Representation in Knesset, according to the Newly Proposed Election System, *Yediot Ha'Galil Weekly Local*, May 5, 1989 (in Hebrew)
- Yitzhak Shamir, 70 Days Have Passed—Where Is Your King? *Maariv Daily*, July 26, 1989 (in Hebrew)
- Thanks to the Many Thousands Who Came to the Kikar Malchei Israel Square (Israel's Kings Square) Despite the Pouring Rain, *Maariv Daily*, November 14, 1988 (in Hebrew)
- Mister Shamir Don't Crawl, *Yediot Aharonot Daily*, November 11, 1989 (in Hebrew)
- Liberty to Civilians or Submission to the Orthodox—For Whom Will the Knesset Vote? Today We Will Know, *Hadashot Daily*, November 15, 1989 (in Hebrew)
- MK Uriel Lynn, We've Had Enough of Waiting! *Yediot Aharonot Daily*, December 29, 1989 (in Hebrew)
- MK Uriel Lynn, The National Responsibility Is Now Placed Upon You, *Yediot Aharonot Daily*, December 15, 1989 (in Hebrew)
- MK Uriel Lynn, I am Too Fed Up to Wait! And I Demand You to Pass the Law Immediately, *Yediot Aharonot Daily*, January 12, 1990 (in Hebrew)

- Tomorrow, Monday, May 28, 1990, We Shall Know Who Votes for and Who against Direct Election of the Prime Minister" *Haaretz Daily*, May 27, 1990 (in Hebrew)
- Four Knesset Members Forgo Partisan Considerations, *Haaretz Daily*, May 28, 1990 (in Hebrew)
- Does Mister Dov Shilansky Stand the Test of Statehood? *Haaretz Daily*, November 21, 1991 (in Hebrew)
- Is MK Corfo a PLO Agent? *Haaretz Daily*, December 2, 1991 (in Hebrew)
- This Might Be Their Finest Hour, Bibi Nethanyahu, Uriel Lynn, Yigal Horowitz, *Haaretz Daily*, December 30, 1991 (in Hebrew)


## Direct Election Law Annulment—2001


Alon, G. (1997) Law for Direct Prime Ministerial Elections Supports Anyone Taking On the Peace Path, *Haaretz Daily*, March 10, 1997 (in Hebrew)

Alon, G. (1998) Plan to Abolish Direct Elections Faces Committee Hearings in Knesset Today, *Haaretz Daily*, June 29, 1998 (in English)

Alon, G. (2000) MKs Line Up to Do Away with Direct Elections, *Haaretz Daily*, November 30, 2000 (in English)

Bar Gefen, L. (2000) Shifting the Electoral Change to the Committee on Constitution, *Y-net Daily—Yediot Aharonot Online*, July 6, 2000 (in Hebrew)

Bar Gefen, L. (2001) Knesset Decides to Return to Previous Elections System, *Y-net Daily—Yediot Aharonot Online*, March 8, 2001 (in Hebrew)

Carmon, A. (1998) An Eternal Dirty Trick, *Haaretz Daily*, June 10, 1998 (in Hebrew)

Carmon. A. (2000) Revocation of the Direct Election Law, *Globes*, June 15, 2000 (in Hebrew)

Lavie, Z. (2000) Democracy Declined and Corruption Flourished, *Globes*, August 1, 2000 (in Hebrew)

Lynn, U. (1995) Not a Principled Struggle, *Haaretz Daily*, June 8, 1995 (in Hebrew)

Rubinstein, A. (2000) The Italian Option, *Haaretz Daily*, November 11, 2000 (in English)

Segal, Z. (2000) Worst of All Governance Methods, *Haaretz Daily*, November 6, 2000 (in Hebrew)

Shadmi, H. (2000a) Beilin versus the Existing Electoral System, *Haaretz*, August 28, 2000 (in Hebrew)

Shadmi, H. (2000b) Burg Demand Free Voting, *Haaretz*, June 13, 2000 (in Hebrew)

Shadmi, H. (2000c) Burg Organized a Meeting of 1,000, *Haaretz Daily*,, September 20, 2000 (in Hebrew)

Steinberg, G.M. (1998) Straight to Knesset, *Haaretz Daily*, June 25, 1998 (in Hebrew)

Vardi, R. (2001) Capital and Political Power in Our Country—It's a Fascinating and Intense Story, *Globes Daily*, March 8, 2001 (in Hebrew)

Verter, Y. (2000) Labor Girds Over Direct Elections Law, *Haaretz Daily*, July 5, 2000 (in English)

# INDEX